LANDSCAPE DETAILING

Volume 1   ENCLOSURE

LANDSCAPE DETAILING

Volume 1   ENCLOSURE

Third Edition   Michael Littlewood

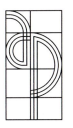

Architectural Press

Architectural Press
An imprint of Butterworth-Heinemann Ltd
Linacre House, Jordan Hill, Oxford OX2 8DP
225 Wildwood Avenue, Woburn, MA 01801-2041
A division of Reed Educational and Professional Publishing Ltd.

A member of the Reed Elsevier plc group

OXFORD   AUCKLAND   BOSTON
JOHANNESBURG   MELBOURNE   NEW DELHI

First published 1984
Second edition 1986
Third edition 1990
Reprinted 1994. 1995, 1997, 1998, 1999, 2000

British Library Cataloguing in Publication Data
Littlewood, Michael
  Landscape Detailing. - Vol 1 Enclosure.-
  3Rev.ed
  I. Title
  712

ISBN 0 7506 1304 1 volume 1
ISBN 0 7506 1303 3 volume 2

Library of Congress Cataloguing in Publication Data
Littlewood, Michael.
  Landscape detailing/Michael Littlewood. -3rd ed.
  p. cm.
  Includes bibliographical references.
  Contents: v. 1. Enclosure - v.2. Surfaces.
  ISBN 0 7506 1304 1 (v. 1) ISBN 0 7506 1303 3 (v.2)
  1. Fences - Design and construction. 2. Garden walks - Design and
  construction. 3. Walls - Design and construction. I. Title.
  TH4965.1.58 1993   92-34847
  717-dc20   CIP

Composition by Scribe Design, Gillingham, Kent
Printed and bound in Great Britain

CONTENTS

Volume 1 ENCLOSURE

FOREWORD

The success of both editions of
Landscape Detailing has resulted in a
review of material and data for the third
edition. In view of the many more details
that have been produced since the
second edition it was felt that the user
would prefer to have them in two volumes
for ease of use. This book covers details
relating to enclosures and the second
relates to surfaces.

Many landscape architects, architects, other
professionals and students responsible for
the production of drawn details and
specifications for landscape construction
works have a need for ready reference.
This book has been produced to meet that
need and it can be extended by additional
sheets. It has been arranged for ease of
copying of sheets and it is sufficiently
flexible for designers to use the details for
their specific requirements.

The range of materials for external works
and their possible combinations for
enclosures would make it impossible to
provide a definitive book of details.

It is not the intention of this book to
supplant the landscape designer's own skill
and experience, which is vital to the
success of any project. This is still essential
in evaluating the site conditions, assessing
the character of the environment and
creating sensitive design solutions.

It is hoped that the book, if used correctly,
will allow the designer to spend more time
on design details, avoiding the need to
produce repetitive drawings for basic
construction elements. It has been found
that the details can be very useful for
costing purposes and to support the
preliminary design when presented to a
client. To assist the designer and to save
further time in writing specifications, check
lists for these have been included in this
edition along with technical guidance notes
and tables.

Design information has been excluded;
many other publications deal with this
subject much more adequately than could
be achieved in this book. General
comments on appearance have been given
only where it was felt appropriate.

ACKNOWLEDGEMENTS

I must give particular thanks to many people who have supported me in some way – no matter how small – and who have encouraged me to complete this third edition, which has been greatly enlarged.

My particular thanks must go to Caroline Mallinder and Paddy Baker of Butterworth-Heinemann – my publishers – both of whom have supported my work and put up with so many frustrating delayed publishing dates. Thank you for being so patient. Also to landscape architects Andrew Clegg, Melissa Bowers, Naila Parveen, Donna Young, Peter Dean and Craig Schofield, all of whom have succumbed to my persistence in drawing the details and reading the text.

My appreciation must also go to Colin MacGregor of NBS for his ready and willing assistance on specification matters as well as Alistair Smythe of *Specification* and Barrie Evans of the *Architect's Journal*. A very special thanks to Doris Evans for typing the text and correcting it so many times.

I am also very grateful to civil engineers John Williamson and Alan Taylor for their advice on retaining walls and to Peter Morrison of Ibstock Building Products Ltd for his kind assistance on brick walls in general.

All of the above have contributed to this book to ensure that it eventually reaches the publishers, after such a long time.

INTRODUCTION

The landscape detail sheets have been produced in an effort to eliminate needless repetition in detailing landscape works covering hard elements. It is possible to use them without alteration, but in some cases minor modifications and additions to dimensions or specifications may be necessary. Lettering has been standardised by the use of a stencil (italic 3.5 mm). When a detail is required which is not available on a detail sheet, the new detail can be drawn by the designer using the standardised format, which will enable it to be added to the original collection of details and to be easily re-used on other projects. Readers are invited to send the publishers copies of their own details which they think would merit inclusion in future editions of this book. Appropriate acknowledgement will be made.

Each sheet portrays a detail without reference to its surroundings. This approach has been adopted because it affords to each detail the maximum number of possibilities for re-use. No attempt has been made to recommend a particular detail for a particular situation. This remains the responsibility of the landscape architect, architect or designer.

There are, of course, a great many other details which might be included on specific projects or in specific situations. In some cases, the detailing of site elements and site structures can be coordinated very carefully with the architect or building designer in order to ensure a uniformity of form and material. In yet other instances, various agencies and organisations may have standard details which must be used on their particular projects.

Notes

The notes which precede each section are intended to give only the briefest outline of main points. For more detailed guidance, the publications listed in Appendices A and B should be consulted.

Specifications

Specifications should not be written without a knowledge of the content of the relevant British Standards in Appendix C. Some British Standards contain alternative specifications which may prove more suitable in a particular case.

The task of writing specifications has now been made very much easier by the use of the word processor. Nevertheless, if a specification is to serve its purpose efficiently it must be concise and accurate, otherwise it could be misunderstood by all the people involved in the project.

To assist the designer and to ensure that he or she makes the minimum of omissions, a check list has been provided after the notes for each chapter or section. Ease of access to a particular section will encourage a contractor to read the specification and conform with its requirements. So many contractors ignore the specifications and use only the bills of quantities. Probably the best way to ensure that the completed specification is satisfactory is for the designer to read it as if he or she were the contractor and could complete the project accordingly.

Reference should be made to two main sources for specifications, namely the NBS of Newcastle-upon-Tyne and the publication *Specification*. Full details of their services are given in the Appendices.

Use of the detail sheets

The collection of detail sheets, as purchased, may if users wish be photocopied, punched and stored in a ring binder. The detail sheets have been laid out in such a way as to facilitate this operation. In the form of individual leaves the details can easily be traced or copy negatives can be made.

The sheets must be used in conjunction with a site layout drawing, preferably at 1:200. These may be more than one sheet,

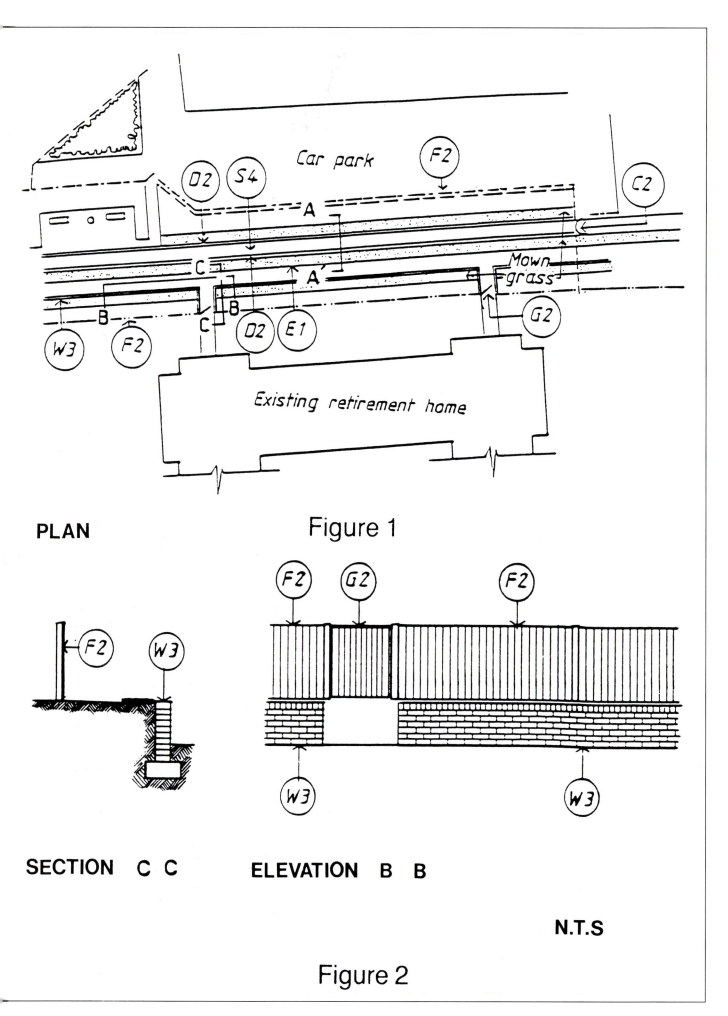

PLAN

Figure 1

SECTION C C   **ELEVATION B B**

N.T.S

Figure 2

depending upon the size of the project. The layout drawings will convey all information on levels, directions of falls and setting-out dimensions. They also indicate the location of the elected details and the deployment of surface finishes. (See Figure 1.) Simple conjunction of details (for example, a fence, a wall and a gate) can be indicated on section and elevation drawings quite easily. (See Figure 2.)

Standards

British Standards and Codes of Practice are referred to where necessary. Users of this book living in countries where British Standards are not used should delete the reference to the British Standard and, if they feel it necessary, either insert a reference to an equivalent national standard or describe what is required in empirical terms.

Production of new detail sheets

Where the use of a detail not included in the original collection of detail sheets is required, the new detail can be produced on A4 tracing paper using a standard format. This will enable it to be added to the original collection and to be easily re-used. New details will be assigned a reference number by the design office, using their own reference system. The title of the new detail, as shown in the centre label at the foot of the drawing, can then be added to the contents list prefacing each section.

Issue of detail sheets

Detail sheets can be used in two ways. A set of photocopies can be issued to the contractor of the selected details, after completion of the title panel reference, and number-stamping each detail with the office stamp. The second method is to trace or copy a batch of details, grouped according to type and identified with key numbers, onto an A1 sheet of tracing paper and include the drawing with the contract set in the normal way.

Design detailing

The creation of good design can only come from the designer, and no amount of drawn details can be a substitute for this fact. The principles must be followed as Fraser Reekie has stated in his book *Design in the Built Environment*:

To make an objective assessment of a design, or to set about the process of designing, consideration has to be given to the three aspects which may be summarised as:

1. Function: The satisfying of requirements of use or purpose;
2. Structure: The physical implementation of function by the best available material(s), construction, manufacture and skills as conditions permit;
3. Appearance: The obtaining of satisfactory visual effects (sometimes referred to as 'aesthetic values').

Other words can be used to describe these three aspects but, on analysis, whatever words are used it will be found that almost every writer on building design, which may be extended to cover the built environment, is dealing with the same three fundamentals.

These three constituent parts of design are closely interrelated and each, to a greater or lesser extent, according to the nature of the subject, influences the others. An urban composition or a building or a detail that is truly well designed is one in the creation of which all three aspects have been fully considered and integrated. Integration may well be the key-word in good design. Not only does it mean the correct combining of parts into a whole but it implies, by association with integrity, soundness and honesty.

COPINGS, CAPPINGS AND BONDS

GUIDANCE NOTES

Copings and cappings

Their primary purpose is to prevent water seepage into the wall from the top, and second, to shed water clear of the face of the wall, both as effectively as possible. Reference should be made to BS 3798: 1964 for copings of clayware, concrete or stone. A minimum weight of 1.5 kN/m^2 is preferred for copings with concrete or stone units. The overhang, if any, of any coping or capping should include a throating recess or a drip not less than 13 mm wide, with the outer drip edge at least 40 mm from the face of the brickwork.

The practice of using a brick on edge coping is acceptable because it is the damp proof course incorporated under the coping that functions as a coping and not the brick on edge. The presence of a damp proof course causes the brick copings to become saturated and susceptible to frost damage. Only bricks that are resistant to such damage should therefore be used. Engineering or concrete bricks are usually preferred. End bricks should be held in position by galvanised metal cramps. Cramps can also be built into the top of the wall at a spacing of 900 mm to secure the coping bricks along the length of the wall. Concrete block walls are often capped with concrete slabs or bricks. Concrete copings may need to be dowelled together for strength, especially in areas susceptible to vandalism. Tile, slate or metal could also be used for copings. A coping for a wall needs to be simple, bold and effective, although random rubble walls look far more convincing when finished with the traditional

method for the locality. It should be remembered that the choice of suitable coping for the situation may decide the choice of brick in the wall and limit the possibilities available to the designer.

Bonds for brickwork

The way bricks are arranged within a wall is known as the bond, and while they do have marginally differing strengths their main virtue is aesthetic. The bond will to some extent depend upon the thickness of the wall. For a one-brick-thick wall the bond is usually of stretchers only and the height is normally under one metre. For higher walls a Flemish or English bond is used which has a double thickness of brick with headers (bricks laid end-on) laid to bind the wall.

DETAIL SHEETS

Copings and cappings
Brick (2)
Concrete
Mixed
Bonds
Brick bonds (5)
Stone
Random rubble masonry patterns
Ashlar stone masonry patterns

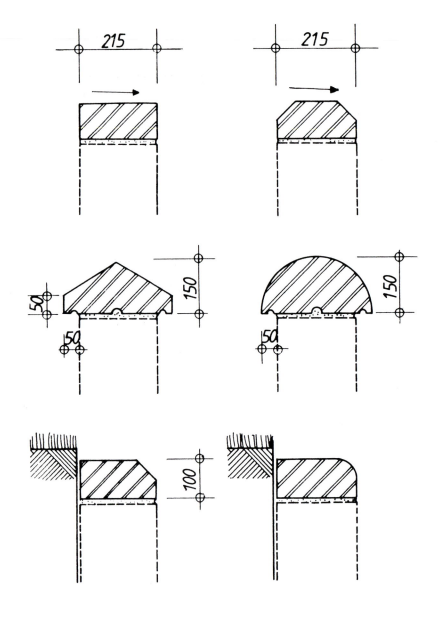

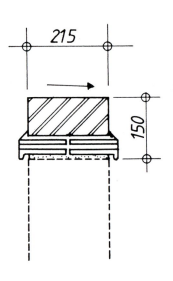

Scale 1:10

COPINGS &
CAPPINGS, brick

2

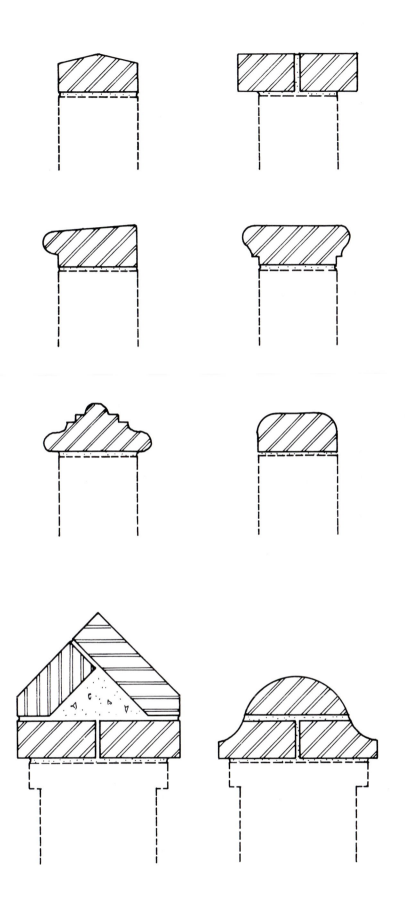

COPINGS &
CAPPINGS, brick

3

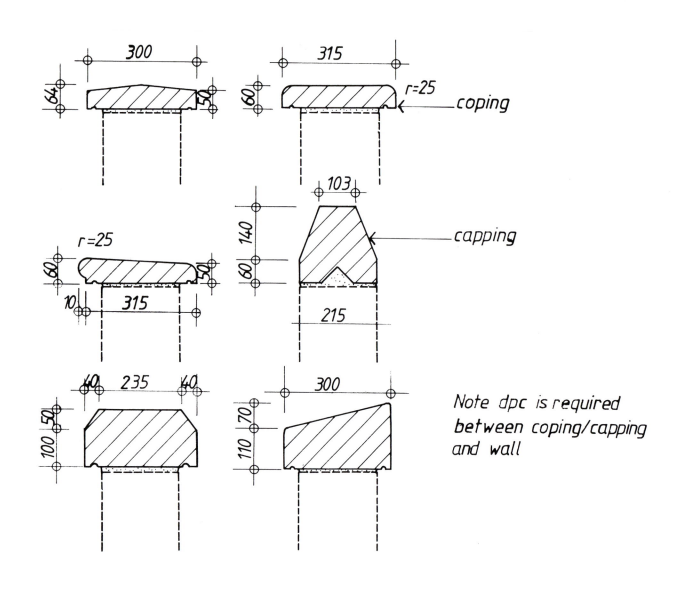

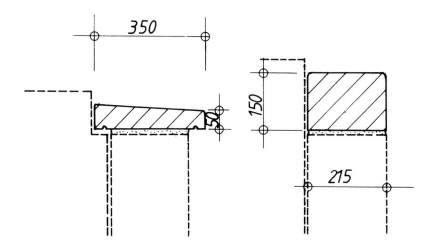

Note dpc is required
between coping/capping
and wall

Scale 1:10

COPINGS &
CAPPINGS, concrete

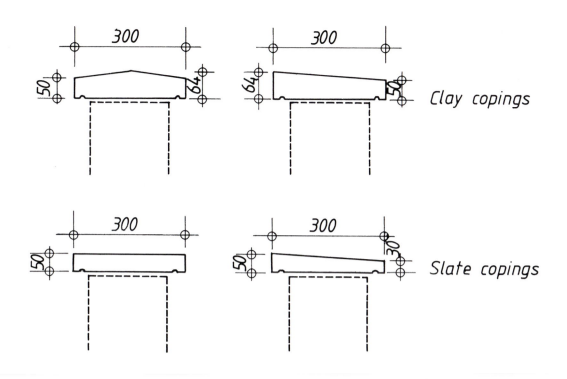

Clay copings

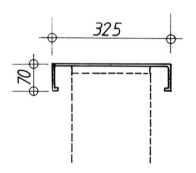

Slate copings

Metal coping

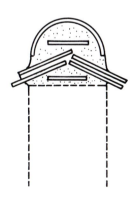
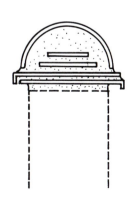

Tile copings

Scale 1:10

COPINGS
mixed

5

Garden wall

Flemish double bond

Scale 1:10

WALLS
brick bonds

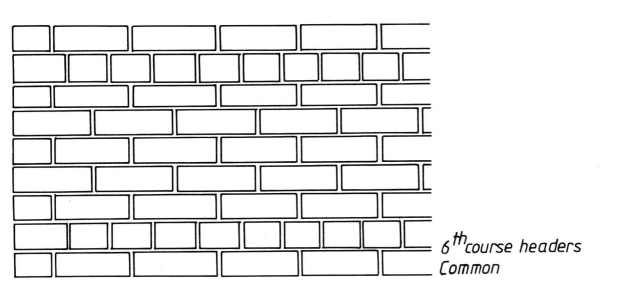

6thcourse headers
Common

6th course flemish headers
Common

Scale 1:10

WALLS
brick bonds

7

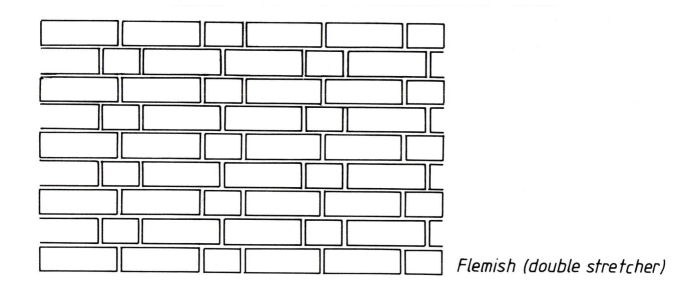

Flemish (double stretcher)

English cross or dutch

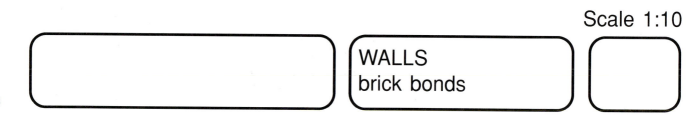

WALLS
brick bonds

Scale 1:10

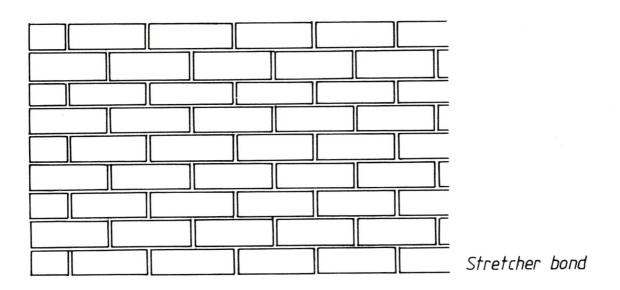

Stretcher bond

1/3 running

Scale 1:10

WALLS
brick bonds

9

Flemish (diagonal)

Flemish (cross)

Scale 1:10

WALLS
brick bonds

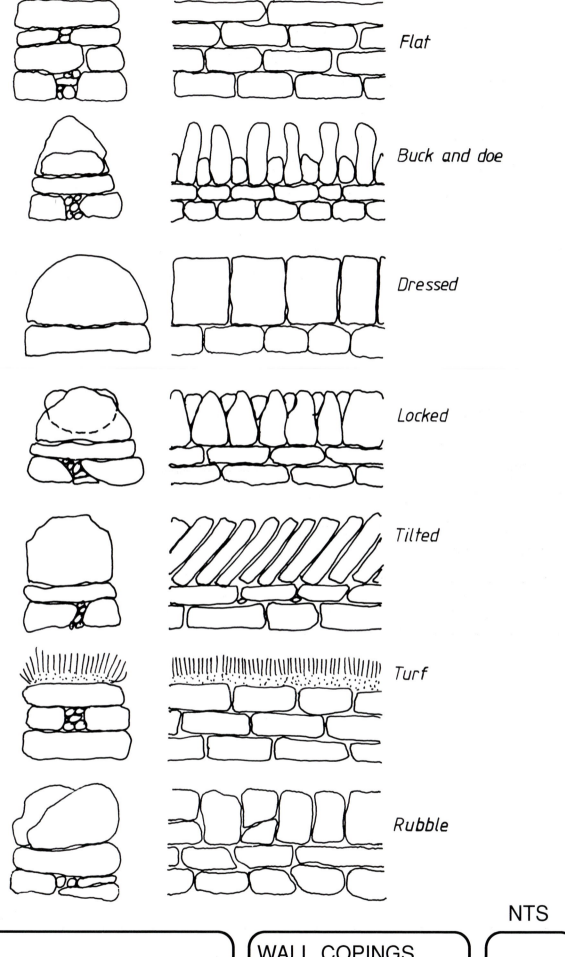

Flat

Buck and doe

Dressed

Locked

Tilted

Turf

Rubble

NTS

WALL COPINGS
stone

11

Uncoursed random with roughly squared rubble

Coursed random with roughly squared rubble

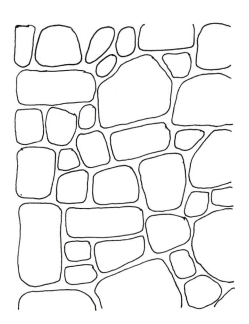

Uncoursed random with rough rubble

ELEVATIONS

Scale 1:10

WALL
Random rubble
masonry patterns

Stone can be up to 600 long
depth   150 / 200 / 250 / 300
height   75 / 100 / 125 / 150

Coursed Ashlar with irregular courses

Coursed Ashlar with regular courses

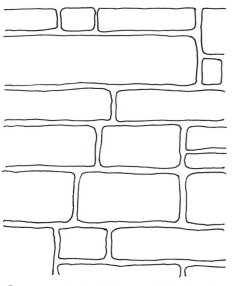

Coursed Ashlar with broken

Random coursed random bond

<u>Note</u>: *Units are precast and dressed before delivery to site*

Scale 1:10

WALL
Ashlar stone
masonry patterns

FREE-STANDING WALLS

GUIDANCE NOTES

Appearance

The choice of materials available today is quite considerable and great care must be taken to ensure that the appearance of any wall is in harmony with the local vernacular of style. Too often, materials are used which bear no relation to either the place where the walls are being built or to the surrounding landscape. Natural stone is generally much more appropriate in rural areas, whereas concrete blocks are better used in urban areas, unless they are rendered or painted. Bricks can be used in almost any locality, provided the selected colour is appropriate to the area.

Natural stone walling should never be used from another part of the country and the local materials and techniques will provide the catalyst for the design. Walls in the open landscape are usually used only as alternatives to fences and hedges where stone is plentiful.

Walls higher than eye level are usually used to form a complete physical and visual barrier and are often more associated with the architecture. Walls below eye level provide partial enclosure and are useful where a view can still be obtained. Dwarf walls are often used as a physical barrier where strength is required by retaining all the visual qualities. Brick walls cannot 'flow' with the landscape in the same way as stone walls, because they cannot take up changes of level without the top of the wall being stepped.

With such a wide choice of bricks available today great care must be taken in their selection, especially over the use of colour and finish. Minor details such as the raking out of joints, for example, will be of less importance in the open landscape scene than in the urban one.

Design factors

Special considerations in the design of external free-standing walls include:

- *Rain exposure*: rain may penetrate the wall from both sides and above, affecting both durability and appearance unless material quality and design detailing take account of the special requirements.
- *Thermal exposure*: damp proof courses in free-standing walls are subject to extremes of temperature, and therefore to high thermal movement.
- *Wind exposure*: in a building, a wall of similar height would be restrained both at the top and bottom by floors and roof and laterally by cross walls. The free-standing wall, in contrast, is an unrestrained vertical cantilever, and is often designed without any structural calculations having been made.
- *Appearance*: there will be two exposed sides to fair-face, unless an applied finish is specified.
- *Foundation design*: because free-standing walls do not carry applied loads there is a tendency to economise on foundation design. This often leads to expensive remedial work.
- *Building in cold weather*: precautions are essential when walls are exposed to wind, rain and frost on both faces.
- *Damp proof courses and movement joints*: detailing may differ from the norm in walls of buildings.
- *Associated planting*: adjacent planting may affect detailing.

Stability

Although in many cases the ratio of height to width (slenderness ratio) is the major factor affecting stability, the list of design criteria should include:

Wall plan shape
Type of bond
Use of reinforcement
Weight of brick and block
Slenderness ratio
Wind load
Movement joints

14

Foundations
Special strength requirements

Appearance

The stability of a free-standing wall can be improved by adding piers, staggering the wall in bays, or increasing the thickness of the wall. The thickness of a free-standing wall can be estimated by reference to appropriate publications given in Appendix B.
All walls over 2,000 mm high should be referred to a structural engineer for checking. Stability calculations for such walls may also be required by the district surveyor or building inspector. Approval is usually required from a local authority when the height above ground level exceeds 1,800 mm.

Brick

Brick is the most commonly used material for building walls. There are three types that are suitable for external use:

- Commons, which are for general-purpose building, have no finish and are particularly subject to weathering.
- Facings, used where appearance is of prime importance, have either a hand finish or a wire-cut weather-resistant finish on the side facings only.
- Engineering bricks are the hardest and most impervious brick available.

Bricks used in free-standing external walls, being exposed on both sides, are more prone to deterioration through frost actions than the same bricks used, for example, in the external walls of a building.
Frost-resistant bricks are generally those with low water absorbencies. However, certain types of stock bricks with absorbencies of up to 20 per cent are frost-resistant because their highly porous structure allows ice to expand within the brick without causing damage. Users should contact the manufacturers to confirm that their bricks are suitable for the degree of exposure intended.
External free-standing brick walls are also subject to deterioration following the reaction of soluble sulphates present in the bricks with the tricalcium aluminate constituent in ordinary Portland cement. The reaction is accompanied by expansion of the mortar and subsequent cracking. Sulphate attack can be avoided by the use of a 'special' quality brick as defined by BS 3921: 1974. The BS limits the soluble salt content of bricks of 'special' quality, but not those of 'ordinary' quality. Alternatively, use a richer mortar mix, e.g. 1:3, or a sulphate-resisting cement.

Thickness

The thickness and height of a brick wall determine the frequency of piers or buttresses used to provide support. None is required if the wall is staggered in a zig-zag way or by bringing the line of the wall forward and backward by the thickness of the brick. Curving or serpentine walls will also support themselves, although they need more space. Single-brick walls look unstable, whereas a double-brick wall looks more safe and solid. In all but exceptionally exposed positions a double-brick wall, unbuttressed, should be satisfactory for heights up to 2.0 metres.

Concrete blocks

These are very strong and, because they are also much larger than bricks, a wall can be constructed more quickly and therefore will be cheaper. The large size of cavity blocks used for walling makes piers unnecessary for a standard wall, but solid concrete blocks are half the thickness and will require the support of piers used with the same frequency as for brick walls. Similarly, concrete foundations are required as well as copings. Concrete blocks are now available in a wide range of finishes and colours to match local brick or stone. The blocks may be utilised in a variety of ways to produce either a decorative or a plain finish. They can easily be combined with other materials, such as brick, to relieve monotony in a long length of wall. Concrete blocks used in free-standing external walls should be type A, as defined in BS 2028,

1364: 1968. A rough surface texture helps reduce weather staining. Special pierced concrete blocks are also available. Calcium silicate bricks should be Class 3 or higher as defined in BS 187: Part 2: 1978.

Stone

Natural stone

Most kinds of stone can be used for wall construction – granite, limestone, slate or sandstone. The two main types of stone-walling are ashlar and rubble walling, of which the latter comprises three groups:

- Random rubble, which is of uncut stone, is laid coursed or uncoursed.
- Squared rubble, which is of roughly dressed stone, is laid regularly coursed, irregularly coursed, or uncoursed.
- Miscellaneous rubble walling uses traditional materials and construction methods.

Most stone walls are built in random rubble. No cutting is done to fit the stones together and when they are placed within the wall there is an adequate distribution of pressure over a maximum area, with no continuous vertical joints. To stabilise the wall, header stones are used approximately every square metre and should ideally run right through the wall. Whether this type of wall is coursed or uncoursed, all joints should be well filled and flushed with mortar. Variation can be achieved by filling some of the joints with soil and growing plants in them. To construct a wall in stone of which one side only is visible, a concrete block wall can be faced with stone, tying the two together with galvanised wall ties. The elements of a natural stone wall are usually thick enough to be self-supporting and do not require any piers or buttresses. Natural stone walls usually have the coping or cappings traditionally used in the area.

Reconstituted stone

Different areas produce different rock, which can be crushed and used as the aggregate in the composition of

reconstituted stone blocks. Reconstituted stone block is easier to transport and lay than natural stone. Walls of these materials must be laid in the same way as for bricks.

Mortars

It is essential that there be a permanent tensile bond between the bricks and the mortar to ensure that free-standing walls resist lateral pressure. In sulphate-free conditions use a relatively weak mortar, e.g. 1:1:6, with clay bricks. If sulphates are present in the bricks a sulphate-resisting cement or a stronger mix should be used, as recommended above. Calcium silicate bricks are generally laid in a weaker mix than clay bricks. Brickwork below ground level and up to 150 mm above ground level should be laid in a 1:3 cement/mortar mix. See Tables 1 and 2.

Damp proof courses

A damp proof course, 150 mm from ground level, is required. The use of any damp proof course near ground level must provide the necessary adhesion across the joint. Only two methods meet this requirement:

1. Two courses of (engineering) bricks, to BS 3921: 1974 or BS 743: 1970, having a water absorption of not more than 7 per cent laid in 1:(1/4):3 mortar.
2. Two courses of 5 mm slates fully half-lapped and bedded in 1:(1/4):3 mortar to BS 743: 1970.

In certain situations where walls are constructed of frost-resistant bricks a damp proof course may not be necessary. A damp proof course is also required under the coping is the coping is of a porous material such as brick on edge. If the coping is of an impermeable material, such as metal, PVC or engineering bricks, no damp proof course is needed. Although natural slate or clay tile is the best damp proof course in this position, a lead core bituminous damp proof course can also be used.
If a damp and mossy appearance to the lower parts of a wall is not objected to, the

damp proof course may be omitted provided that the bricks be of 'special' quality and a strong mortar mix (e.g. 1:3) is used. The same applies to the damp proof course under the coping.

Expansion joints

Expansion or movement joints are necessary to accommodate thermal and moisture expansion. They must be constructed in such a way as to ensure a complete separation over the full height of the wall, including the damp proof course and coping/capping, but not the foundations. A 10 mm joint should be provided every 12 m for clay, bricks and concrete blocks and every 6 m for calcium silicate (sand lime) bricks. Expansion joints may be left open but are more commonly filled with a proprietary flexible mastic jointing compound.

Foundations

The depth and width of a foundation will vary according to the type of subsoil. On average subsoils a depth of 450–600 mm is usually sufficient; on shrinkable clay the depth may have to be 900 mm or greater. A maximum width of 525 mm for unreinforced concrete foundations for 225 mm wide walls is advised, but site conditions will determine a final size after consultation with an engineer. A concrete mix of 1:6 is used in all the details, although other mixes may be equally suitable. Where a wall is below 500 mm in height, foundations can be omitted altogether. The topsoil should be removed and the brickwork built off the top of the subsoil, which should be thoroughly compacted. Where more than 150 mm of topsoil has to be removed, the level of the excavation can be made up with well-consolidated granular material. The depth of facing brickwork below ground should not exceed 200 mm.

TABLE 1. MORTAR MIX GROUPS FOR BRICKWORK AND BLOCKWORK

	Group 1	Group 2	Group 3	Group 4
Cement:lime:sand	1:0–¼:3	1:½:4–4½	1:1:5–6	1:2:8–9
Cement:premixed lime and sand (proportions of lime to sand given in parentheses)	1:3 (1:12)	1:4–4½ (1:9)	1:5–6 (1:6)	1:8–9 (1:4½)
Cement:sand and air entrainer	–	1:3–4	1:5–6	1:7–8
Masonry cement:sand	–	1:2½–3½	1:4–5	1:5½ –6½

Note
Specify the mortar by group or by type and proportions, including any special requirements, e.g.
Group 3 as clause 460 with sulphate-resisting cement.
1:1:6 cement:lime:sand.
1:5–6 white cement:selected white sand.

TABLE 2. MINIMUM QUALITY OF MORTARS FOR BRICKWORK AND BLOCKWORK IN VARIOUS SITUATIONS

The mortar groups given are the weakest of those recommended in BS 5628: Part 3, table 13. Higher-strength mortars may be required for environmental (see notes below) or structural reasons. Also, for work below ground, if the soil or ground water contains sulphates it may be necessary to use a stronger mortar mix (i.e. containing more cement) and/or sulphate-resisting cement. If mortar is susceptible to sulphate attack then so also may be concrete bricks and blocks used in the same location.

Masonry condition or situation	Clay silicate	Calcium Brick	Block	Concrete
Work below or near external ground level				
• low risk of saturation with or without freezing	3	3	3	3
• high risk of saturation without freezing	2*	3	3	2
• high risk of saturation with freezing	2*	2	3	2
Brick dpcs	1	NS	NS	NS
Unrendered external walls (other than chimneys, cappings, copings, parapets, sills)				
• low risk of saturation	3	4†	3	4†
• high risk of saturation	2**	3	3	3
Rendered external walls (other than chimneys, cappings, copings, parapets, sills	3*	4†	3*	4†
Internal walls and inner leaves of cavity walls	4†	4†	4†	4†
Unrendered parapets (other than copings or cappings)				
• low risk of saturation, e.g. low parapets on some single-storey buildings	3	3	3	3
• high risk of saturation	2*	3	3	2
Rendered parapets (other than copings or cappings)	3**	3	3	3
Copings, cappings and sills	1	2	2	2
Free-standing boundary and screen walls (other than copings or cappings)				
• with coping	3*	3	3	3
• with capping	2	3 SRC	3 SRC	2
Earth-retaining walls (other than copings or cappings)				
• with waterproofed retaining face and coping	2*	3	2	2
• with coping or capping but no waterproofing on retaining face	1*	2	2	2
Manholes, inspection chambers, culverts				
• surface water	1SRC	3	3	2
• foul drainage (continuous contact with walling)	1 SRC	2	2	NS
• foul drainage (occasional contact with walling)	1 SRC	2	2	NS

NOTES
†   Where group 4 mortar is used it is essential that the walling under construction is fully protected from saturation and freezing. Alternatively, specify group 3.
*   If clay bricks with a normal soluble salt content (as defined in BS 3921) are specified, sulphate-resisting cement should be used.
**   If clay bricks with a normal soluble salt content (as defined in BS 3921) are specified, sulphate-resisting cement should be used or the mortar changed to the next stronger group.
NS not suitable.
SRC sulphate-resisting cement.

TABLE 3. FREE-STANDING BRICK WALLS: CONSTRUCTIONAL DETAILS

| Thickness (mm) | Max. height (m) | Piers | | Expansion joints | | Mass concrete founds | | Notes |
		Size (mm)	Spacing (m)	Preferred spacing (m)	Max. spacing (m)	Min. width (mm)	Min. depth (mm)	
112	1.2	225 × 112	4.5	9	9	337	150	Expansion joint at every second pier position: 12 mm joint between two No. 225 × 112 mm piers
112	1.8	337 × 225	4	8	9	337	150	Expansion joint at every second pier position: 12 mm joint between two No. 225 × 225 mm piers
112	2.4	337 × 225	2.6	7.9	9	337	150	Expansion joint at every third pier position: 12 mm joint between two No. 225 × 225 mm piers
225	1.8	–	–	6	9	675	225	
337	2.75	–	–	6	9	1,012	337	

SPECIFICATION CHECK LIST

Brick/block walling

General
Specification may be by reference to a standard by proprietary name(s) or both. Clause headings should describe the use and/or location of the brick/blockwork in a helpful way, e.g.

FACING BRICKWORK ABOVE DPC
FACING BLOCKWORK FOR WALLS
ENGINEERING BRICKWORK FOR
MANHOLES

The clause heading need not be absolutely precise but more a confirmation that the clause is the correct one for the situation identified and/or cross-referenced on the drawings or in the schedule of work.

For foundations see separate section.

Type of walling
Select type of walling required, e.g.

Facing brickwork
Second-hand facing brickwork
Facing blockwork
Reconstituted stonework
Common brickwork
Common blockwork
Engineering brickwork

Drawings
State drawing references

Materials

Clay bricks
BS 3921 designates clay bricks according to frost resistance and soluble salt content.
Calcium silicate bricks
BS 187 classes 3 to 7 can be used in any situation with the exceptions of:

Cappings, copings and sills	Minimum class 4
Manholes with foul effluent in continuous contact with the brickwork	Minimum class 7
Damp proof courses	Not suitable

See BS 5628: Part 3, table 13.

Concrete bricks and blocks
BS 6073: Part 1 does not specify functional properties such as thermal conductivity, nor does it give recommendations as to suitability for particular purposes.
Concrete bricks and blocks should not be used in contact with ground from which there is danger of sulphate attack unless they have been specifically made for this purpose, i.e. with sulphate-resisting cement and/or a certain minimum cement content – see BRE Digest 250.
For detailed guidance on durability see BS 5628: Part 3, table 13.

Reconstituted stonework
This clause is for proprietary blocks which simulate natural stone rubble walling, e.g. rough hewn brought to courses, Ashlar coursed and bonded as shown on drawings.
Provide details of make, manufacturer's reference, size, colour and finish.

Special shapes
Bricks should be to BS 4729 as shown in drawings. Specify detail of special shapes for blocks.

Mortar
State mix for mortar. Where mortar is specified by group number select any mortar in that group, using the same mortar throughout any one type of facing work. For guidance on selection see BS 5628: Part 3, table 13 or BRE Digest 160. In general, stronger bricks and blocks and more severe exposure conditions require mortars of higher strength, i.e. with a greater cement content. When coloured mortar is required, it is better to specify coloured ready-mixed material. Site mixing using pigments is rarely satisfactory;

adequate control of colour consistency being very difficult.

Samples
Indicate if any samples of bricks or blocks are to be seen for approval prior to commencement of works.

Damp proof course
State type of damp proof course required for both wall and coping.

Workmanship

Foundation
Provide details on type and size of foundation.

Laying
State details of wall construction.

Bond
Describe the type of bond required. See illustrations of brick and block bonding. To reduce the number of types of brickwork, one type can cover more than one bond if these are in different thicknesses and the brickwork is identical in other respects.

Mortar
Give details on the use of mortar and its strength

Joints
This item applies only to facework, including fair-facework. Wall faces which are to be plastered or which will not be visible in the finished work are covered by general clauses.
Profiles may be specified as:

Flush
Weathered
Recessed square
Bucket handle
Approved

Movement joints
Describe type and material of movement joint required along with frequency.

Features
Insert details of any unusual requirements,

cross referring where appropriate to other sections.

Damp proof course
Ensure bricks are to BS 3921 Engineering Class. Give details of mortar, mix, bond and joints.

Copings
Describe the type of coping required and type of mortar as copings are vulnerable to frost action.

Control samples
The specification of control samples should be related to the size and importance of the job. It may be difficult to justify control samples on small jobs. Insert type, item(s) of walling reference, location, minimum size and any features to be included, i.e. copings, etc.

Inclement weather
State procedure for work in wet and cold weather, storage of bricks/blocks and any other materials. Describe remedial works where mortar has failed.

Appearance
State requirements to achieve uniform appearance with consistent joints cut bricks/blocks.

Cleanliness
Describe method for keeping work clean.

Jointing
Specify method of jointing and profile.

Pointing
State procedure for pointing and profile.

Protection
Give details of how work is to be protected both during and after construction.

Natural stone walling

General
Specification may be by reference to a standard or proprietary names or both. This section deals with the construction of walling using natural stone blocks of varying sizes. The stone may be used as it comes out of the quarry or can be roughly dressed. Rubble stonework is principally used in external walls built from local granite, whinstone, limestone or sandstone. Rubble walls may be stone faced both sides, or stone faced one side and backed with bricks or blocks separated by a cavity. This section does not cover the repair, renovation or cleaning of existing stonework. If ashlar dressings are required they should be specified separately. For brickwork and blockwork used in association with rubble walling use separate specification.

Type of walling
Use this to briefly describe the type of walling required, e.g.

Random rubble uncoursed
Random rubble brought to course
Squared rubble uncoursed
Squared rubble snecked
Squared rubble coursed
Kentish rag
Lakeland

Materials

Stone: Insert the stone required, e.g.

Portland Roach
Clipsham
Darley Dale
Springwell

Visit the quarry and select stone with regard to proven durability, weather resistance and suitability for local atmospheric conditions and the nature of the work.
For advice on selection see BS 5390, BRE Digest 269 and *Stone in Building* published by The Architectural Press. For sources and availability see the *Natural Stone Directory.*
Size of stones will vary with type and quarry, but generally allow 150–180 mm for thickness. Stones used in rubble walling are usually small enough to be manhandled. State type of finish required, e.g. 'as found' or hammered, tooled or sawn.

Type of joints
State either

Flush or
Bucket Handle

Features
Insert brief details of any unusual requirements, e.g. wall laid to batter against concrete block wall.

Mortar
Insert proportions of mix required, including any special requirements, e.g. 1:3:12 white cement:lime:crushed stone.
See BS 5390, clause 23 for mortar mixes. Consult local specialists for advice on composition and proportions of mortar mixes to suit the type of stone, method of walling and exposure conditions.

Accessories
Wall ties, fastenings, damp proof courses, etc, should be specified.

Workmanship

Operatives
State that work is to be executed by skilled masons. Request evidence of previous experience and work.

Appearance
Include clause requesting inspection of samples of dressed stone before delivery to site.

Inclement weather
State procedure for work in wet and cold weather, storage of stone and any other materials. Describe remedial works where mortar has failed.

Control samples
A panel will only be necessary to verify that the contractor can provide the standard of workmanship required and/or to check aspects of design. For simple panels, one square metre should be sufficient. List any features which are to be included in the panel.

Laying
Describe procedure for laying generally including size, shape and colour of stones, quoins, jambs and bonders.

Courses and joints
Specify how coursed work and joints are to be undertaken.

Protection
Give details of how work is to be protected during and after construction.

DETAIL SHEETS

Brick
Brick (low) (2)
Brick (medium) (2)
Brick (high) (4)
Brick with piers
Brick rat trap bond
Brick serpentine
Brick with stone plinth
Concrete
Concrete
Concrete block (low)
Concrete block (high)
Concrete block (gravity)
Stone
Cornish hedge (stone)
Hedge bank and fence
Stone hedge
Natural stone: mortared/coursed
Ashlar: mortared/coursed
Natural stone: mortared/uncoursed
Natural stone, dry

*Only certain bricks have an acceptably visual finish to the back stretcher face. This could be rendered

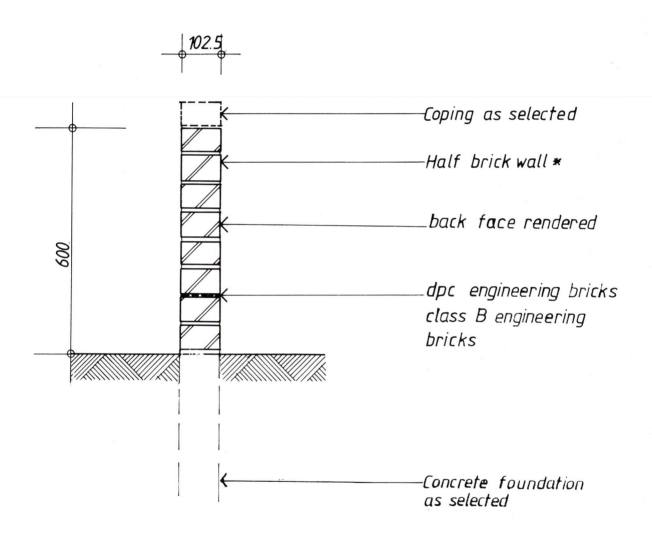

102.5

600

Coping as selected

Half brick wall *

back face rendered

dpc engineering bricks
class B engineering
bricks

Concrete foundation
as selected

Scale 1:10

WALL
brick (low)

23

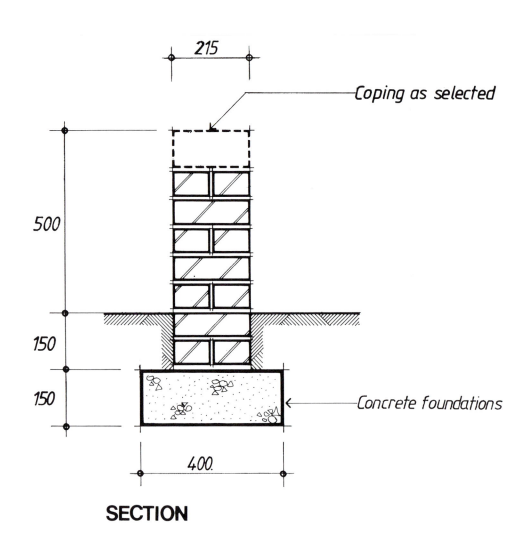

215

Coping as selected

500

150

150

Concrete foundations

400.

SECTION

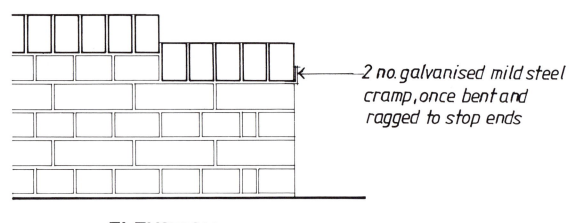

2 no. galvanised mild steel cramp, once bent and ragged to stop ends

ELEVATION

Scale 1:10

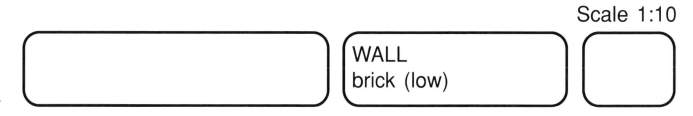

WALL
brick (low)

24

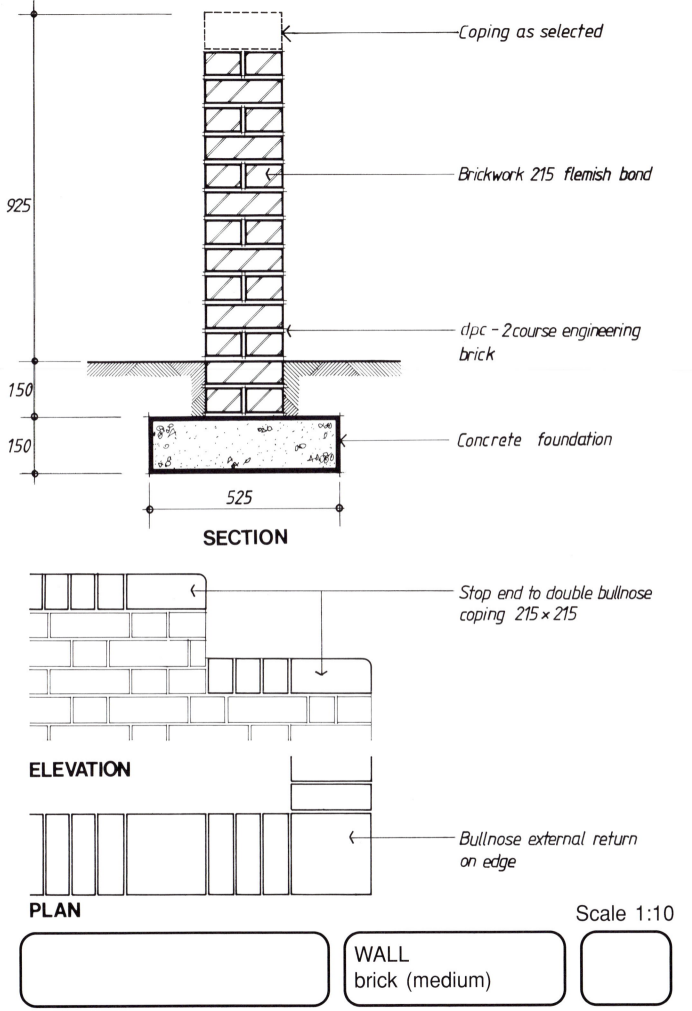

Coping as selected

Brickwork 215 flemish bond

925

dpc – 2 course engineering brick

150

150

Concrete foundation

525

SECTION

Stop end to double bullnose coping 215 × 215

ELEVATION

Bullnose external return on edge

PLAN

Scale 1:10

WALL
brick (medium)

25

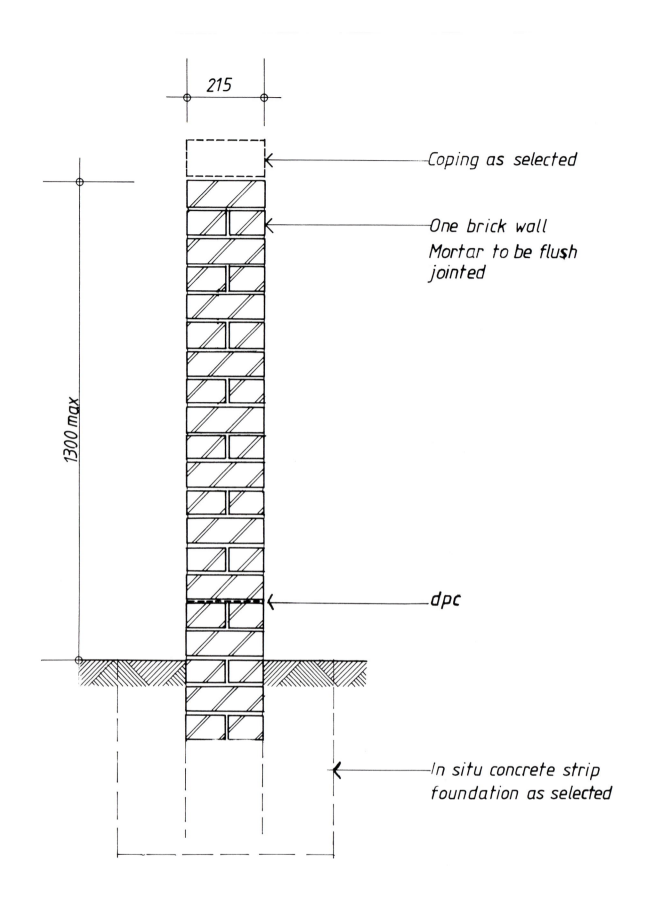

215

Coping as selected

One brick wall
Mortar to be flush
jointed

1300 max

dpc

In situ concrete strip
foundation as selected

Scale 1:10

WALL
brick (medium)

26

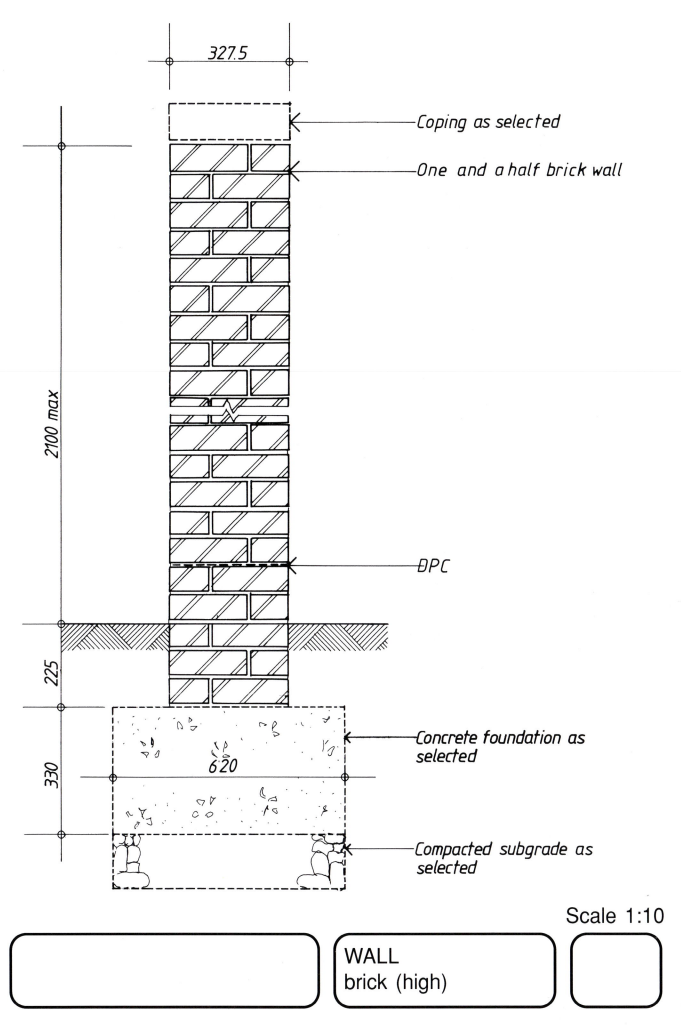

327.5

Coping as selected

One and a half brick wall

2100 max

DPC

225

330

620

Concrete foundation as selected

Compacted subgrade as selected

Scale 1:10

WALL
brick (high)

27

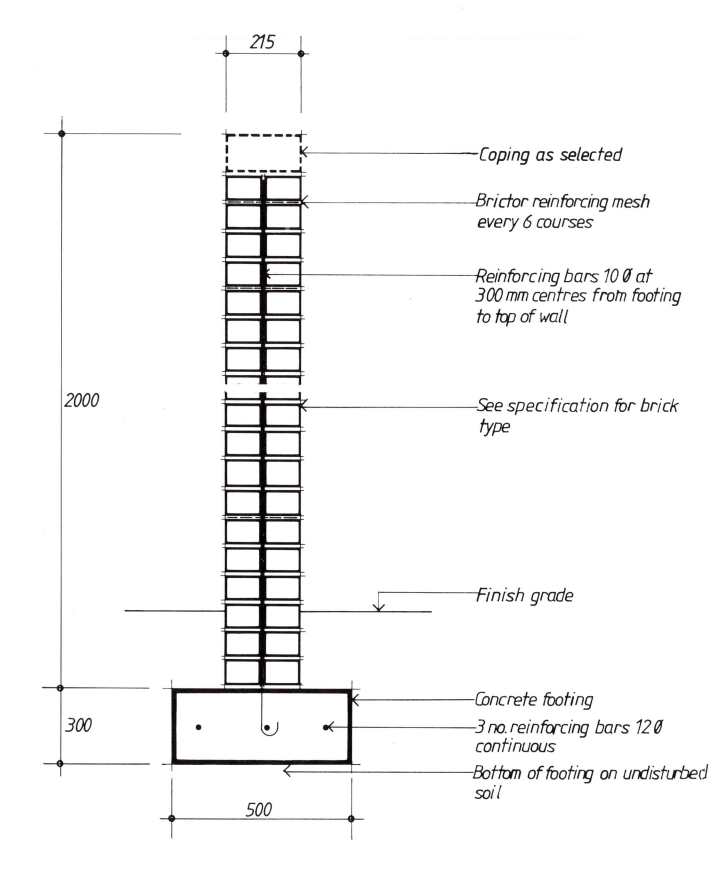

215

2000

300

500

Coping as selected

Brictor reinforcing mesh every 6 courses

Reinforcing bars 10 Ø at 300 mm centres from footing to top of wall

See specification for brick type

Finish grade

Concrete footing

3 no. reinforcing bars 12 Ø continuous

Bottom of footing on undisturbed soil

SECTION

Scale 1:10

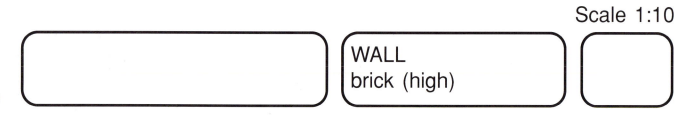

WALL
brick (high)

28

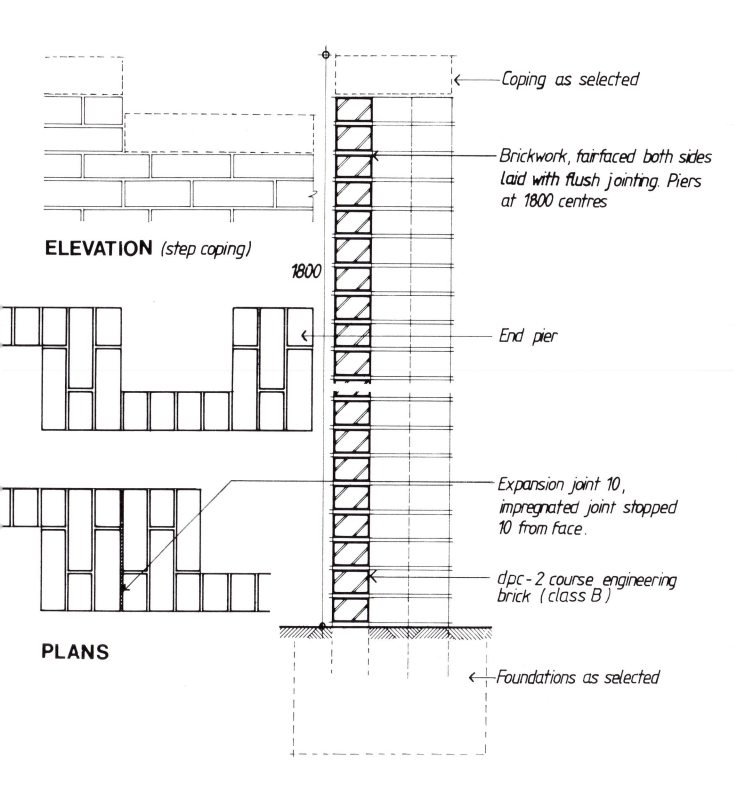

ELEVATION *(step coping)*

PLANS

1800

SECTION

Coping as selected

Brickwork, fairfaced both sides laid with flush jointing. Piers at 1800 centres

End pier

Expansion joint 10, impregnated joint stopped 10 from face.

dpc - 2 course engineering brick (class B)

Foundations as selected

Scale 1:10

WALL
brick (high)

29

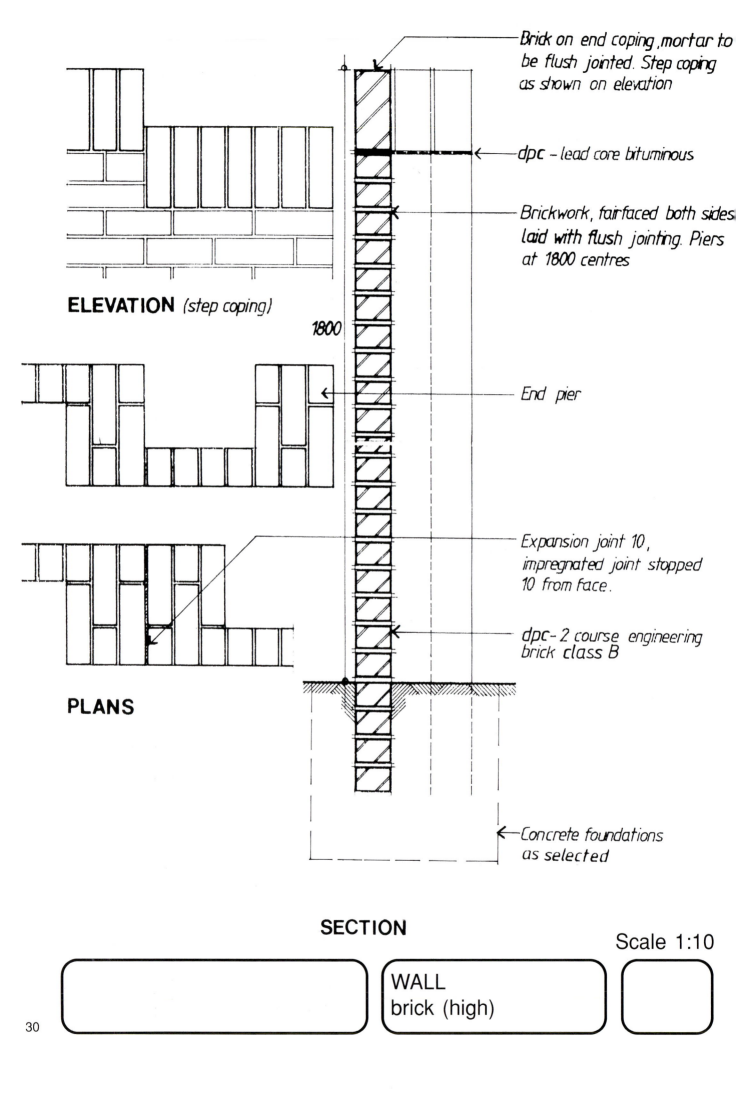

ELEVATION (step coping)

PLANS

Brick on end coping, mortar to be flush jointed. Step coping as shown on elevation

dpc – lead core bituminous

Brickwork, fairfaced both sides laid with flush jointing. Piers at 1800 centres

1800

End pier

Expansion joint 10, impregnated joint stopped 10 from face.

dpc- 2 course engineering brick class B

Concrete foundations as selected

SECTION

Scale 1:10

WALL
brick (high)

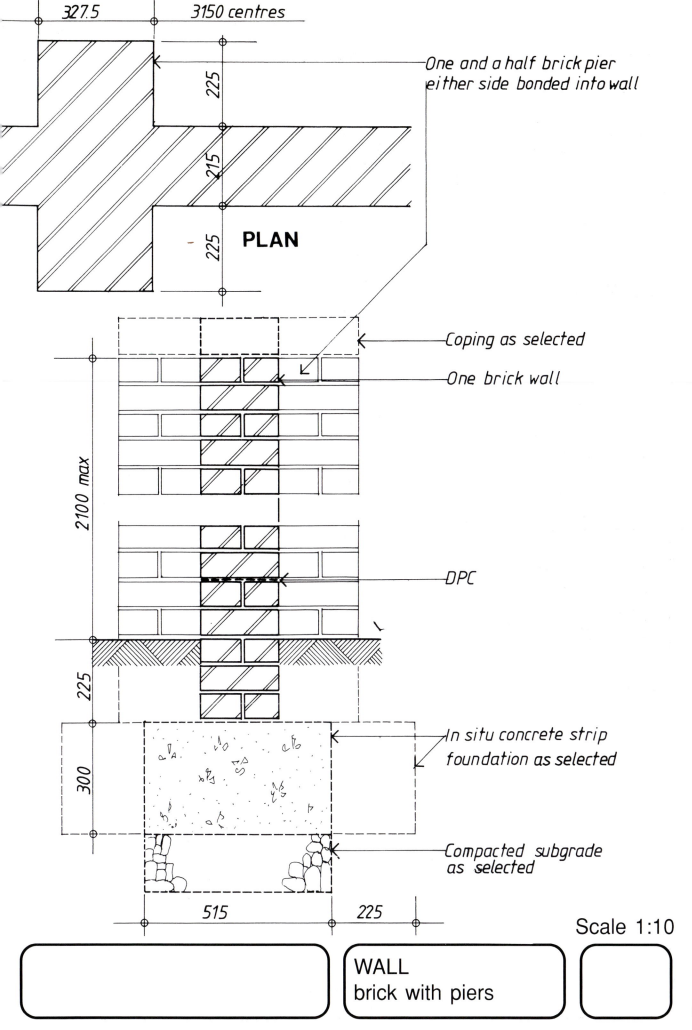

327.5

3150 centres

225

215

225

PLAN

One and a half brick pier either side bonded into wall

Coping as selected

One brick wall

2100 max

DPC

225

300

In situ concrete strip foundation as selected

Compacted subgrade as selected

515

225

Scale 1:10

WALL
brick with piers

31

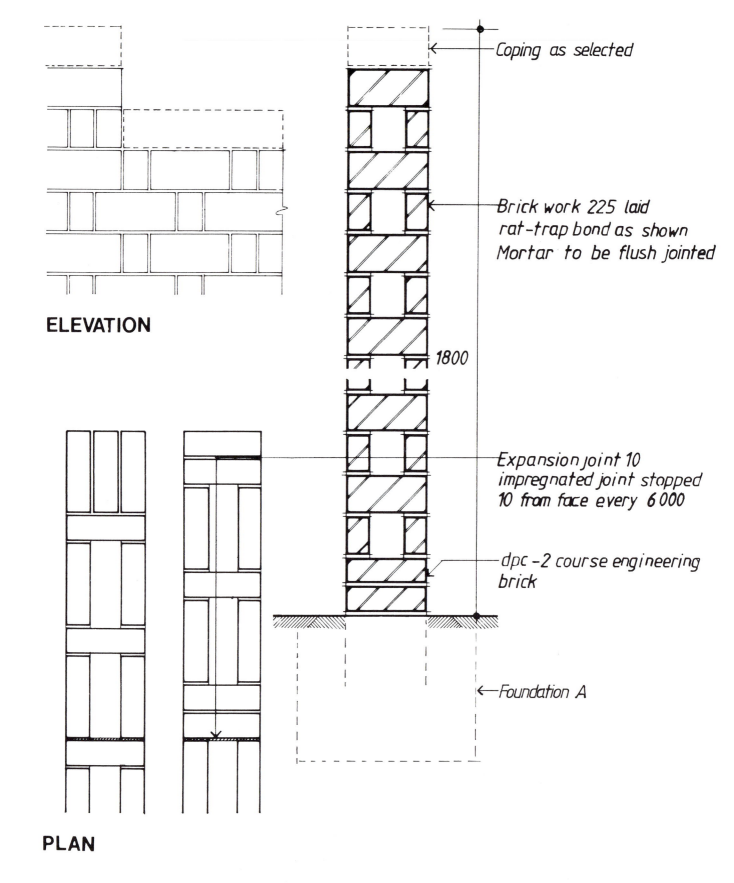

ELEVATION

PLAN

SECTION

Coping as selected

Brick work 225 laid
rat-trap bond as shown
Mortar to be flush jointed

1800

Expansion joint 10
impregnated joint stopped
10 from face every 6 000

dpc -2 course engineering
brick

Foundation A

Scale 1:10

WALL
brick rat trap bond

32

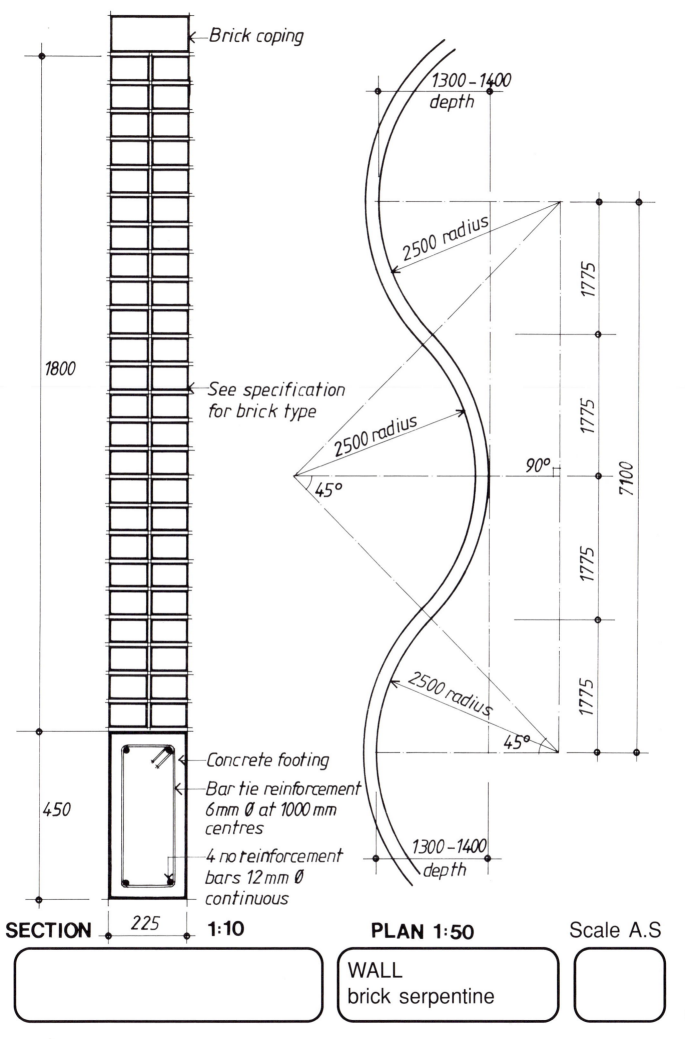

← Brick coping

1300-1400 depth

2500 radius

1800

See specification for brick type

2500 radius

45°

90°

1775

1775

1775

1775

7100

450

Concrete footing

Bar tie reinforcement 6mm Ø at 1000 mm centres

4 no reinforcement bars 12 mm Ø continuous

2500 radius

45°

1300-1400 depth

SECTION 225 **1:10**

PLAN 1:50

Scale A.S

WALL
brick serpentine

33

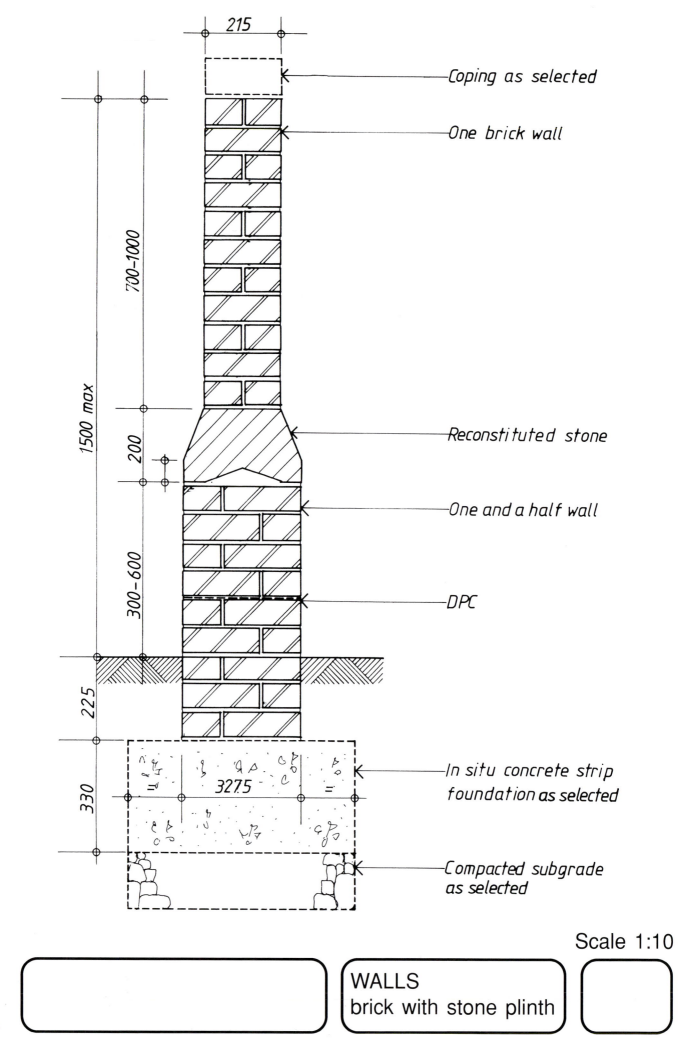

215

Coping as selected

One brick wall

700-1000

1500 max

200

Reconstituted stone

One and a half wall

300-600

DPC

225

330

327.5

In situ concrete strip foundation as selected

Compacted subgrade as selected

Scale 1:10

WALLS
brick with stone plinth

34

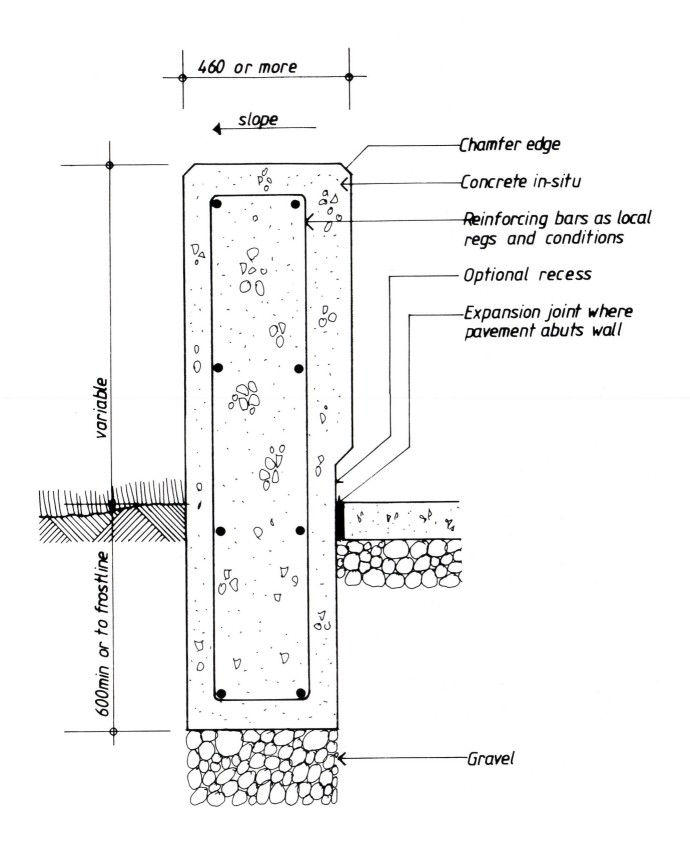

460 or more

slope

Chamfer edge

Concrete in-situ

Reinforcing bars as local
regs and conditions

Optional recess

Expansion joint where
pavement abuts wall

variable

600min or to frostline

Gravel

Scale 1:10

WALLS
contrete

35

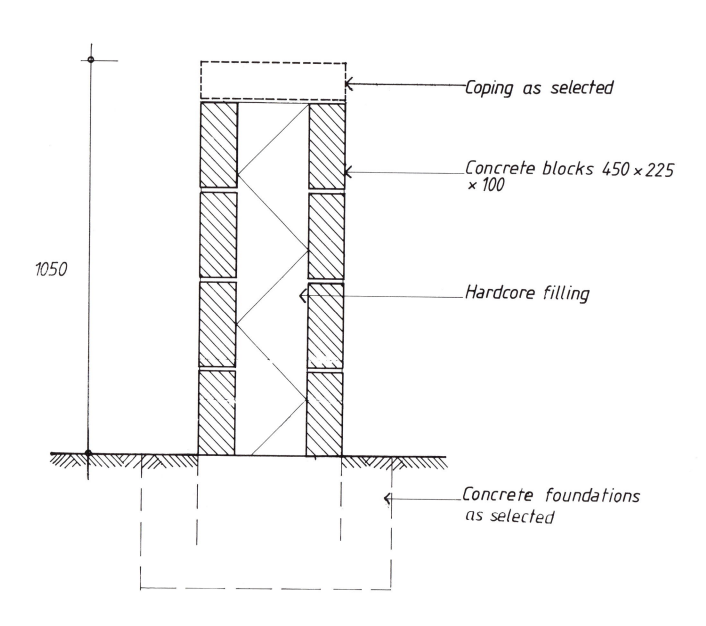

500

1050

Coping as selected

Concrete blocks 450 × 225 × 100

Hardcore filling

Concrete foundations as selected

Scale 1:10

WALL
concrete block (low)

36

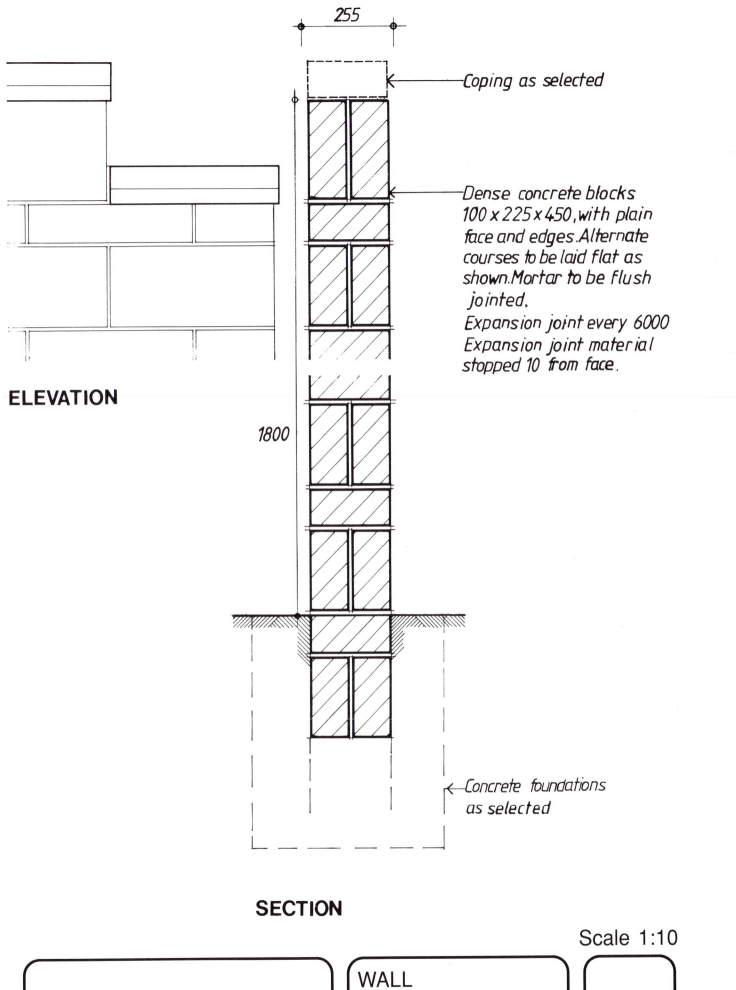

255

Coping as selected

ELEVATION

Dense concrete blocks
100 x 225 x 450, with plain
face and edges. Alternate
courses to be laid flat as
shown. Mortar to be flush
jointed.
Expansion joint every 6000
Expansion joint material
stopped 10 from face.

1800

Concrete foundations
as selected

SECTION

Scale 1:10

WALL
concrete block (high)

37

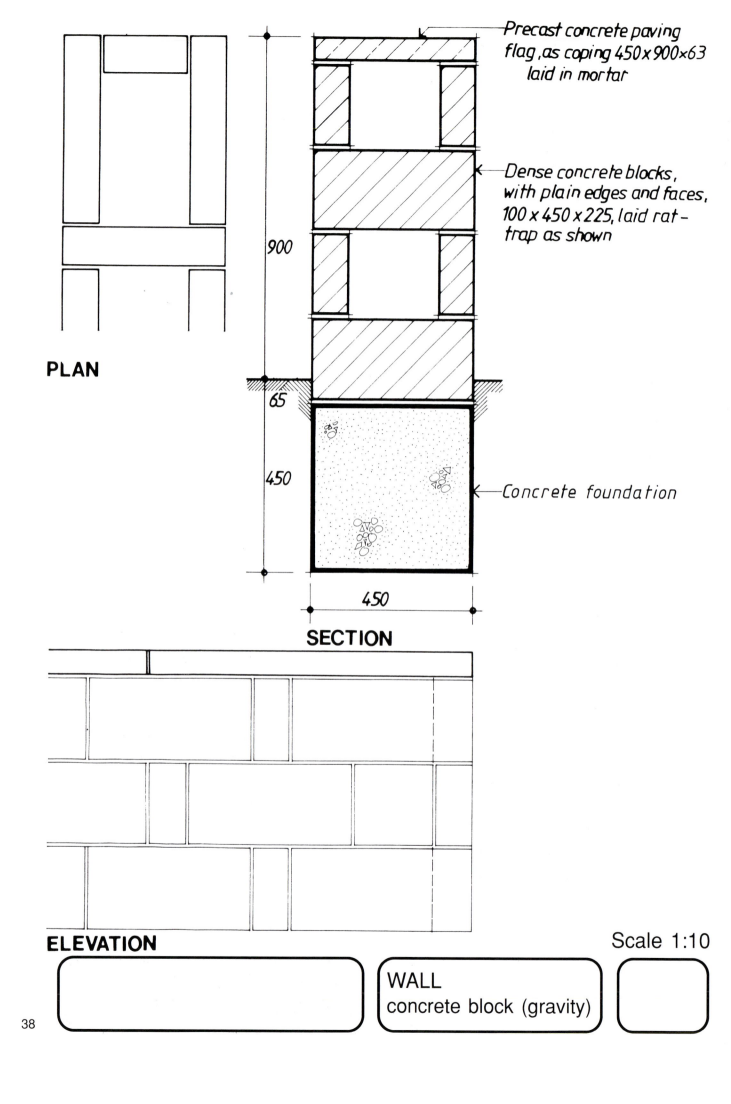

PLAN

Precast concrete paving
flag, as coping 450 x 900 x 63
laid in mortar

Dense concrete blocks,
with plain edges and faces,
100 x 450 x 225, laid rat-
trap as shown

900

65

450

Concrete foundation

450

SECTION

ELEVATION

Scale 1:10

WALL
concrete block (gravity)

38

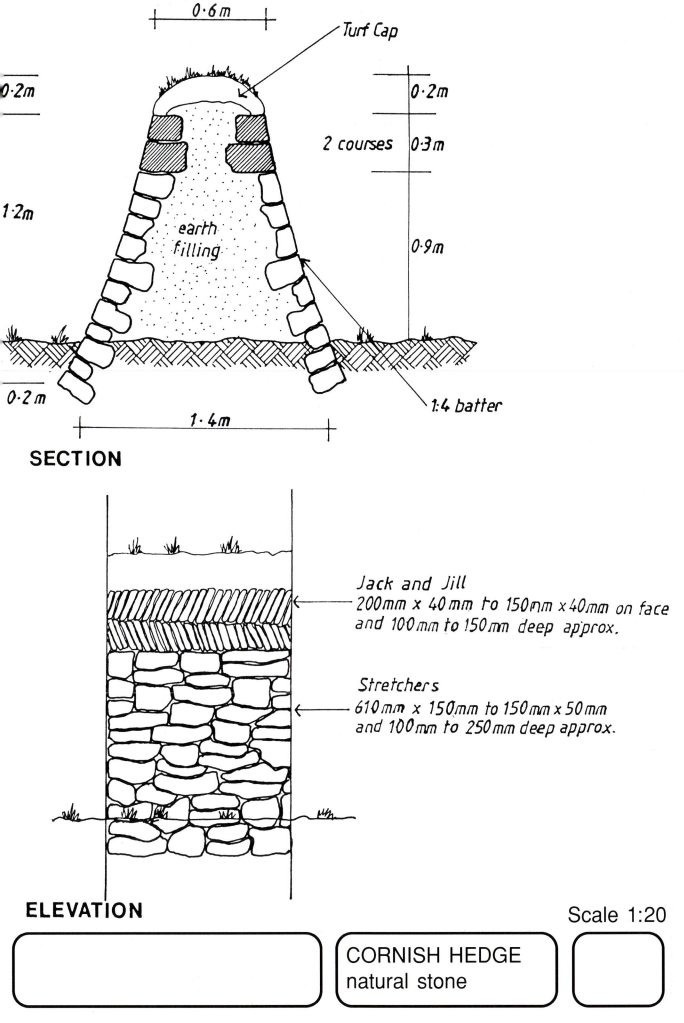

0·6 m

Turf Cap

0·2m

0·2m

2 courses   0·3m

earth filling

1·2m

0·9m

0·2 m

1·4m

1:4 batter

SECTION

Jack and Jill
200mm x 40mm to 150mm x 40mm on face
and 100mm to 150mm deep approx.

Stretchers
610mm x 150mm to 150mm x 50mm
and 100mm to 250mm deep approx.

ELEVATION

Scale 1:20

CORNISH HEDGE
natural stone

39

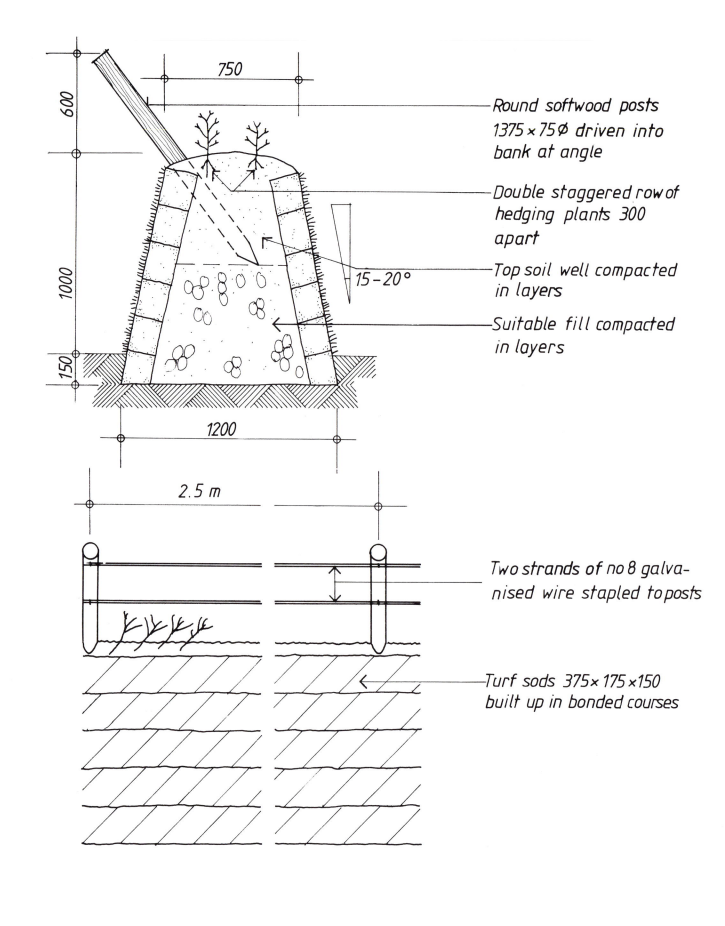

750

600

Round softwood posts
1375 × 75∅ driven into
bank at angle

Double staggered row of
hedging plants 300
apart

1000

15 – 20°

Top soil well compacted
in layers

Suitable fill compacted
in layers

150

1200

2.5 m

Two strands of no 8 galvanised wire stapled to posts

Turf sods 375 × 175 × 150
built up in bonded courses

Scale 1:20

WALLS
hedge bank + fence

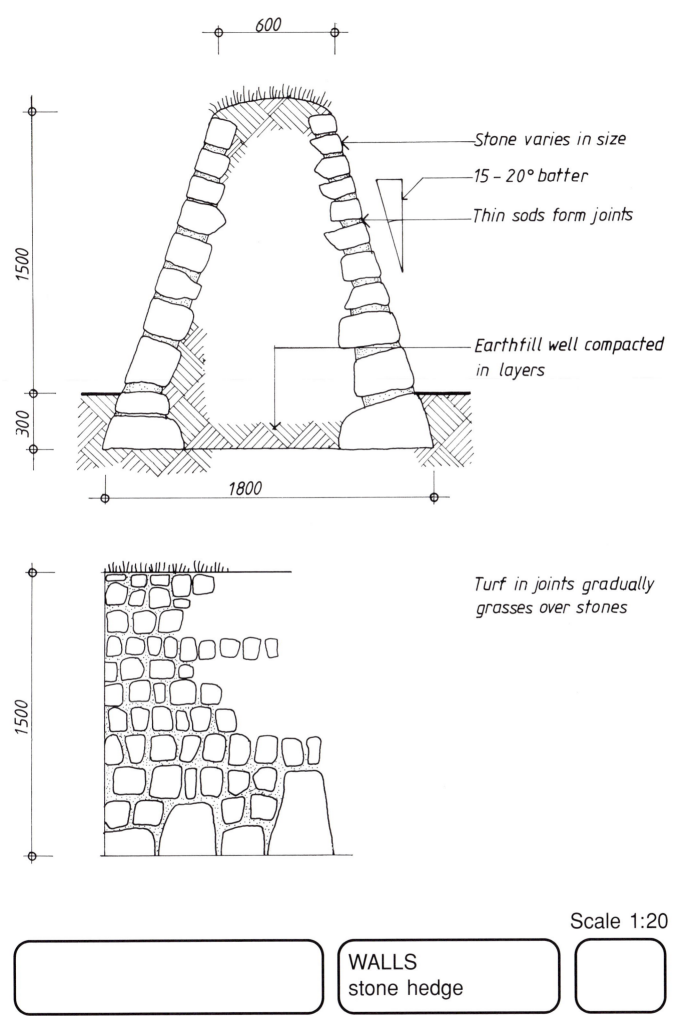

600

1500

300

1800

Stone varies in size

15 – 20° batter

Thin sods form joints

Earthfill well compacted
in layers

Turf in joints gradually
grasses over stones

1500

Scale 1:20

WALLS
stone hedge

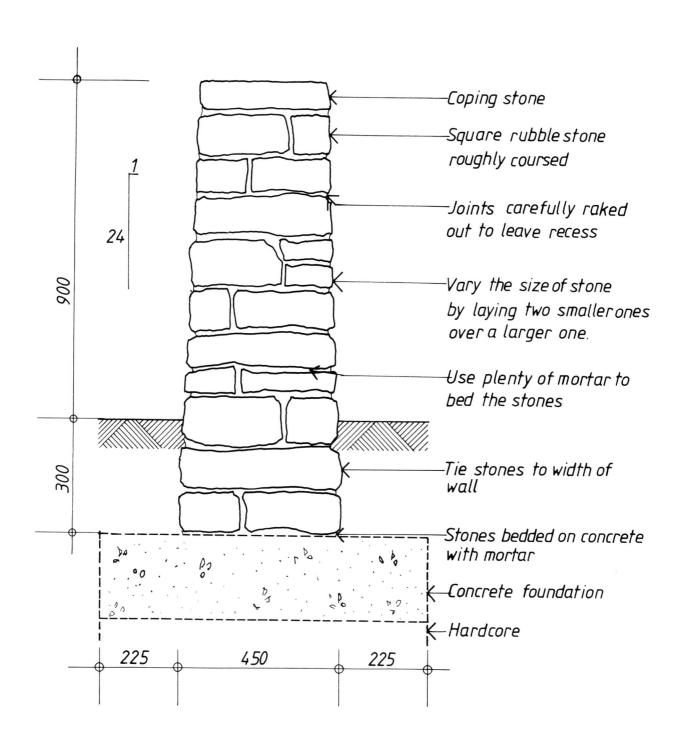

Coping stone

Square rubble stone
roughly coursed

Joints carefully raked
out to leave recess

Vary the size of stone
by laying two smaller ones
over a larger one.

Use plenty of mortar to
bed the stones

Tie stones to width of
wall

Stones bedded on concrete
with mortar

Concrete foundation

Hardcore

1

24

900

300

225   450   225

Scale 1:10

WALL
natural stone
mortared/coursed

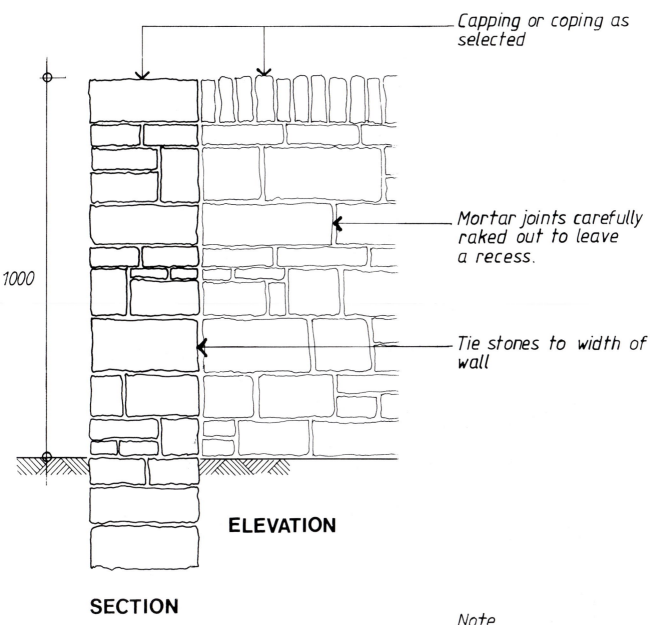

Capping or coping as
selected

Mortar joints carefully
raked out to leave
a recess.

Tie stones to width of
wall

1000

ELEVATION

SECTION

<u>Note</u>

Units are precast
and dressed before
delivery to site

Scale 1:10

WALL
ashlar mortared/
coursed

43

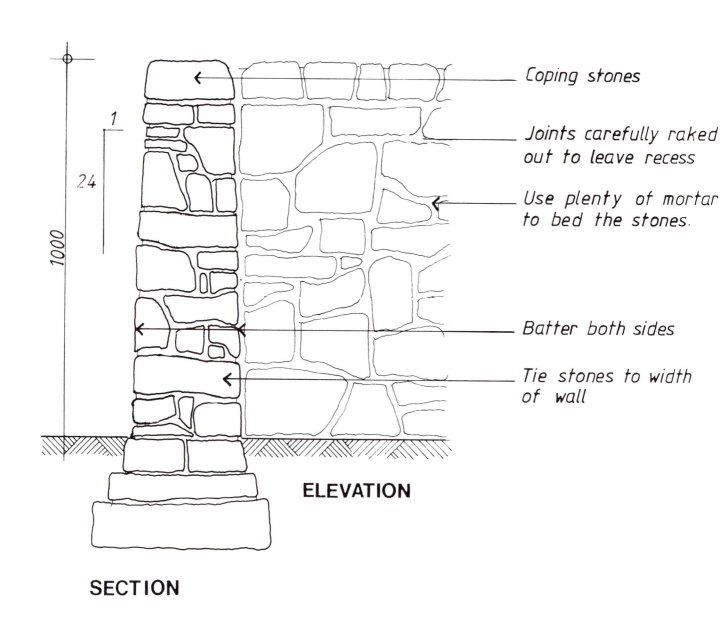

1

24

1000

SECTION

ELEVATION

Coping stones

Joints carefully raked
out to leave recess

Use plenty of mortar
to bed the stones.

Batter both sides

Tie stones to width
of wall

Scale 1:10

WALL
natural stone
mortared/uncoursed

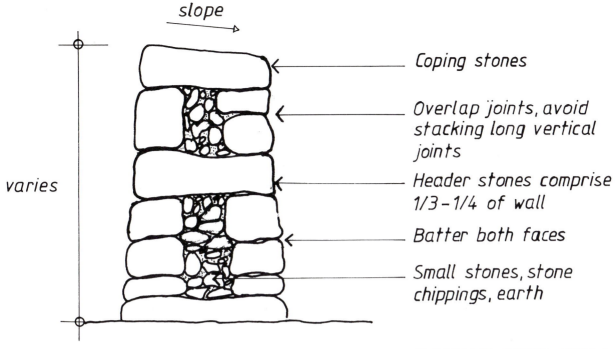

slope →

Coping stones

Overlap joints, avoid stacking long vertical joints

Header stones comprise 1/3 – 1/4 of wall

Batter both faces

Small stones, stone chippings, earth

varies

DOUBLE TIER WALL

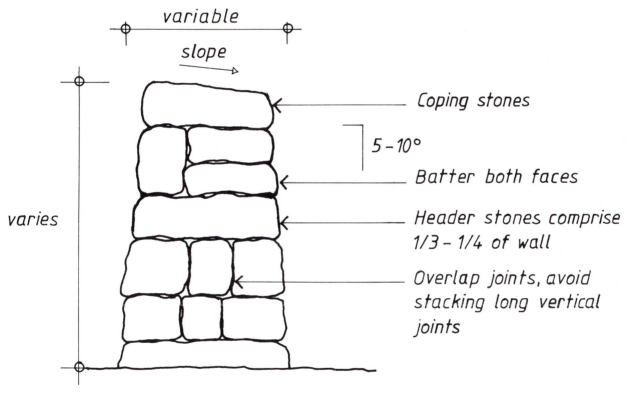

variable

slope →

Coping stones

5 – 10°

Batter both faces

Header stones comprise 1/3 – 1/4 of wall

Overlap joints, avoid stacking long vertical joints

varies

SINGLE TIER WALL

Scale 1:10

	WALL natural stone, dry	

45

SCREEN WALLS

GUIDANCE NOTES

Appearance

Scale, texture and pattern should decide the type of open screen unit required. Since any large area would become boring, an open screen is usually more successful when used sparingly as a decorative element in a solid wall or in short lengths. These walls look their best when there is strong contrast of light and shade and especially when used with large foliage plants.

This type of walling is quite easy to erect and reinforcement is not usually necessary. Concrete blocks are available in several standard designs, but in general they are approximately 300 mm square, and 90 mm thick. Colour and finish vary according to the manufacturer. Alternatively, a screen wall can be achieved using bricks and perforated bricks.

Foundations

Screen blocks can be mortared directly onto the concrete foundations of 1:6 mix. They should be 200 mm wider than the wall (100 mm each side) and at least 200 mm deep, depending upon the wall height and ground conditions. Soft ground may necessitate thicker foundations. Alternatively, lay two courses of ordinary concrete blocks on a hardcore bed, with a flat coping stone on top.

Mortar

This should be workable, but not sloppy. Protective measures should be taken to prevent spillage onto the block faces. A 1:5 mortar mix should be used.

Joints

These should be 9 mm throughout.

Piers

Pilaster or pier blocks are needed at each end of a free-standing wall and at 300 mm centres, depending upon the height of the wall. Walls above four courses high should be reinforced with rods set into the foundations. The cavity must then be filled with mortar and capped with a special capping block.

Coping

A special coping block should be placed on top of the screen blocks to provide a suitable finish.

Design notes

Infinite combinations of texture, pattern and perforation make brick modules a unique and challenging design material for screen walls, adding visual interest. They improve microclimatic conditions as they allow breezes into a garden and discourage wind turbulence and frost pockets, which often occur on the leeward side of solid walls. Before designing a perforation or texture it is useful to review the available sizes and possible placement of bricks within a wall. Brick bonds are used primarily to strengthen the wall and tie the bricks together; they also create various patterns which provide the system for designing perforations. The simplest way to pierce a wall is to leave out one or more of the brick units in a standard bonding pattern, using loose bricks as temporary spacers. There are few materials which offer brick's colour, pattern and texture possibilities. From pattern-to-pattern placement, the variations in brick garden walls are limited only by the designer's imagination. Additional variety can be achieved by breaking from ordinary coursing and/or orientations. These variations can also be constructed much more efficiently if the voids conform to a brick module. In such cases, temporary brick fillers can be used to support the courses above, and brick cutting can be minimised.

Construction types

Because free-standing brick walls are vertical structures subject to wind loads, the resistance to wind loads is the primary design consideration. The wall height-to-thickness ratio is usually the major factor affecting lateral stability, but wall shape and/or reinforcement can make thinner walls acceptable.

Structural analysis for the specific design and wind conditions is necessary to

determine the safest and most economical thickness. But, as a rule, solid brick walls under 2.0 m high are 100 mm (one wythe, or tier of brick units), 200 (two wythe), or 300 mm (three wythe) thick. See extract from BS 5628 Part 3 attached.
They are built in one of five ways:

1. Straight with continuous footings.
2. Straight with continuous footings and pier supports.
3. Reinforced 'thin fences' with footing support only at piers.
4. Staggered.
5. Serpentine or chevron-shaped.

When designing perforated walls it is assumed that the reduction in brick weight is offset by the reduction in wind load. Consequently, the same methods used to calculate thickness for solid, free-standing walls are acceptable. All five types can be designed with perforations as long as the dimensions and reinforcing normally required are still accommodated. The required wall thickness can also influence the choice of an economical and effective perforation pattern.
Because straight walls on a continuous footing rely only on the height-to-width ratio for lateral stability, they must be thicker than the other four types.
Straight walls buttressed by piers and supported on footings are often 100 mm thick with 300 mm or 400 mm square piers. The minimum required frequency of supports is determined by wind loads, and the reduced thickness of the wall usually results in lower costs.
'Thin fence' construction is seldom used. Foundations occur only at pilasters, or piers, which support 100 mm thick, steel-reinforced brick panels. No. 2 and larger steel bars are used, their exact size and frequency determined by wind load and distance between piers. Reinforcing requirements could be difficult to meet on a wall with a continuous perforation pattern. However, perforations within a limited area – particularly at the top – usually pose no problem.
Staggered walls less than 2.0 m high can be built only 100 mm thick if they are offset

200 mm every 1800 mm. A wall higher than 2.0 m can also be only 100 mm thick, but it requires more than 300 mm offset. The shape of serpentine and chevron walls provides additional lateral resistance to wind loads; a 100 mm thick wall is often sufficiently strong. However, the geometry of the wall should be analysed to ensure that it provides the required lateral stability.

Water resistance

Often bricks are used to cap a wall rather than a solid stone or cast top. Flashing the horizontal joint below prevents water from penetrating and freezing the mortar. Some perforation patterns can leave vertical joints similarly vulnerable, and these should be avoided when possible. If a large void has vertical joints open to the weather, it is wise to flash the horizontal joint below. Joints should be completely filled to resist water penetration; weathered, concave, and flush joints are acceptable.

Mortars and joints

The use of Designations 1 and 2 mortars (1–3 and 1–4(1/2)) will greatly increase wall strength and durability – particularly at ground level (if no damp proof course is possible) and at coping and capping levels. A movement joint may be necessary at the normal centres (max. 6 cm and max. 3 cm from a corner). This will interrupt the bond and stability and would be best placed where a stiffener or pier occurs.
FL quality bricks should always be used for cappings and copings and preferably where they are in the ground or below a damp proof course.

SPECIFICATION CHECK LIST

See previous chapter.

DETAIL SHEETS

Concrete block screen (3)
Perforated screen (2)

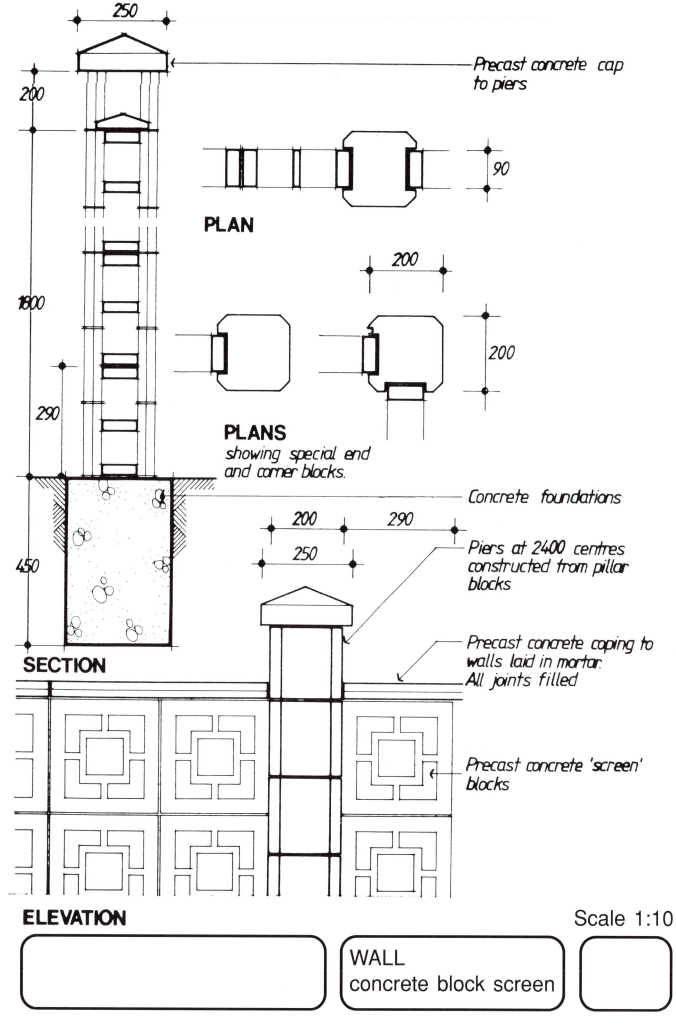

250

Precast concrete cap
to piers

200

PLAN

90

1800

200

200

290

PLANS
showing special end
and corner blocks.

Concrete foundations

200   290

250

Piers at 2400 centres
constructed from pillar
blocks

450

SECTION

Precast concrete coping to
walls laid in mortar.
All joints filled

Precast concrete 'screen'
blocks

ELEVATION

Scale 1:10

WALL
concrete block screen

48

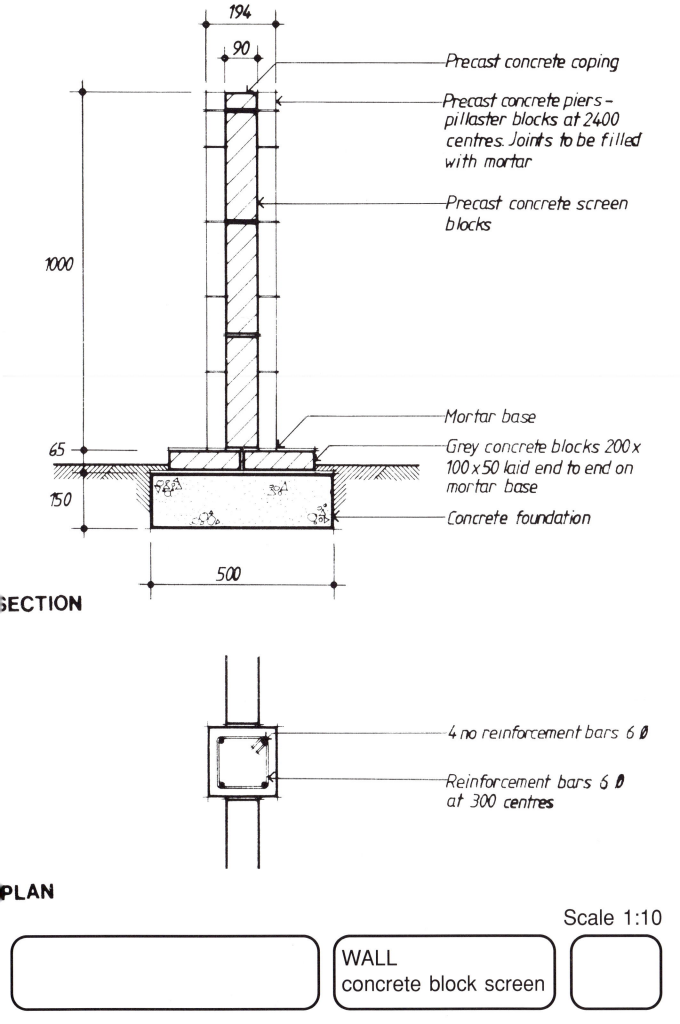

194

90

Precast concrete coping

Precast concrete piers - pillaster blocks at 2400 centres. Joints to be filled with mortar

Precast concrete screen blocks

1000

Mortar base

Grey concrete blocks 200 x 100 x 50 laid end to end on mortar base

65

150

Concrete foundation

500

SECTION

4 no reinforcement bars 6 Ø

Reinforcement bars 6 Ø at 300 centres

PLAN

Scale 1:10

	WALL concrete block screen	

49

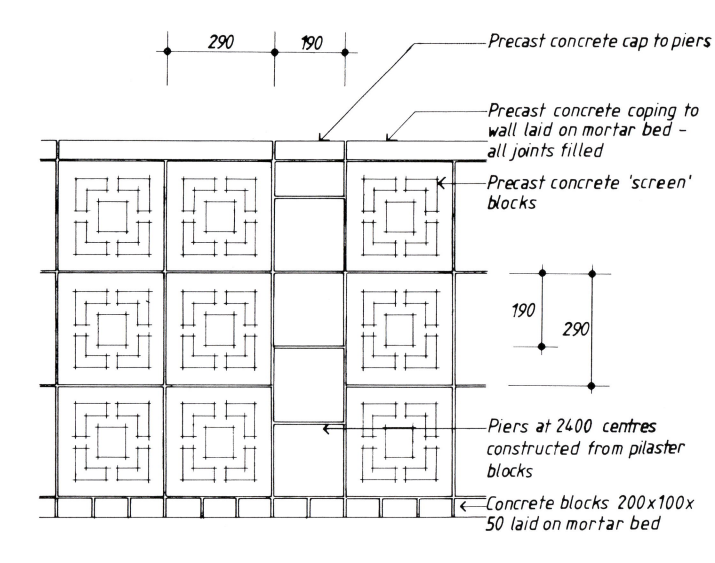

290 | 190

Precast concrete cap to piers

Precast concrete coping to
wall laid on mortar bed –
all joints filled

Precast concrete 'screen'
blocks

190 | 290

Piers at 2400 centres
constructed from pilaster
blocks

Concrete blocks 200 x 100 x
50 laid on mortar bed

ELEVATION

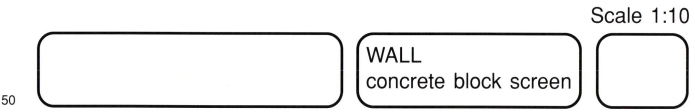

WALL
concrete block screen

Scale 1:10

50

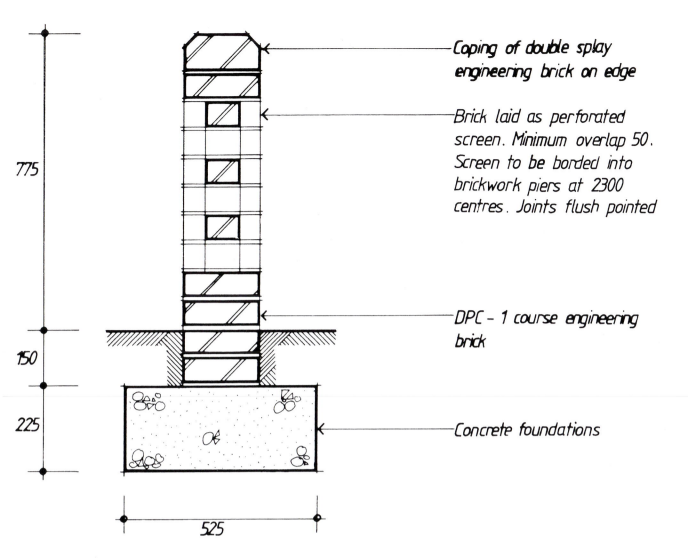

775

150

225

525

Coping of double splay engineering brick on edge

Brick laid as perforated screen. Minimum overlap 50. Screen to be bonded into brickwork piers at 2300 centres. Joints flush pointed

DPC - 1 course engineering brick

Concrete foundations

SECTION

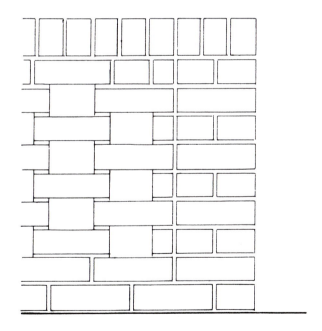

ELEVATION

Scale 1:10

WALL
perforated screen

51

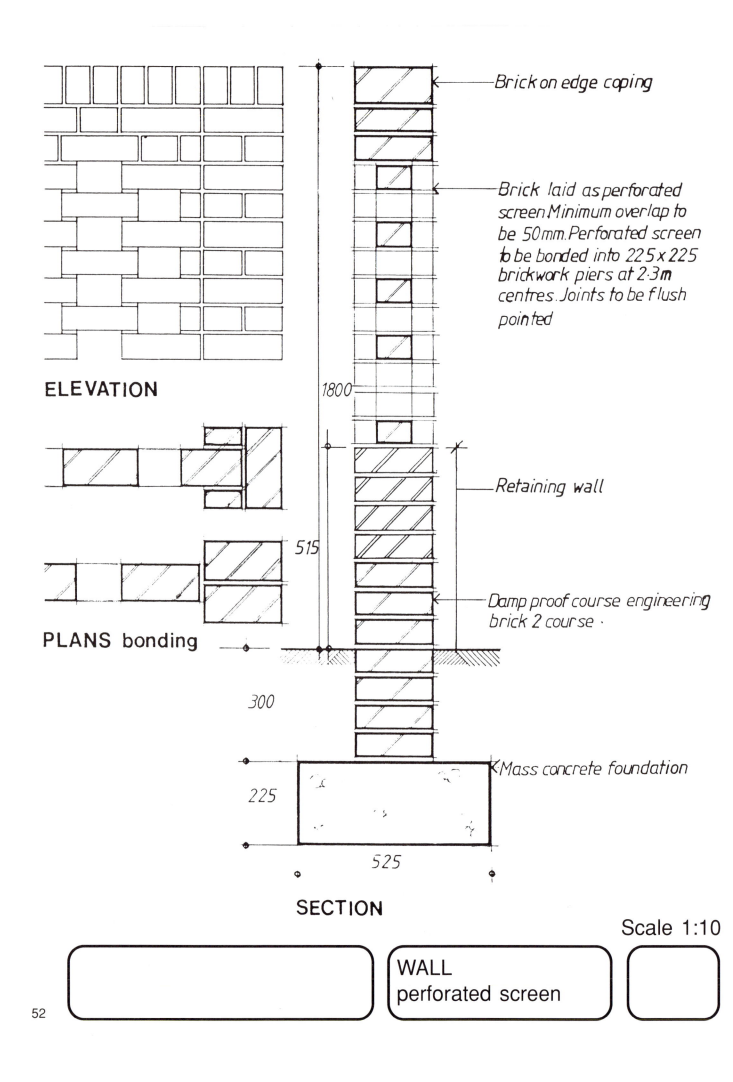

ELEVATION

PLANS bonding

Brick on edge coping

Brick laid as perforated screen. Minimum overlap to be 50mm. Perforated screen to be bonded into 225 x 225 brickwork piers at 2·3m centres. Joints to be flush pointed

Retaining wall

Damp proof course engineering brick 2 course ·

Mass concrete foundation

1800

515

300

225

525

SECTION

Scale 1:10

WALL
perforated screen

52

RETAINING WALLS

GUIDANCE NOTES

Design procedure

Soils cannot stand more steeply than their natural angle of repose, so that it is often necessary to construct a retaining wall. After an analysis of subgrade conditions and soil profile has been done, the normal design process is:

- Estimate the forces exerted by the material to be restrained on the back of the wall.
- Determine profile of retaining wall and base so that the structure will be stable and not fail by overturning or sliding.
- Analyse the wall itself in terms of structural stability.
- Check the bearing pressure under the base.
- Design structural elements.
- Decide drainage method in backfill.
- Allow for movement and settlement.
- Decide on finishes to wall. (The service of a structural consultant will be required on all walls over 1000 mm high.)

Basic categories of retaining structures

Retaining structures basically fall into two general categories: flexible and rigid construction.

Flexible construction

Flexible construction includes dry stone walls, crib walls, gabion walls and other types of walls that are not rigid structures. The base, or footing, for a flexible wall need not go below the frost line if the depth has a suitable bearing, i.e. undisturbed ground or a compacted sub-base. Typically, a setting bed of sand or compacted granular material is used to improve drainage and provide a level surface. The advantage of flexible construction is that it will tolerate a certain amount of differential settlement without being affected significantly.

Rigid construction

Rigid construction is used where any movement of the structure cannot be tolerated or when aesthetic considerations require it, such as in association with buildings or in formal landscape designs. Typically, rigid construction implies the use of concrete and masonry in a gravity wall or reinforced cantilevered wall type of construction.

Types of retaining walls

Three major types of structural solutions are gravity walls, cantilevered walls and crib walls. Each one has several variations that may be considered, depending upon the criteria used for selection.

Gravity walls

Gravity walls depend upon their mass (i.e. weight and volume) for stability. Regardless of their size, the ratio of the base width to height is approximately constant, varying from about 0.40 to 0.45 for a horizontally loaded wall. Gravity walls are constructed of concrete, stone masonry, or concrete faced with stone or brick. Gravity walls less than 1.5 m high are usually built vertically at the front and back or with a slight batter. In such cases, the base width should be at least 0.4 m

Gravity walls built of stone laid without mortar, called dry stone walls, are useful in many situations where the retained heights are low (less than 3 m), the stone is easily available and is suitable for the local landscape character.

Concrete block walls

Block walls are of three main varieties:

1. *Plain blocks*, which have a comparatively smooth grey concrete surface.

2. *Profiled blocks*, in which the block is cast in a mould to give it an irregular surface, to either a geometric or a natural pattern. Their advantage over plain blocks is that marking from atmospheric pollution is less visible.
3. *Exposed aggregate blocks* composed of aggregates chosen for their colour and texture which are exposed by removing the cement skin – their advantage over the two previous types is that the greater part of the surface is of a natural material.

Cantilevered walls

Reinforced concrete
A cantilevered wall consists of a base and a stem, which are securely tied together by reinforcing rods extending from the base up through the stem. Reinforcing rods running laterally through the stem provide longitudinal reinforcement in the wall. The weight of the backfill on the base counteracts the forward pressure of the retained height and helps to keep the wall from overturning and sliding. This only applies when the back of the wall can be constructed under the retained material. In most instances this type of wall can be replaced by an embankment.
Reinforced concrete cantilevered construction is particularly useful for long lengths of wall where standard metal forms can be re-used with great economy in construction. Liners can be used to achieve a variety of finishes and join patterns in the face of the wall. A veneer of brick or stone can be applied to the wall by using standard metal fasteners.

Reinforced masonry and concrete
A two-brick retaining wall is especially suitable for low-wall construction. It has the finished appearance of brick but the structural stability of a cantilevered wall. It can be laid up without any formwork, using only brick and grout.
The vertical reinforcement bars must be placed within about 10 mm of the brick on the tension side (i.e. the retained earth side) so that the bars will be bonded to the grout and must extend the full height of the wall. The bricks should be laid with no headers projecting into the grout and in successive tiers of about 200 mm. The space should then be filled each time with grout, followed by puddling with a grout stick. All joints behind the wall should be fully grouted. Solid concrete units or stone units may also be used besides brick.

Reinforced concrete block
A concrete block retaining wall using a cantilever and grout design can be laid up without any framework. The vertical reinforcement bars must be placed within about 10 mm of the inside face of the blocks on the tension side (i.e. the retained earth side) so that the bars will be bonded to the grout. The cells are filled with grout, which should be thoroughly puddled during pouring.

Crib walls

Concrete
A concrete crib wall is constructed of precast reinforced concrete units laid up in interlocking stretchers and headers to form vertical bins which are filled with crushed stone or other granular material. They are a particularly utilitarian solution for retaining fills in situations where excavation is not necessary. Reinforced projecting lugs on the headers are typically used to lock the headers and stretchers together.
Backfilling should follow closely the erection of units, and the cribbing should not be laid up higher than 1 m above the backfilled portion.

Timber
Crib walls may be built of timber when the appearance of wood is desired in the design. All timber units should be pressure-treated with a suitable preservative. New or used railway sleeper ties were commonly used in early crib wall construction and continue to be used for low walls. However, timber units cut to size and pressure-treated with copper salts or other non-bleeding preservatives are now widely available.

Other wall types

Timber
Since the timber wall's resistance to overturning depends upon one-half of its height being below finished grade, it is often not economical or practical to use this timber design for retained heights greater than 1.5 m. The timber units in the horizontal wall can be of variable length but should be at least 1.5 m long. Low timber walls are especially useful for raised planting beds and boxes.

The retained height should never be greater than eight to ten times the thickness of the timbers and at least 50 per cent of their overall length should be buried below the lower ground level in average soil; for poor soil 70 per cent and very soft soil amost 100 per cent. For example, 150 mm thick timber retaining wall could comfortably retain a 1200 mm high vertical bank provided that the timbers had an overall length of at least 2000 mm.

Gabions
Gabions are rectangular baskets in standard sizes made of galvanised steel wire or polyvinyl-coated (PVC) wire hexagonal mesh which are filled with stone and tied together to form a wall. Each gabion has a lid and is sub-divided into 1 m cells. After being filled with stone, the lid is closed and laced to the top edges of the gabion. Each gabion is then laced to the adjacent gabions.

Gabion walls, being flexible, can adapt to ground settlement. Their permeability allows water to drain through, making gabions especially suitable along stream and river banks where variations in water depths occur between flood and dry weather conditions. Volunteer vegetation establishes itself quickly in gabions, softening the structure's appearance in the landscape while also adding durability.

Materials

Retaining walls can be constructed of a wide choice of materials, such as brick, block, concrete, stone or timber. Combinations of these materials are used in some instances, but in the interests of simplicity these have not been included.

Brick

Choice of bricks
Retaining walls can be constructed of ordinary clay bricks (BS 3921: 1974). If there is any likelihood of the brickwork becoming frozen after being saturated by high rainfall, frost-resistant clay bricks (special quality) should be used. Where ordinary clay bricks are proposed, the manufacturer's advice should be sought.

Copings/cappings
The comments in the chapter on free-standing walls apply equally to brick retaining walls. The coping selected should be effective in throwing the water clear of the exposed surfaces of the wall.

Mortars
Sulphate-resisting cement in a mortar of 1:(1/4):3 (cement:lime:sand) should be used up to and including the ground damp proof course, and above if the retaining face is not effectively waterproofed where aggressive sulphate ground conditions are found. When clay bricks of ordinary quality are used in high-rainfall areas, mortar with sulphate-resisting cement should be used for the whole wall. It is advisable to use the same mortar for brickwork below the damp proof course.

Expansion joints
Retaining walls are less susceptible to horizontal movement than free-standing walls, and although CP 121 suggests that vertical joints be provided at 12 m centres in long runs of clay brickwork walling, and at 7.5–9.0 m centres in calcium brickwork, these could be extended to 15 m and 12 m, respectively. A water bar included in the joint will prevent staining of the face. When brick on edge cappings are used, expansion or movement joints should be provided at about half the normal spacing.

Precast concrete
Concrete blocks used for the construction of retaining walls are normally reinforced and laid on foundations as for bricks.

Foundations

To simplify the shuttering of the wall, the bottom 75 mm should be constructed with the foundations. Reinforcement using starter rods should be placed in the foundations and run up into the wall. A damp proof course will not be necessary.

Expansion joints

A 12 mm open joint should be provided at 5.0 mm intervals in unreinforced walls and at 10 m intervals in reinforced walls. Except in battered walls, joints should form an integral pattern in unreinforced walls to avoid cracks caused by shrinkage. Joints should be filled with approved material and pointed with non-hardening polysulphide sealant.

Natural stone

This makes a good solid retaining wall, especially when a batter is used. Construction is similar to that described in the chapter on free-standing walls. The type of stone available and the local style should determine the overall appearance. Alternatively, stone can be used to face a concrete block wall or an *in-situ* concrete wall. It is most important to ensure that soil is level with the top of the wall, not only to allow vegetation to grow over and down but also to provide a better appearance. Copings should be selected to conform to the local character and style.

Timber

Retaining walls of timber should be built of hardwood or naturally resistant wood (redwood or cedar). All timbers should still be treated with fungicidal and insect-repellent preservatives. Softwood when used must be pressure-impregnated with preservative by a vacuum process. Consideration should be given to the shrinkage of timbers, especially where joints are used.
For horizontal timbers, vertical supports tied back into the bank with metal rods set into concrete should be used. All exposed timbers should be stained with a proprietary coloured stain.

All edges of timber should be chamfered and end grains protected by cappings which should slope 10–20° to shed water. Fixings must be of galvanised mild steel or stainless steel.

Concrete

In-situ concrete

All reinforced concrete should be grade C30 with 20 mm maximum aggregate size and the back face of the wall should be lined with a bituminous damp-proof membrane. All reinforcement overlaps should be a nominal 40 diameter and the minimum concrete cover should be 40 mm. The bearing capacity of the soil must also be taken into account. As a general guide, in a wall approximately 1,700–2,000 mm high the thickness of a reinforced wall will not be less than 150 mm and mass concrete 300 mm.
If above 1.0 m in height, *in-situ* reinforced concrete retaining walls should generally be designed by a structural engineer. *In-situ* mass concrete walls without reinforcement are double the thickness of reinforced walls. Only in exceptional circumstances will it pay not to use reinforcement, but there are occasions when a heavy structure is required.

Drainage

To prevent the build-up of water pressure behind a retaining wall, a hydraulic drain should be provided near the base on the retaining side. The size will depend on ground conditions, but an average of 100–150 mm diameter is generally used. The drain must be surrounded by granular sulphate-free material, extending to the surface where possible. Weep-holes should discharge at least 150 mm above ground level and at intermediate levels if necessary. Care should be taken to ensure that the drainage is not allowed to become blocked through build-up of silt.

Reinforcement

In grouted cavity retaining walls reinforcement will vary according to the size of the wall.

TABLE 4: SOIL TYPES AND THEIR PROPERTIES

Division	Soil description	Value as a foundation material*	Frost action	Drainage
Gravel and gravelly soils	Well-graded gravel, or gravel–sand mixture, little or no fines	Excellent	None	Excellent
	Poorly graded gravel, or gravel–sand mixtures, little or no fines	Good	None	Excellent
	Silty gravel, gravel–sand–silt mixtures	Good	Slight	Poor
	Clayey gravels, gravel–clay–sand mixtures	Good	Slight	Poor
Sand and sandy soils	Well-graded sands, or gravelly sands, little or no fines	Good	None	Excellent
	Poorly graded sands, or gravelly sands, little or no fines	Fair	None	Excellent
	Silty sands, sand–silt mixtures	Fair	Slight	Fair
	Clayey sands, sand–clay mixtures	Fair	Medium	Poor
Silts and clays LL <50†	Inorganic silts, rock flour, silty or clayey fine sands, or clayey silts with slight plasticity	Fair	Very high	Poor
	Inorganic clays of low to medium plasticity, gravelly clays, silty clays, lean clays	Fair	Medium	Impervious
	Organic silt–clays of low plasticity	Poor	High	Impervious
Silts and clays LL <50	Inorganic silts, micaceous or diatomaceous fine sandy or silty soils, elastic silts	Poor	Very high	Poor
	Inorganic clays of high plasticity fat clays	Very poor	Medium	Impervious
	Organic clays of medium to high plasticity organic silts	Very poor	Medium	Impervious
Highly organic soils	Peat and other highly organic soils	Not suitable	Slight	Poor

*Consult soil engineers and local building codes for allowable soil-bearing capacities.
†LL indicates liquid limit.
Source: Douglas S. Way, *Terrain Analysis: A Guide to Site Selection Using Photographic Interpretation*, Douglas S. Way, Columbus, Ohio, 1972.

Cover to reinforcement
Grouted cavity walls: minimum cover to all reinforcement = 10 mm. Pocket Walls: minimum cover to all reinforcement = 40 mm. Quetta bond: minimum cover to all reinforcement = 10 mm. Buttressed wall or other wall with reinforcement positioned in the joints: minimum cover to main reinforcement = 25 mm.
The above recommendations are in accordance with SP 91(8), to which reference should be made for further information.

SPECIFICATION CHECK LIST

Check with consultant engineer all walls over one metre high regarding ground conditions, size of wall, drainage, etc.

Brick/block/stone faced

Use the check list for free-standing walls where retaining walls are to be faced with brick, block or stone, or built entirely of these materials.
Add details of reinforcing, waterproofing rear of unit walls, drainage and weep holes. Provide details of:

- Foundation type and size.
- Wall construction.
- Waterproofing and drainage.
- Coping type.

Concrete
Where the material is to be concrete *in-situ* or concrete block, both may have to be reinforced and therefore it is advisable to check with consultant engineer regarding type and method of reinforcing.

Timber
Where timber is to be used check the type of hardwood is suitable without any preservation. Where softwood is specified ensure that it is treated and to the appropriate grade. Ensure all hardware is galvanised. State details of finished appearance and where timber is to be stained specify manufacturer, colour and number of coats.

DETAIL SHEETS

General
Reinforcement
Foundations
Joints
Brick
Brick (low) (3)
Brick (high)
Concrete
Battered concrete
Concrete block (2)
Cobble blocks
Concrete crib (2)
Stone
Stone faced
Mortared/coursed
Uncoursed/dry
Gabions – stepped
Gabions – batter
Gabions and plants
Timber
Board (low)
Board (medium)
Angled – horizontal (2)
Stepped
Crib – square
Crib – round
Crib – round (live)
Angled – vertical
Rail sleeper and steel
Timber and steel
Timber and mesh

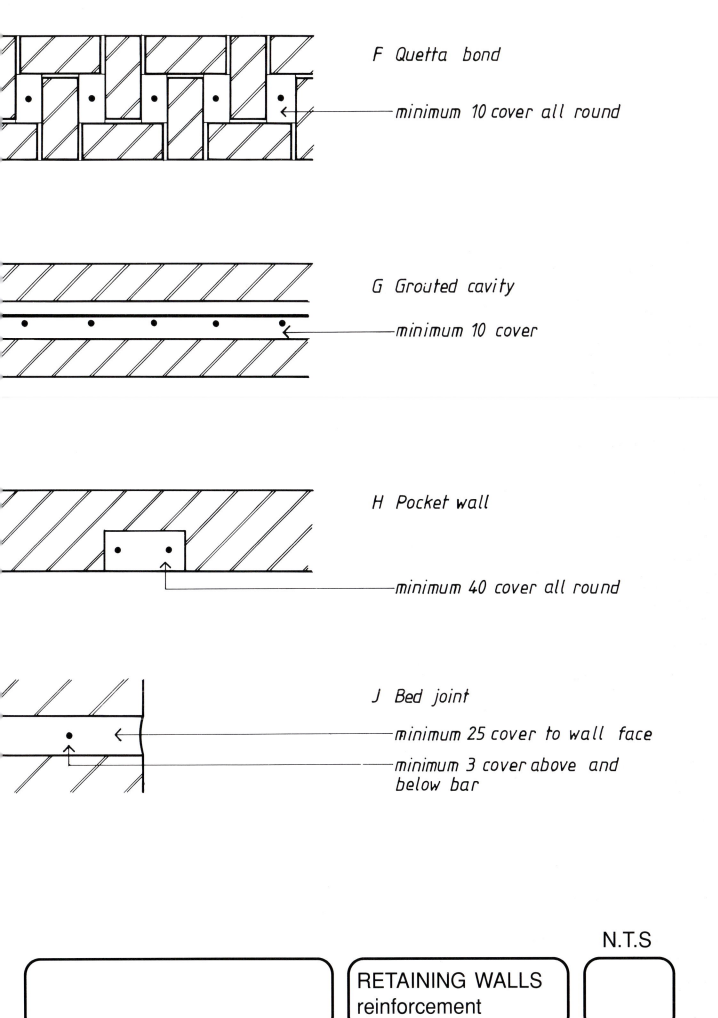

F Quetta bond

minimum 10 cover all round

G Grouted cavity

minimum 10 cover

H Pocket wall

minimum 40 cover all round

J Bed joint

minimum 25 cover to wall face

minimum 3 cover above and below bar

N.T.S

RETAINING WALLS
reinforcement

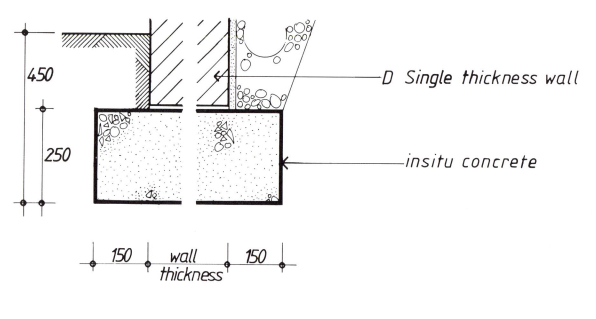

450

250

D Single thickness wall

insitu concrete

150 | wall thickness | 150

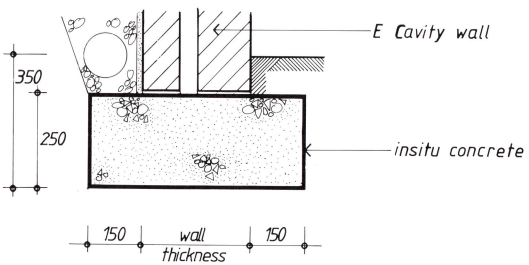

350

250

E Cavity wall

insitu concrete

150 | wall thickness | 150

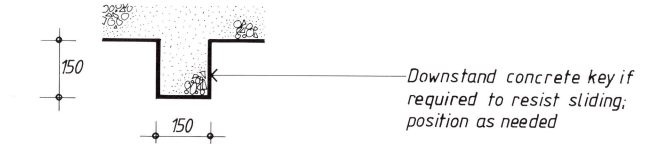

150

150

Downstand concrete key if
required to resist sliding;
position as needed

N.T.S.

RETAINING WALLS
foundations

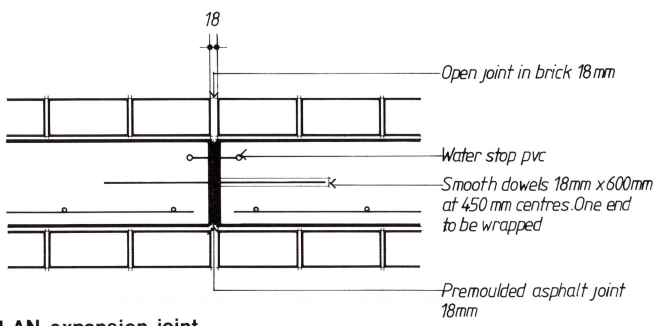

Open joint in brick 18 mm

Water stop pvc

Smooth dowels 18mm x 600mm
at 450 mm centres. One end
to be wrapped

Premoulded asphalt joint
18mm

PLAN expansion joint

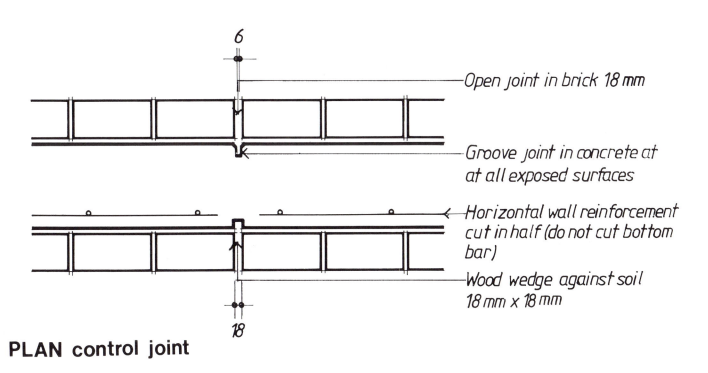

Open joint in brick 18 mm

Groove joint in concrete at
at all exposed surfaces

Horizontal wall reinforcement
cut in half (do not cut bottom
bar)

Wood wedge against soil
18 mm x 18 mm

PLAN control joint

Scale 1:10

RETAINING WALL
joints

61

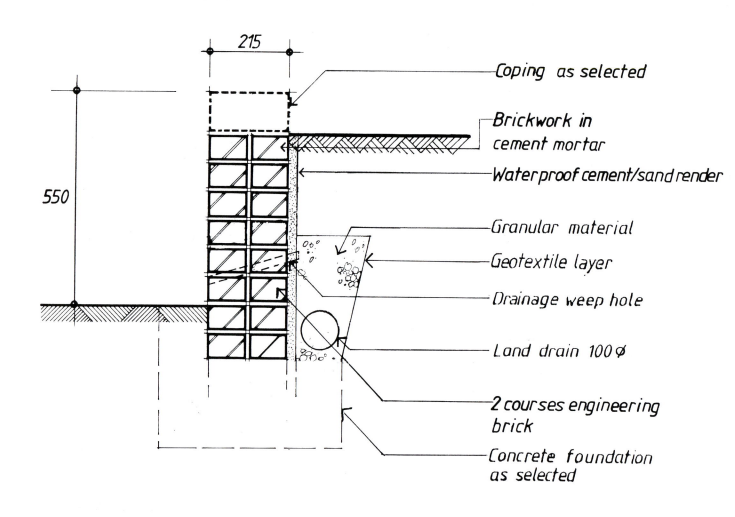

215

550

Coping as selected

Brickwork in cement mortar

Waterproof cement/sand render

Granular material

Geotextile layer

Drainage weep hole

Land drain 100 ⌀

2 courses engineering brick

Concrete foundation as selected

SECTION

Scale 1:10

RETAINING WALL
brick (low)

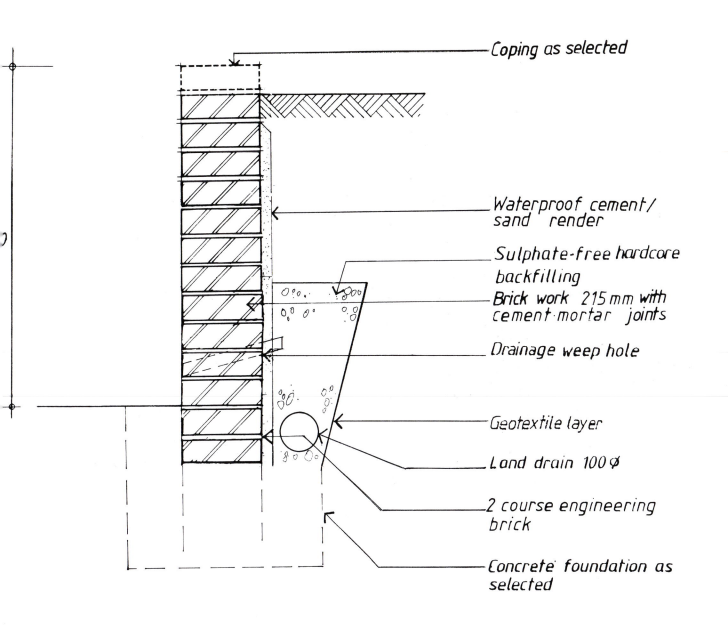

Coping as selected

Waterproof cement/ sand render

Sulphate-free hardcore backfilling

Brick work 215 mm with cement mortar joints

Drainage weep hole

Geotextile layer

Land drain 100 Ø

2 course engineering brick

Concrete foundation as selected

SECTION

Scale 1:10

RETAINING WALL
brick (low)

63

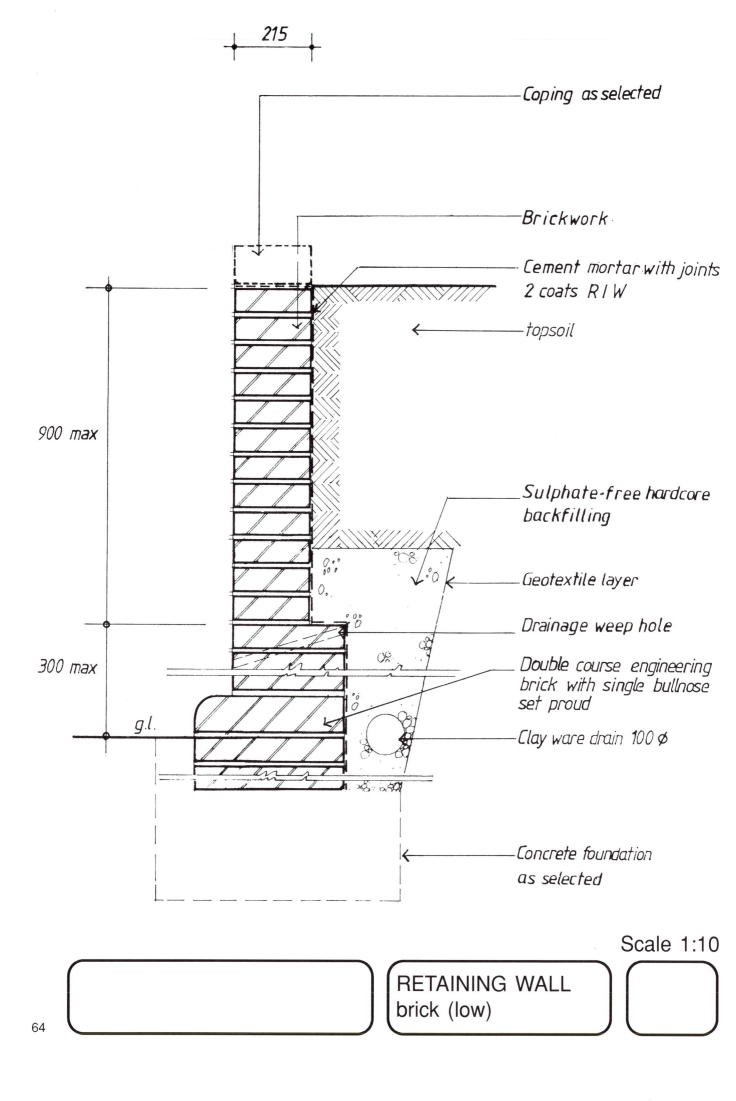

215

Coping as selected

Brickwork

Cement mortar with joints
2 coats R I W

topsoil

900 max

Sulphate-free hardcore
backfilling

Geotextile layer

Drainage weep hole

300 max

Double course engineering
brick with single bullnose
set proud

g.l.

Clay ware drain 100 ∅

Concrete foundation
as selected

Scale 1:10

RETAINING WALL
brick (low)

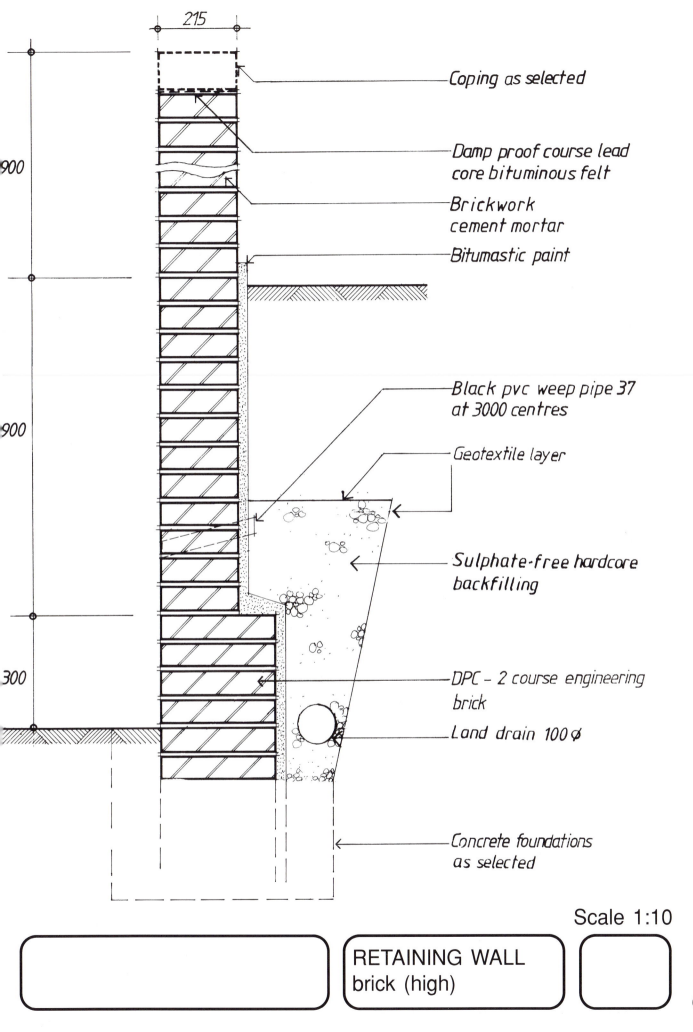

215

Coping as selected

Damp proof course lead
core bituminous felt

Brickwork
cement mortar

Bitumastic paint

Black pvc weep pipe 37
at 3000 centres

Geotextile layer

Sulphate-free hardcore
backfilling

DPC – 2 course engineering
brick

Land drain 100 ⌀

Concrete foundations
as selected

900

900

300

Scale 1:10

RETAINING WALL
brick (high)

65

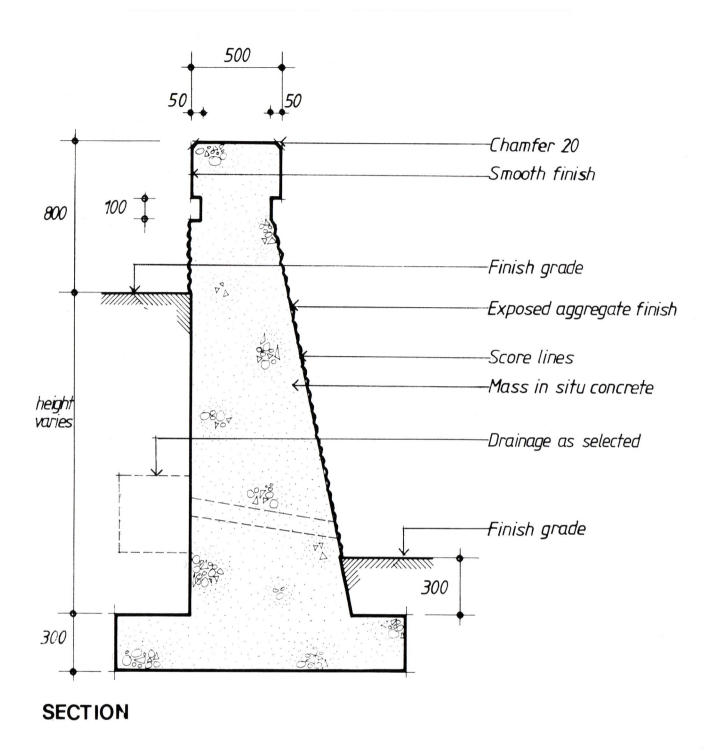

500

50 50

100

800

height
varies

300

Chamfer 20

Smooth finish

Finish grade

Exposed aggregate finish

Score lines

Mass in situ concrete

Drainage as selected

Finish grade

300

SECTION

Scale 1:20

RETAINING WALL
battered concrete

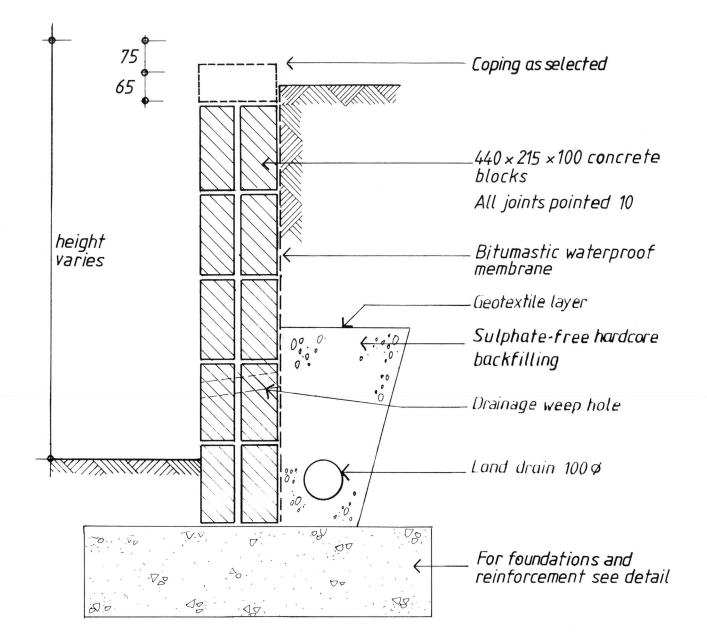

75

65

height
varies

Coping as selected

440 × 215 × 100 concrete
blocks

All joints pointed 10

Bitumastic waterproof
membrane

Geotextile layer

Sulphate-free hardcore
backfilling

Drainage weep hole

Land drain 100 ∅

For foundations and
reinforcement see detail

SECTION

Scale 1:10

RETAINING WALL
concrete block

67

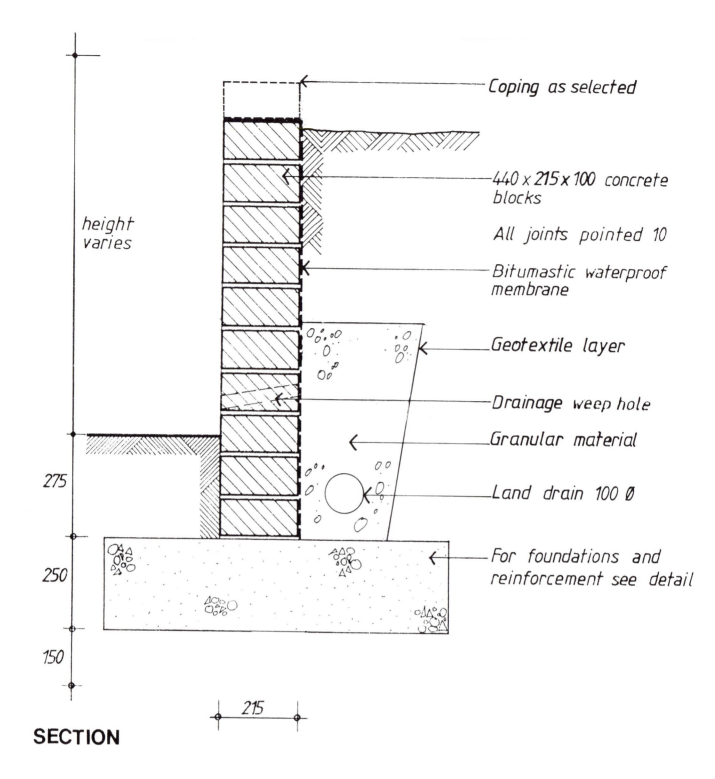

Coping as selected

440 x 215 x 100 concrete blocks

All joints pointed 10

Bitumastic waterproof membrane

Geotextile layer

Drainage weep hole

Granular material

Land drain 100 Ø

For foundations and reinforcement see detail

height varies

275

250

150

215

SECTION

Scale 1:10

RETAINING WALL
concrete block

68

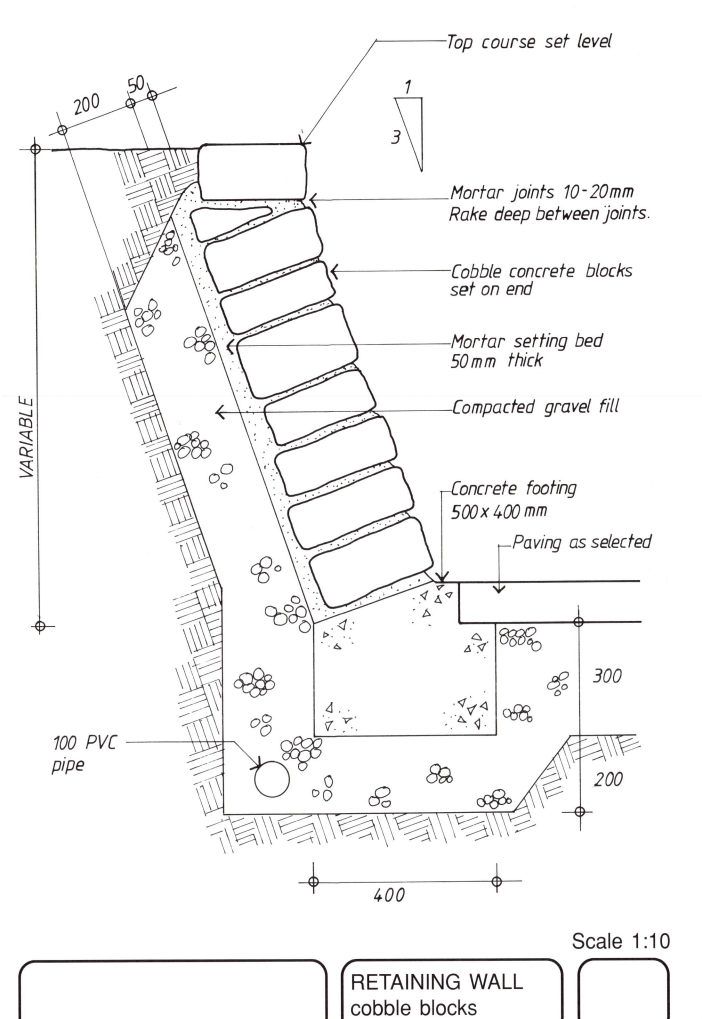

Top course set level

1
3

Mortar joints 10-20mm
Rake deep between joints.

Cobble concrete blocks
set on end

Mortar setting bed
50 mm thick

Compacted gravel fill

Concrete footing
500 x 400 mm

Paving as selected

200   50

VARIABLE

100 PVC
pipe

300

200

400

Scale 1:10

RETAINING WALL
cobble blocks

69

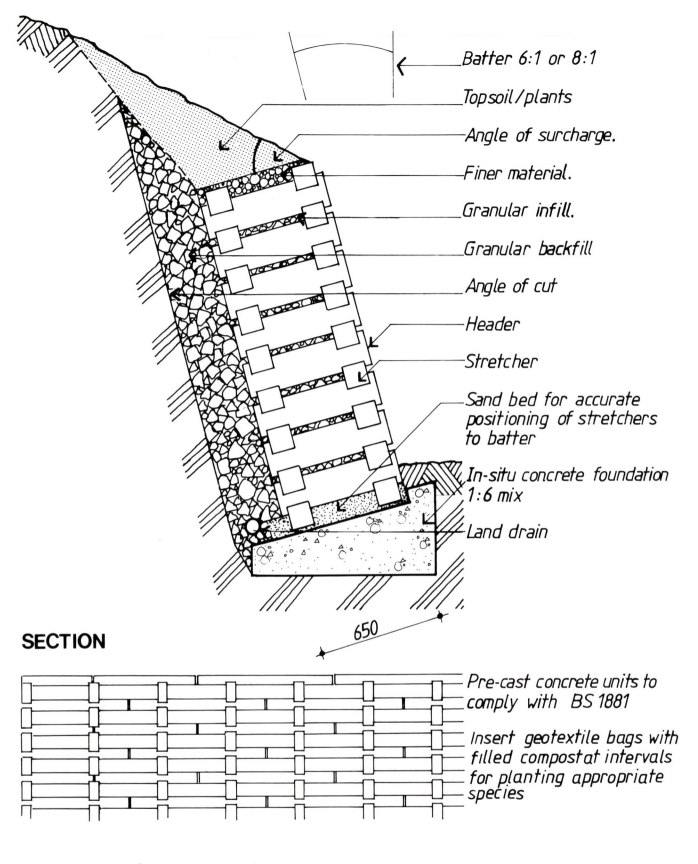

Batter 6:1 or 8:1

Topsoil/plants

Angle of surcharge.

Finer material.

Granular infill.

Granular backfill

Angle of cut

Header

Stretcher

Sand bed for accurate
positioning of stretchers
to batter

In-situ concrete foundation
1:6 mix

Land drain

SECTION

650

Pre-cast concrete units to
comply with BS 1881

Insert geotextile bags with
filled compost at intervals
for planting appropriate
species

ELEVATION (not to scale)

Scale 1:20

RETAINING WALL
concrete crib

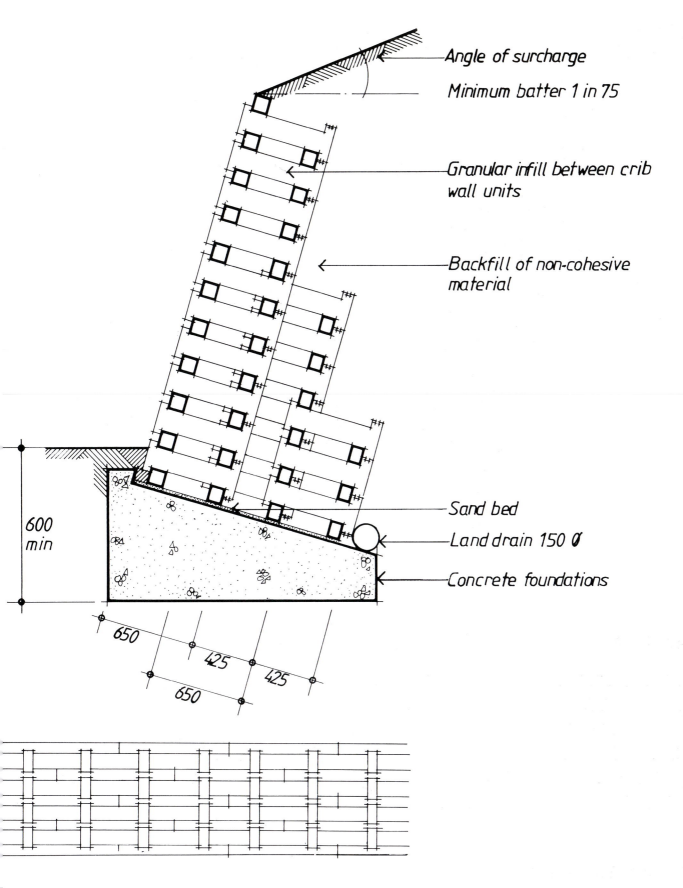

Angle of surcharge

Minimum batter 1 in 75

Granular infill between crib
wall units

Backfill of non-cohesive
material

Sand bed

Land drain 150 ∅

Concrete foundations

600
min

650

425

650

425

ELEVATION

Scale 1:20

RETAINING WALL
concrete crib

71

SECTION

200

50

450

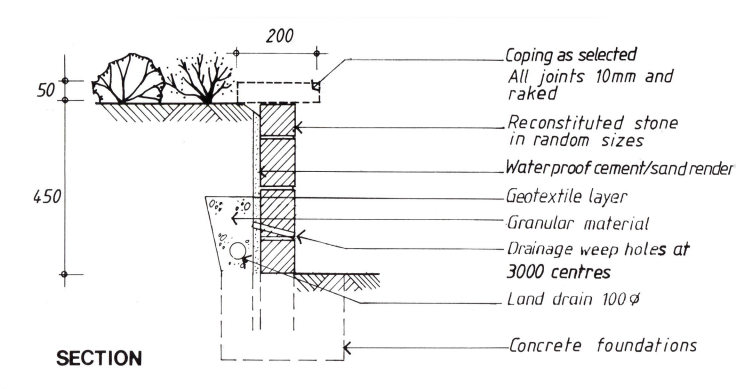

Coping as selected
All joints 10mm and
raked

Reconstituted stone
in random sizes

Waterproof cement/sand render

Geotextile layer

Granular material

Drainage weep holes at
3000 centres

Land drain 100 ⌀

Concrete foundations

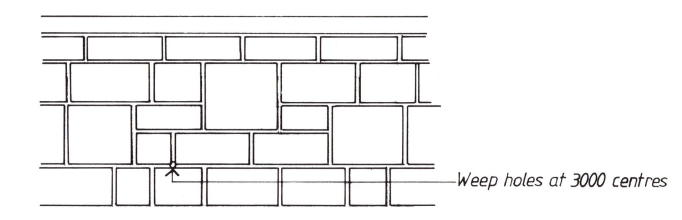

Weep holes at 3000 centres

ELEVATION

Scale 1:10

RETAINING WALL
stone faced

72

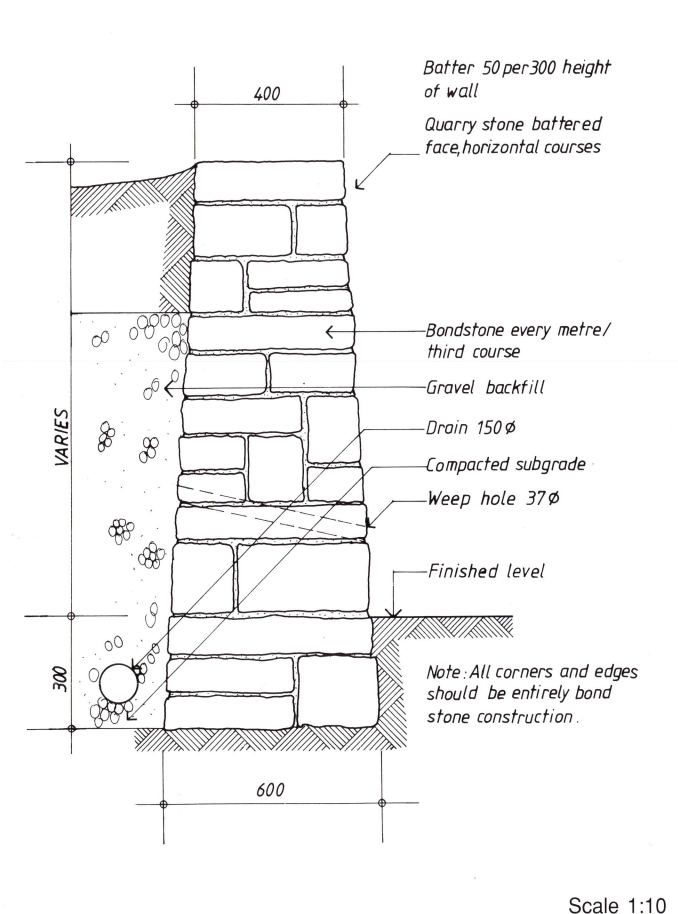

400

Batter 50 per 300 height of wall

Quarry stone battered face, horizontal courses

Bondstone every metre/ third course

Gravel backfill

Drain 150 ø

Compacted subgrade

Weep hole 37 ø

Finished level

Note: All corners and edges should be entirely bond stone construction.

VARIES

300

600

Scale 1:10

RETAINING WALL
natural stone
mortared/coursed

73

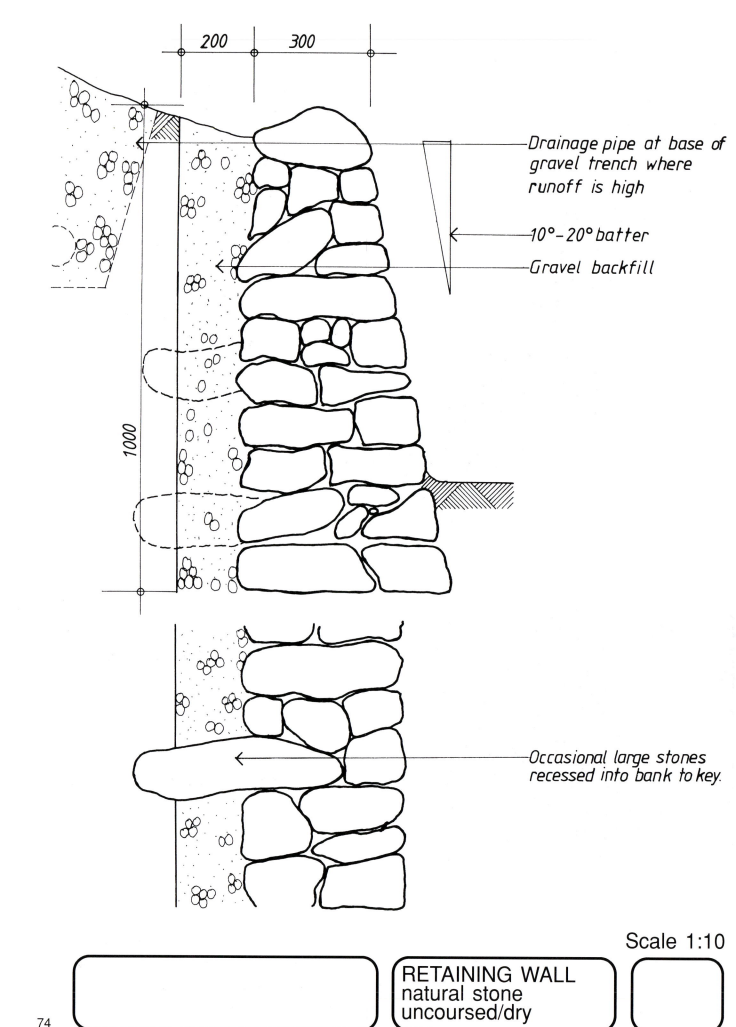

200   300

Drainage pipe at base of
gravel trench where
runoff is high

10°-20° batter

Gravel backfill

1000

Occasional large stones
recessed into bank to key.

Scale 1:10

RETAINING WALL
natural stone
uncoursed/dry

74

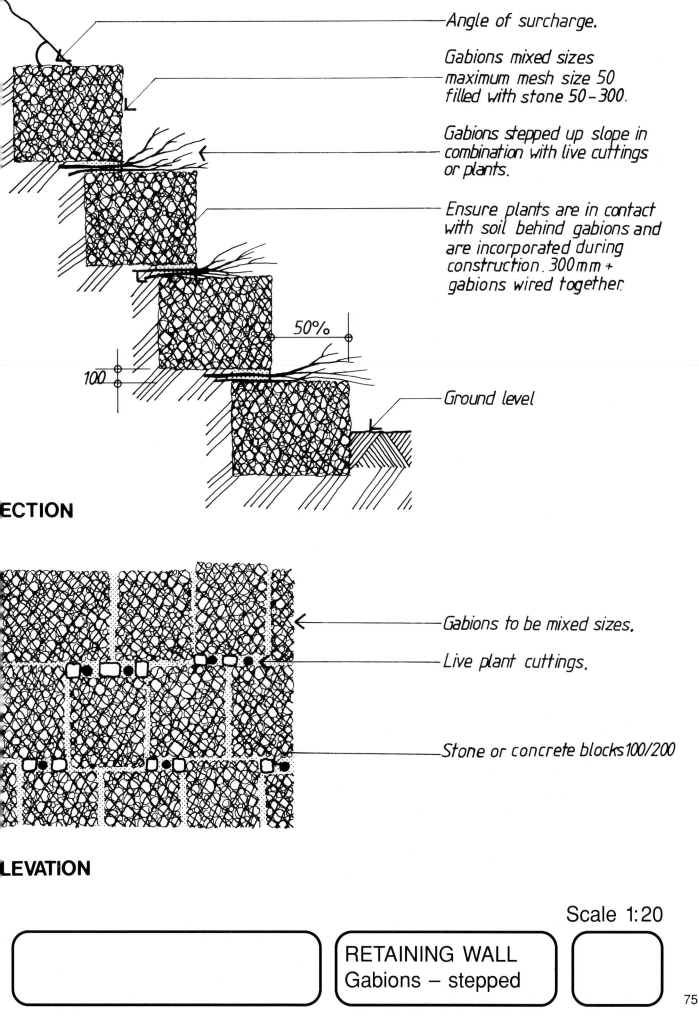

Angle of surcharge.

Gabions mixed sizes maximum mesh size 50 filled with stone 50-300.

Gabions stepped up slope in combination with live cuttings or plants.

Ensure plants are in contact with soil behind gabions and are incorporated during construction. 300 mm + gabions wired together.

50%

100

Ground level

ECTION

Gabions to be mixed sizes.

Live plant cuttings.

Stone or concrete blocks 100/200

LEVATION

Scale 1:20

RETAINING WALL
Gabions – stepped

75

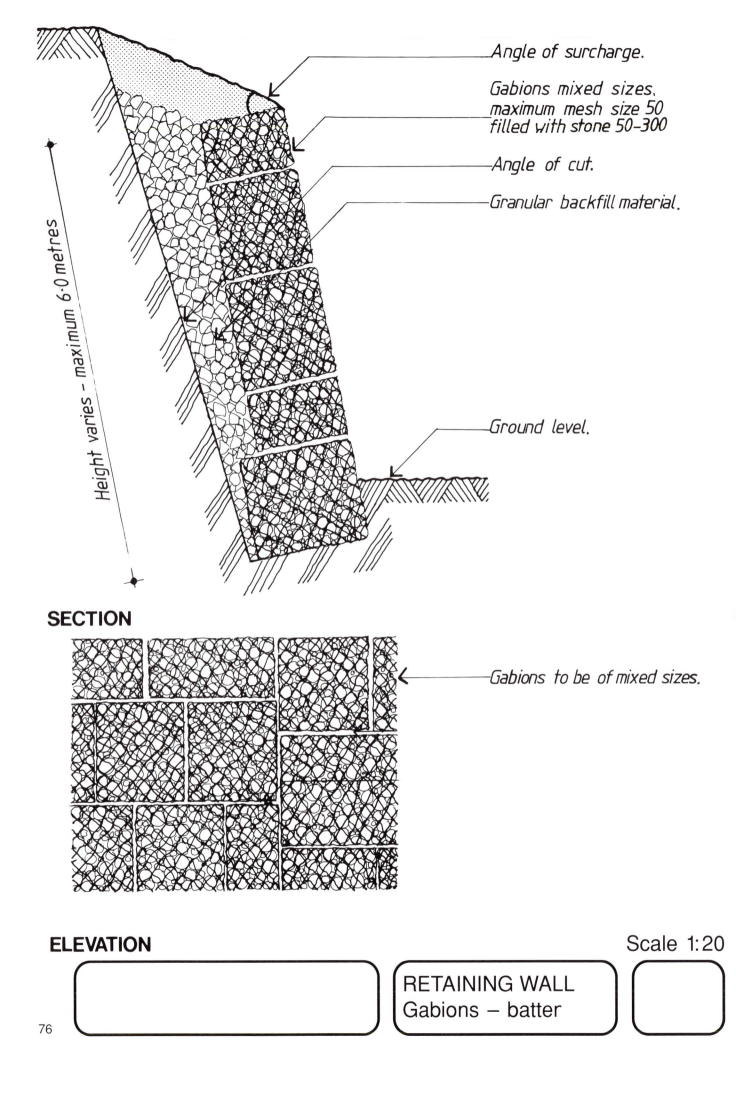

Angle of surcharge.

Gabions mixed sizes,
maximum mesh size 50
filled with stone 50–300

Angle of cut.

Granular backfill material.

Ground level.

Height varies – maximum 6·0 metres

SECTION

Gabions to be of mixed sizes.

ELEVATION

Scale 1:20

RETAINING WALL
Gabions – batter

76

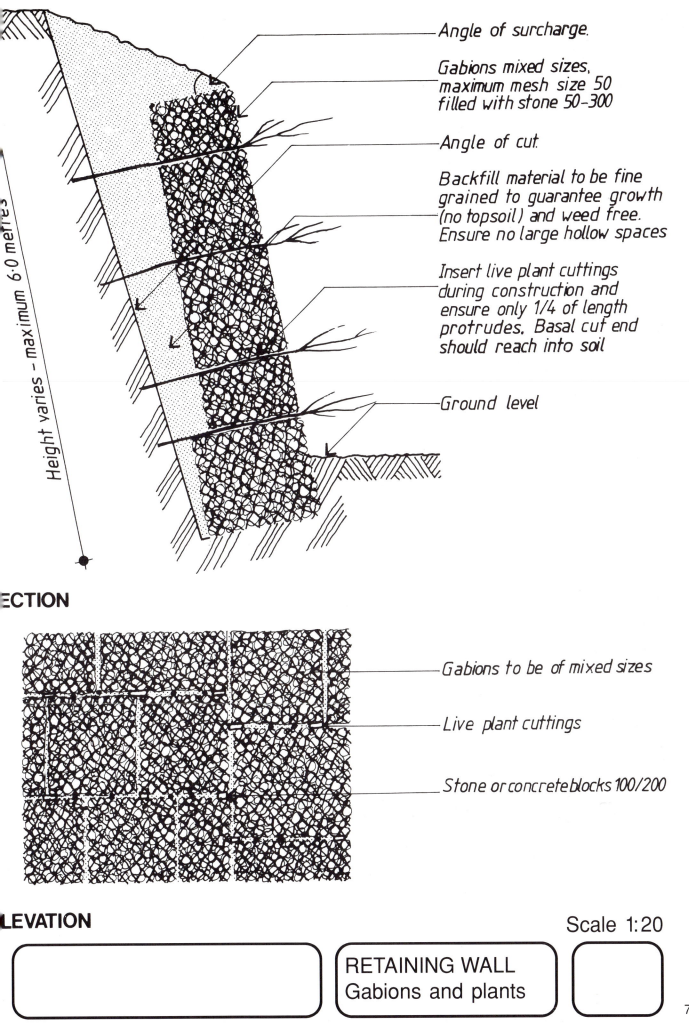

Angle of surcharge.

Gabions mixed sizes, maximum mesh size 50 filled with stone 50-300

Angle of cut.

Backfill material to be fine grained to guarantee growth (no topsoil) and weed free. Ensure no large hollow spaces

Insert live plant cuttings during construction and ensure only 1/4 of length protrudes. Basal cut end should reach into soil

Ground level

Height varies – maximum 6·0 metres

ECTION

Gabions to be of mixed sizes

Live plant cuttings

Stone or concrete blocks 100/200

LEVATION

Scale 1:20

RETAINING WALL
Gabions and plants

77

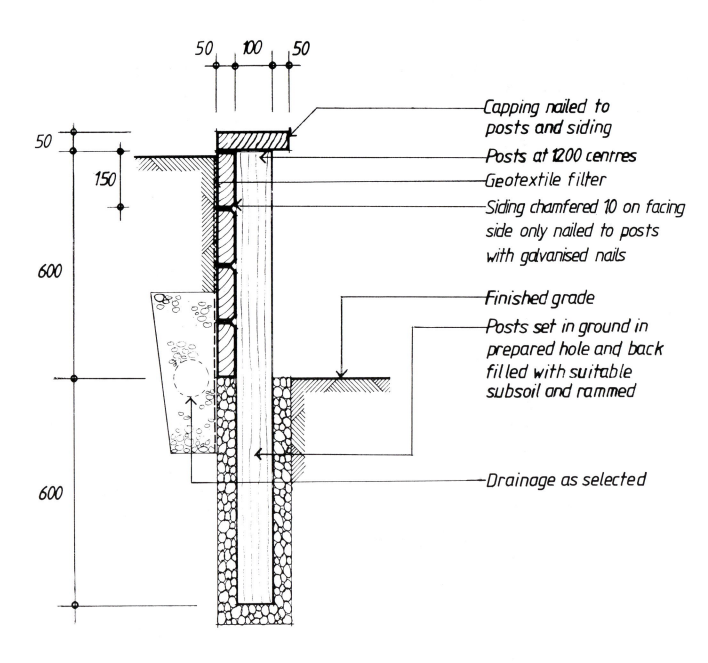

50 | 100 | 50

50

150

600

600

Capping nailed to
posts and siding

Posts at 1200 centres

Geotextile filter

Siding chamfered 10 on facing
side only nailed to posts
with galvanised nails

Finished grade

Posts set in ground in
prepared hole and back
filled with suitable
subsoil and rammed

Drainage as selected

SECTION

RETAINING WALL
timber (low)

Scale 1:10

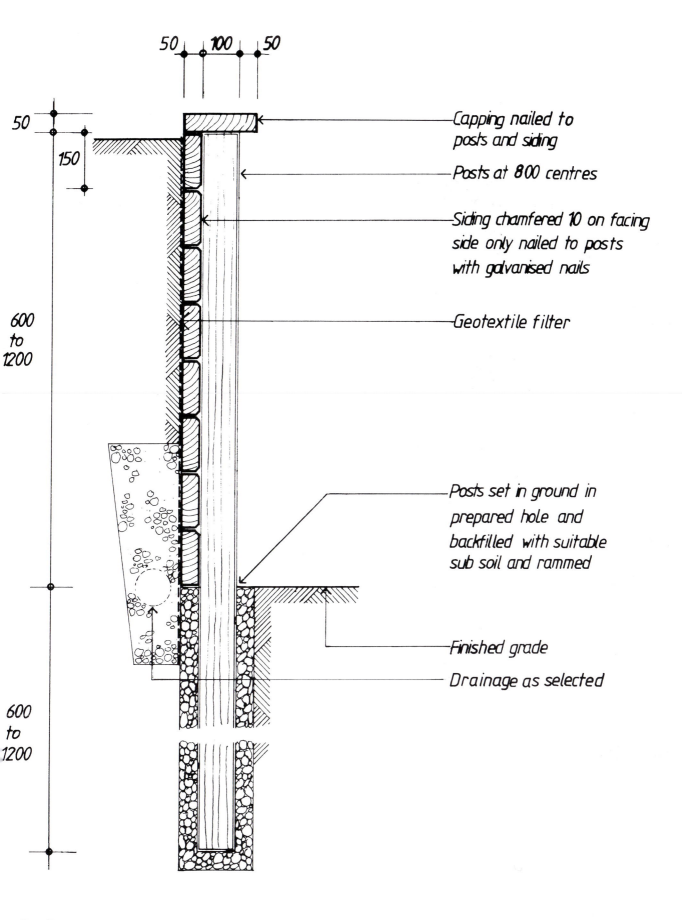

50 | 100 | 50

50

150

600
to
1200

600
to
1200

Capping nailed to
posts and siding

Posts at 800 centres

Siding chamfered 10 on facing
side only nailed to posts
with galvanised nails

Geotextile filter

Posts set in ground in
prepared hole and
backfilled with suitable
sub soil and rammed

Finished grade

Drainage as selected

SECTION

RETAINING WALL
timber (medium)

Scale 1:10

79

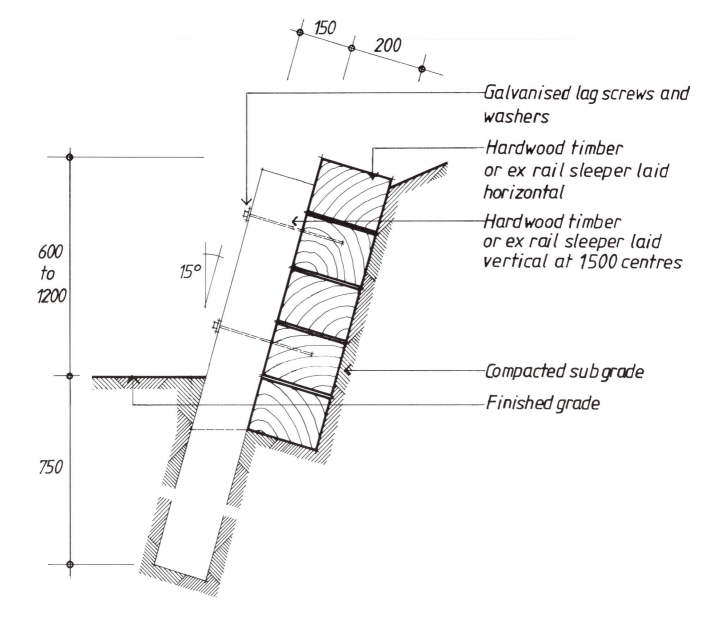

150

200

Galvanised lag screws and washers

Hardwood timber
or ex rail sleeper laid
horizontal

Hardwood timber
or ex rail sleeper laid
vertical at 1500 centres

600
to
1200

15°

Compacted subgrade

Finished grade

750

SECTION

Scale 1:10

RETAINING WALL
timber angled –
horizontal

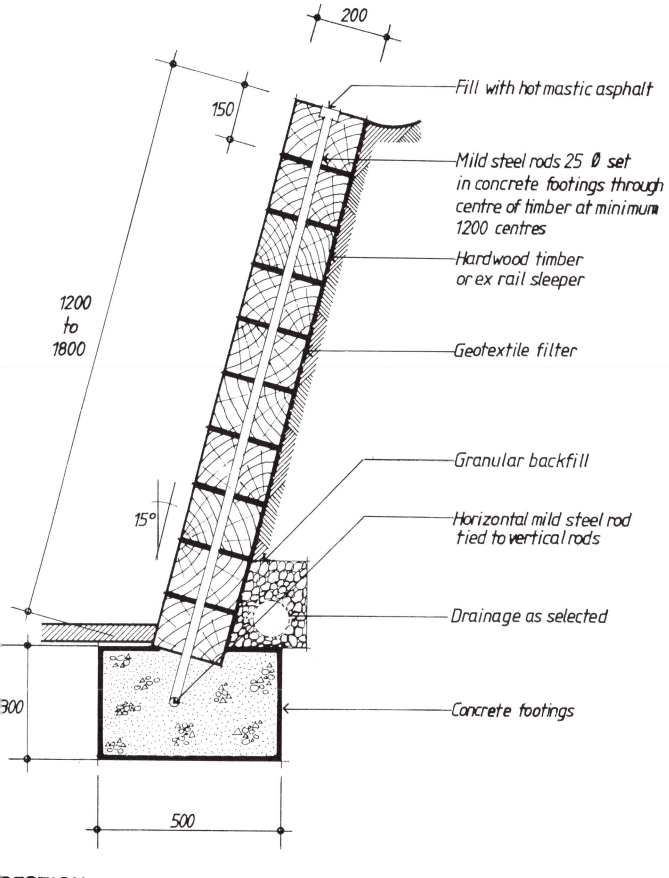

200

150

1200
to
1800

15°

300

500

Fill with hot mastic asphalt

Mild steel rods 25 Ø set
in concrete footings through
centre of timber at minimum
1200 centres

Hardwood timber
or ex rail sleeper

Geotextile filter

Granular backfill

Horizontal mild steel rod
tied to vertical rods

Drainage as selected

Concrete footings

SECTION

Scale 1:10

RETAINING WALL
timber angled

81

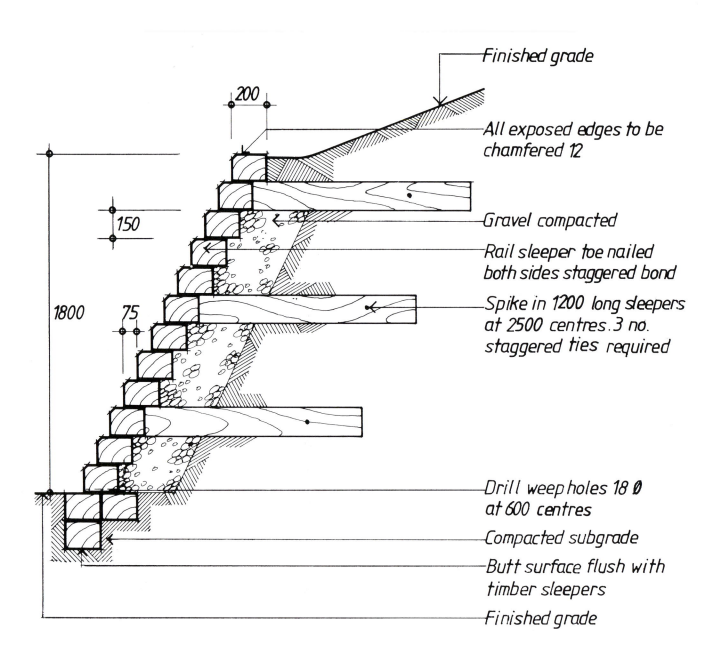

Finished grade

All exposed edges to be chamfered 12

Gravel compacted

Rail sleeper toe nailed both sides staggered bond

Spike in 1200 long sleepers at 2500 centres. 3 no. staggered ties required

Drill weep holes 18 Ø at 600 centres

Compacted subgrade

Butt surface flush with timber sleepers

Finished grade

200

150

1800

75

SECTION

Scale 1:20

RETAINING WALL
timber stepped

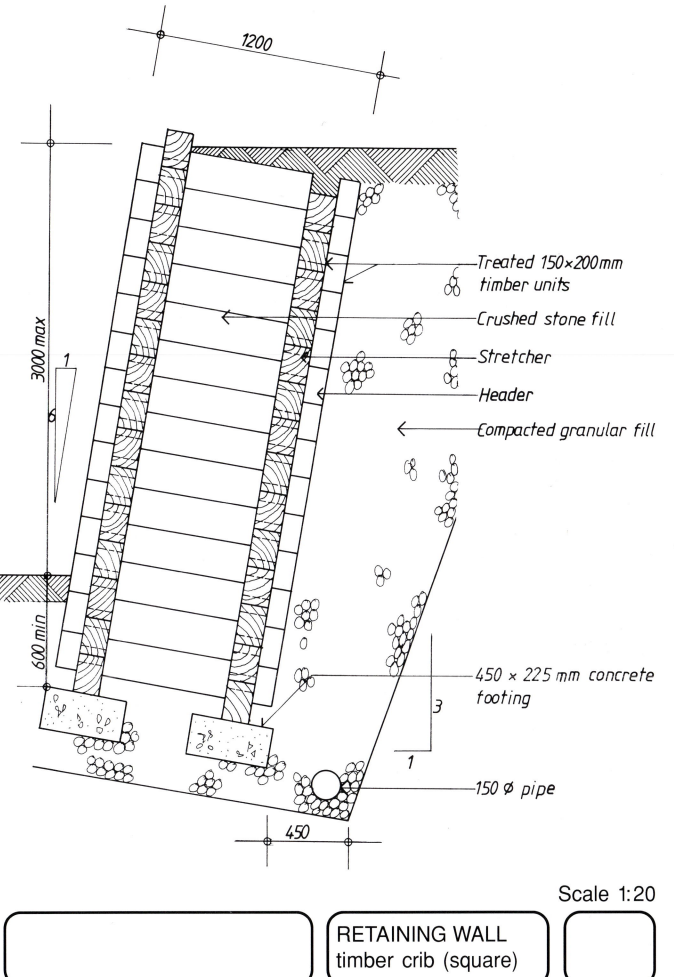

1200

3000 max

1

6

Treated 150×200mm timber units

Crushed stone fill

Stretcher

Header

Compacted granular fill

600 min

450 × 225 mm concrete footing

3

1

150 ø pipe

450

Scale 1:20

RETAINING WALL
timber crib (square)

83

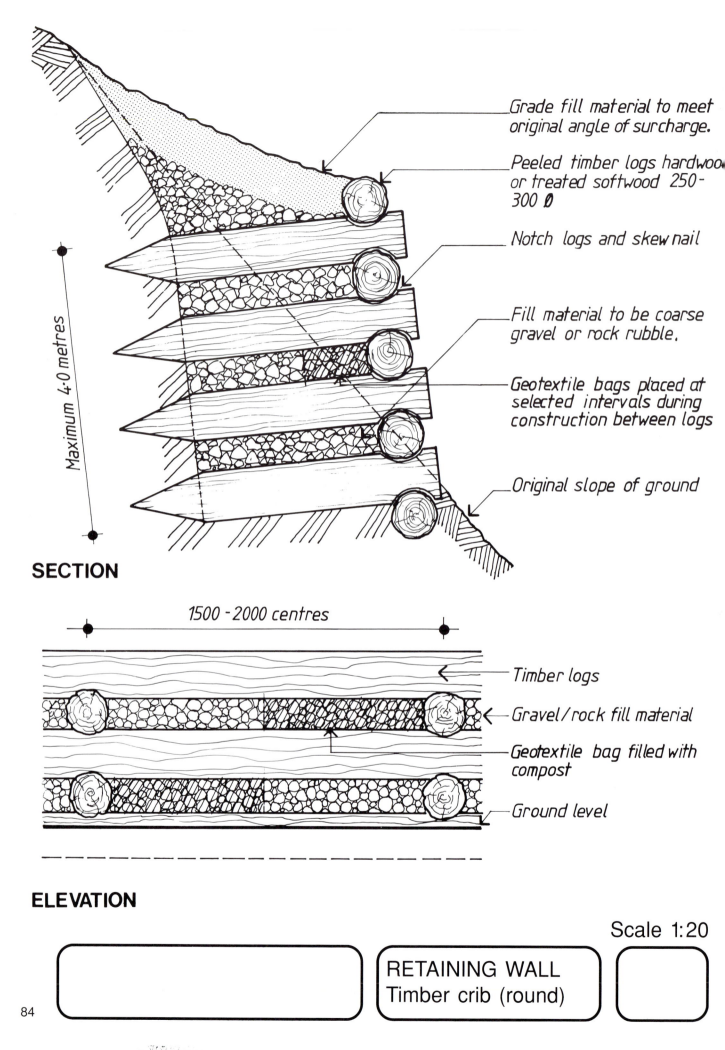

Grade fill material to meet original angle of surcharge.

Peeled timber logs hardwood or treated softwood 250-300 Ø

Notch logs and skew nail

Fill material to be coarse gravel or rock rubble.

Geotextile bags placed at selected intervals during construction between logs

Original slope of ground

Maximum 4.0 metres

SECTION

1500 - 2000 centres

Timber logs

Gravel / rock fill material

Geotextile bag filled with compost

Ground level

ELEVATION

Scale 1:20

RETAINING WALL
Timber crib (round)

84

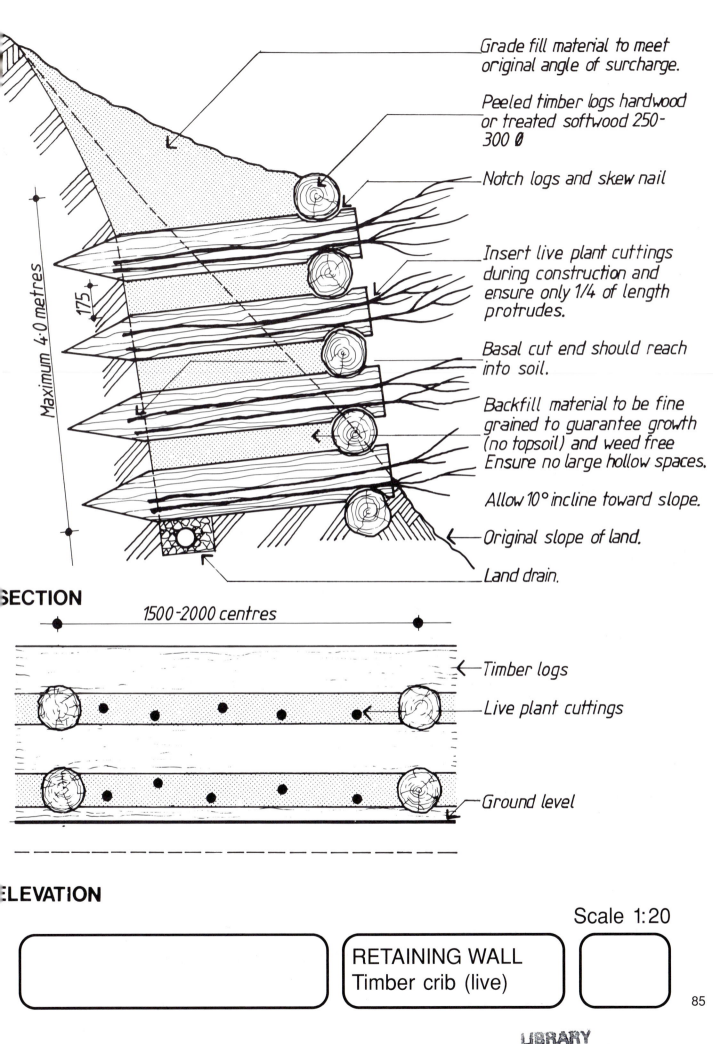

Grade fill material to meet original angle of surcharge.

Peeled timber logs hardwood or treated softwood 250-300 Ø

Notch logs and skew nail

Insert live plant cuttings during construction and ensure only 1/4 of length protrudes.

Basal cut end should reach into soil.

Backfill material to be fine grained to guarantee growth (no topsoil) and weed free Ensure no large hollow spaces.

Allow 10° incline toward slope.

Original slope of land.

Land drain.

Maximum 4·0 metres

175

SECTION

1500-2000 centres

Timber logs

Live plant cuttings

Ground level

ELEVATION

Scale 1:20

RETAINING WALL
Timber crib (live)

85

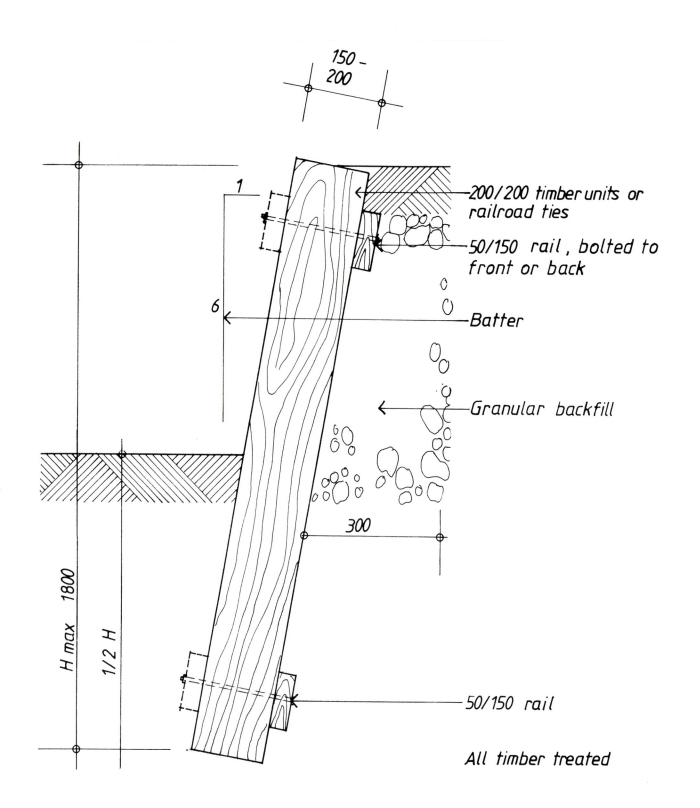

150 - 200

1

6

200/200 timber units or railroad ties

50/150 rail, bolted to front or back

Batter

Granular backfill

300

H max 1800

1/2 H

50/150 rail

All timber treated

Scale 1:10

RETAINING WALL
Timber angled – vertical

86

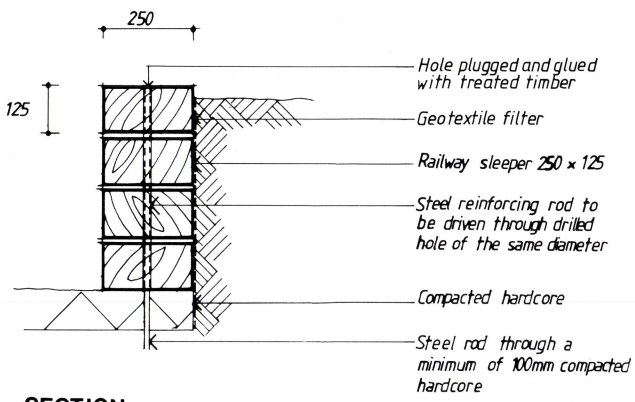

250

125

Hole plugged and glued with treated timber

Geotextile filter

Railway sleeper 250 × 125

Steel reinforcing rod to be driven through drilled hole of the same diameter

Compacted hardcore

Steel rod through a minimum of 100mm compacted hardcore

SECTION

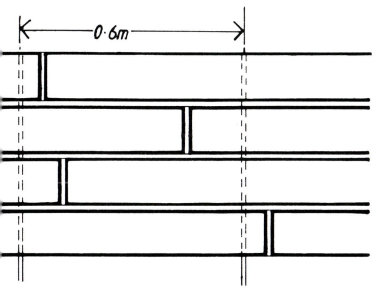

0·6m

ELEVATION

Scale 1:10

RETAINING WALL
railway sleeper

87

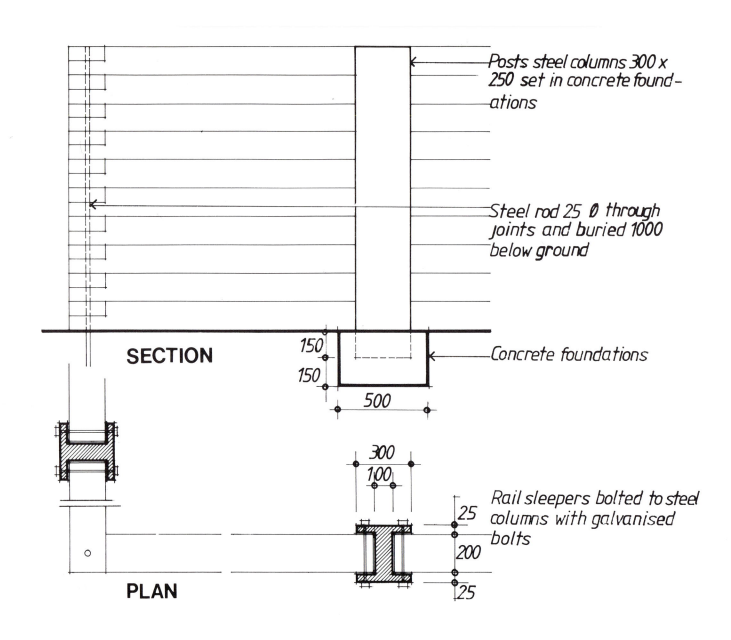

SECTION

Posts steel columns 300 x 250 set in concrete foundations

Steel rod 25 ∅ through joints and buried 1000 below ground

150
150

Concrete foundations

500

PLAN

300
100

25

Rail sleepers bolted to steel columns with galvanised bolts

200

25

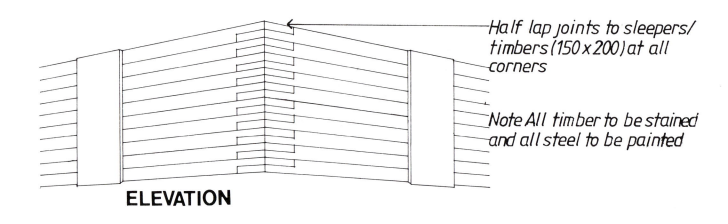

Half lap joints to sleepers/ timbers (150 x 200) at all corners

Note All timber to be stained and all steel to be painted

ELEVATION

Scale 1:20

RETAINING WALL
timber & steel

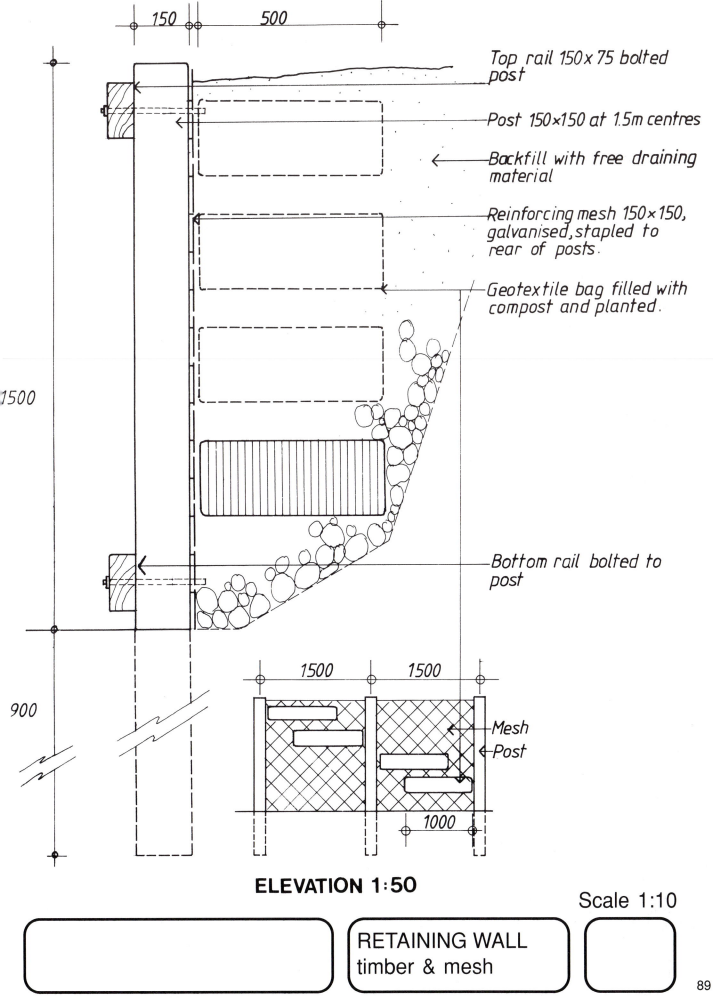

150   500

Top rail 150 x 75 bolted post

Post 150×150 at 1.5m centres

Backfill with free draining material

Reinforcing mesh 150×150, galvanised, stapled to rear of posts.

Geotextile bag filled with compost and planted.

Bottom rail bolted to post

1500

900

1500   1500

Mesh

Post

1000

ELEVATION 1:50

Scale 1:10

RETAINING WALL
timber & mesh

89

FENCES

GUIDANCE NOTES

Timber

Standards

BS 1722 covers many kinds of fencing. Each part of the Standard specifies in detail not only the materials required but also the method of erection. Fences are also classified according to variable characteristics, e.g. height, number of wires or rails, post material.
These are listed in table 1 of each part of the Standard, together with examples of typical uses of each type.

Part 4   Cleft chestnut pale
Part 5   Close boarded and oak pale
Part 6   Wooden palisade
Part 7   Wooden post and rail
Part 11   Woven wood

There are, of course, many other types of fencing not yet covered by the British Standard, such as wattle, etc.
The type and height of a fence should be determined by its situation and location – urban or rural.

Fence types

Cleft chestnut spile
The timber from chestnut coppice woodland is cleft by hand with a billhook usually on site after the coppice has been cut, and consists of cleft spiles driven not less than 300 mm into the ground usually at six per metre spacing. It is connected to each other by one or two lines of galvanised wire twisted round each spile and then between end and intermediate posts.

Chestnut pale
This is made by a machine to BS 1722: Part 4 and comes in rolls for easy erection and dismantling. The pales are connected together by two or three lines of galvanised wire being spaced from 50 to 100 mm apart according to quality. Round posts are used for support. This type of fencing is recommended only for temporary use, the driven spile being far more satisfactory for permanent fences.

Close boarded and oak pale
Oak is the best timber but is expensive, especially if hand split. Machine sawn is less weatherproof and subject to warping. Softwood is cheaper but requires to be treated. Construction consists of squared posts and triangular arris or rectangular rails which generally have toned ends set into mortises formed in the longest faces of the post. Pales or feathered edge boards are fixed vertically and lapped 13–19 mm, with galvanised rails/bolts. Additional refinements are capping and gravel boards which provide protection. BS 1722: Part 5 covers this type.

Horizontal palisade
The boards have feathered edge and lapped or plain section and jointed or spaced apart like louvres. They are fixed horizontally directly to the posts whose maximum spacing is 2.0 m, depending upon the width and thickness of the board and its spacing.

Vertical palisade
Boards are either spaced apart or butt jointed and are usually fixed to the rails on one side, although boards on both sides with the equivalent size spaces between them are quite common.

Post and rail
This fence consists of square or rectangular section posts and one or more horizontal rails in which the parts can be mortised together without the aid of nails. Sawn or wrot timber versions which are subject to warping need to be bolted or mortised and pinned together or held by metal straps and brackets. Part 7 of BS 1722 covers this type.

Interwoven
This consists of panels formed from thin slats of wood woven horizontally between framed uprights. The panels are supported between wooden posts. Quality and durability depend upon timber used – oak and cedar lasting well compared to treated softwood, which becomes brittle and may disintegrate much more quickly. Part 11 of the BS covers this type.

Wattle

Hazel handles are made from hazel coppice using single rods often woven continuously *in-situ* and following the configuration of the ground. Wattle handles and panels are made from the osier-willow rods woven in groups of four or five, all in the round and are usually 2 m long by 0.6–1.8 m high in increments of 150 mm. Wattle fencing has a limited life of approximately six years, especially in exposed positions. It should be secured to supporting posts between battens.

Preservation

The most common fencing timbers are oak, sweet chestnut and cedar. These need no preservation when used above ground. Where these timbers are used as posts, the ends should be impregnated with creosote. All softwood used in fencing should be preservative-impregnated by a vacuum process.

Post spacing

Posts should be spaced at 2,700 mm maximum centres for mortised fencing and 1,800 mm maximum centres for nailed fencing.

Depth of insertion

Under normal exposure conditions a post insertion depth of 500 mm is sufficient for a 1.0 m high fence, and 750 mm for a 1.8 m high fence. If a concrete surround is used, these dimensions can be reduced to 400 mm and 650 mm, respectively, because of the greater face area given by the concrete in certain locations.

Fixings

All fixings for fencing should be galvanised. In public areas, drive screws or wood screws should be used. Where bolts are used the nuts should be recessed into the post or the projecting threads should be burred over.

Finish

Suitable timbers, such as oak, cedar, sweet chestnut or larch, can be left unfinished. Otherwise use a two-coat application of wood dye or a coloured preservative (e.g. Cuprinol). Some brush-applied preservatives are not compatible with vacuum preservation processes which include water repellents. Opaque oil paint systems can be satisfactorily used on vacuum-impregnated timber provided that the preservative does not contain a water repellent. Where a water repellent has been used, loss of adhesion of the paint film may result unless a special primer is used. The paint manufacturer should be consulted.

Changes in level

These are accommodated by stepping each panel when using fences made from prefabricated panels. Posts at the steps will have to be increased in length. Where post and rail fencing is used, changes in level are accommodated by inclining the rails in the mortises, while keeping the posts vertical.

Metal

Metal fencing can be conveniently divided into two groups. The first comprises those types made up from stiff metal sections of flats and round or square bars, forming rigid barriers. The second group comprises wire mesh of flexible material supported by posts and sometimes framed in panels; woven, wire, chain link and welded mesh. BS 1722 lists the following:

Part 1   Chain Link
Part 2   Woven Wire
Part 3   Strained Wire
Part 8   Mild Steel Bar
Part 9   Mild Steel Vertical Bar
Part 10 Anti-Intruder
Part 12 Steel Palisade
Part 13 Tennis Court

The first group includes the painted iron railing that is found around many eighteenth-century parks, estates and large gardens and in urban areas provides a substantial see-through barrier. Metal post and rail or continuous bar fencing is used for boundary enclosure, mainly in rural areas. It is much lighter than timber and less obtrusive. Vertical bar railings are primarily urban in character because of their strong verticality.

The second group comprises chain link, wire mesh and line wire, all of which are strained between concrete, metal or timber posts, with straining posts at changes of direction and at the ends. This type of fence is used more for security and is more functional than aesthetic, although if used in frames it could be made to look considerably better. Wire mesh can also be used for supporting climbing plants. Strained wire fences are most commonly used in rural areas as a barrier against farm animals and in urban areas as a temporary fence between private gardens. The main objective is to ensure that the posts (structural members) are reduced to the minimum while keeping the wires taut. The lighter they are, the cheaper the cost and the better the appearance.

Netting fencing should be used over large boundary runs where timber is too expensive, or where the site is to be defined but any views retained within it. Posts can be timber but concrete is better, since they must support stressing wires along the top and bottom of the mesh. Chain link fencing, which is wire or wire covered with coloured plastic, is the strongest mesh. Plastic netting is less tensile than chain link but is ideal for more general garden use, for infilling decorative panels and to support climbing plants. Decorative fences can be made in a combination of materials, such as translucent fibreglass sheets and timber, or bamboo, etc.

Sizes of members

The materials used almost exclusively for metal fencing are wrought iron and mild steel. BS 1622: Parts 8 and 9 can be used as a guide for sizes and spacing of members. Space between vertical members should not be less than 100 mm or more than 120 mm.

Intermediate posts

An insertion depth of 600 mm is suitable for a fence up to 1.8 m high. Spacing should be 2.7 m maximum. A wing plate parallel to the fence line should be welded to each standard. Standards should have a bearing plate welded to the base. Standards for fences incorporating strained wire should have stays fixed at 60° to the horizontal at corners and ends. Because of the small face dimension of metal members, a concrete surround to the standard should always be used.

Preservation and finish

BS 1722: Part 8 specifies a range of ex-works finishes, the usual finish being a red-oxide primer or hot-dip galvanising after fabrication. The finish coating should be paint, applied as two undercoats and one gloss top coat.

Changes in level

Prefabricated metal fencing is accommodated to changes in level by stepping the panels or fabricating special inclined panels. With either method, the profile of the ground must be known in advance of fabrication.

Rigid fencing types

Continuous bar fencing
Rails can be flat section or round bars and the overall height 1,070, 1,220 or 1,370 mm. Standards can be flat, L or T section. This type of fence is also obtainable in hurdle form.

Vertical bar unclimbable fencing
This fence is also simple, consisting of either round or square vertical bars and flat top and bottom rails. Both square and round versions can be obtained in either rigid or self-adjusting forms for sloping ground lines. The tops of the fence type vary in design and can be pointed, blunt, bowed, interlaced and spear-head. Portable hurdles are obtainable in 2 m lengths.

Vertical bar wall fencing

A swarf version of vertical bar fencing is made for fixing on top of low walls, in heights from the top of the wall of 600, 750 and 900 mm.

Steel angle unclimbable fencing

Substitution of all the components in the vertical bar fence with steel angles for standards, pales and rails results in a similar type of fence with additional rigidity, as the angle pales are more resistant to bending than vertical bars. Heights range from 1,220 mm to 2,440 mm.

Corrugated steel pale fencing

This consists of corrugated steel pales fixed to angle section rails. The tops of the pales are single pointed or splayed to give triple points. The corrugated pales have much greater strength than other types and it is made in heights from 1,525 mm to 3,050 mm.

Post and rail fencing

A number of variations occur in this fence type, which is in the form of horizontal rails of stout tubular section supported by steel standards or cast iron pillars. This type of fence is useful where a strong, robust quality is required.

Post and chain barrier

This is useful for marking the boundary and forming a mild deterrent to possible trespassers. Chains can be plain link or ornamented with spikes and links. Chains are attached to each standard by eyes or hooks or they can pass through intermediate standards and be fixed intermittently. Thicknesses of chain are usually 9.5 mm diameter, but chains are also available in 6.4 mm and 7.9 mm diameter metal. As alternatives to metal, posts can be in concrete or timber.

Flexible fencing types

Although these notes are primarily concerned with metal fencing, the materials described below can be used with posts of timber or concrete in place of steel.

Chain link fence

Anti-intruder chain link fences (with cranked tips) are also available. The BS specifies various gauges of steel wire that may be used for stated purposes and allows for the alternative use of mild steel, aluminium or plastic-coated steel.

Woven wire rectangular and square mesh fence

This fence type is widely used in agriculture and is often called pig wire. It is a more open type of fence than chain link and hexagonal mesh.

Welded mesh fence

A mesh formed of wires welded together to form a rectangular mesh and of stout gauge with or without PVC bonding. It is also used in framed panels, the framing being in timber or steel sections. In the heavier gauges it can form a very strong unclimbable fence.

Post and wire

The use of spring steel or high tensile steel requires supporting timber posts at only up to 18 m centres with strainers up to 1 m apart with or without droppers at 1.8 m centres, depending upon the purpose of the fence.

Expanded metal fence

Expanded metal is made by slitting sheet metal and stretching strands so formed at right angles to the plane of the sheeting, resulting in a diamond mesh. A flattened form is available. There are a large number of mesh sizes available in aluminium, brass, copper and stainless steel as well as ordinary steel. Expanded metal is usually framed in metal or timber when used for fencing.

Perforated metal sheeting

A large range of patterns is available in this material, which is highly decorative for garden screens. The patterns depend on the shape of the perforations or cut-out portions of the sheeting.

Hexagonal mesh wire fence

Hexagonal mesh is of small-gauge wire, galvanised during manufacture. It cannot

93

compare with chain link in permanency and strength. Hexagonal mesh is commonly used for rabbit-proof enclosures around young plantations. Standards can be of angle steel section, peeled larch or chestnut poles. It can be strengthened by the addition of a few lines of galvanised wire.

Finish and painting of metal fencing

A steel fencing requires protection from corrosion, and unless specified to be galvanised the fencing will arrive on-site with a temporary coating, usually of one coat black varnish, although some makers supply fencing coated with boiled linseed oil. The fencing must be treated more adequately without delay, and the general treatment consists of one coat corrosion-inhibiting priming coat (no red oxide), one or two undercoats and a finishing coat of oil paint. If a galvanised finish is required it should be specified to be in accordance with the requirements of BS 443: 1969, for woven wire, or BS 729: 1971, as applicable.

Plastic-coated chain link fencing has become available in a number of colours, the best for weathering being black.

Concrete fencing

Members are always reinforced with mild steel bars. There is no British Standard covering concrete fences as a whole, although concrete posts in composite fencing are dealt with in appropriate parts of BS 1722.

The two most popular concrete fences are:

- *Concrete post and panel fence*: This consists of reinforced concrete posts grooved to receive concrete slabs 38 mm or 50 mm thick and 150, 225 or 300 mm wide, which are placed one on top of the other between posts and in the grooves, to make up a panel.
- *Concrete palisade fence*: This fence is similar to its traditional timber counterpart, consisting of posts and rails and palisades. Fixings are all concealed and the finish is in plain concrete. No gates are available.

SPECIFICATION CHECK LIST

General

Refer to the relevant British Standard for the selected fence, either timber or metal. Information should be given in all the clauses to comply with SMM 7 and to provide checks for any site supervision.

Timber types

For timber fences BS 1722 covers the following parts:

Part 4   Cleft chestnut pale
Part 5   Close boarded and oak pale
Part 6   Wooden palisade
Part 7   Wooden post and rail
Part 11   Woven wood

Cleft chestnut pale
Type: Use table 1 from the British Standard and select reference (e.g. CW 135).
Posts and struts: From tables 2 and 3 state either concrete or timber posts, struts and size.
Centres of posts: BS 1722: Part 4 specifies the following maximum centres for intermediate posts:

Height of fence (mm)	Concrete posts (m)	Timber posts (m)
900, 1,050	3.00	2.50
1,200, 1,350	2.75	2.25
1,500, 1,800	2.25	2.00

Straining posts: 70 m in straight runs and at all ends, corners, changes of direction and acute variations in level.
Setting posts: See table 1 of the British Standard. Insert the method and depth.
Other requirements: If barbed wire is required, the details can be given here (e.g. two lines of barbed wire). BS 1722: Part 4 specifies that the posts should be increased by 150 mm in height for each line of barbed wire.

Close boarded

Type: Use table 1 from the British Standard and select reference (e.g. BCM 120). The type reference indicates whether oak or other timber is to be used, material of posts, height and whether posts are mortised or recessed to receive rails.

Height: State size. Part 5 specifies heights of 1,050, 1,200, 1,500, 1,650 and 1,800 mm.

Boards/rails: See Guidance Notes. BS 1722: Part 5 specifies feather-edged boards and arris (triangular section) or rectangular rails. Insert e.g. softwood feather-edged boards on 75 × 50 mm arris rails.

Posts: Specify concrete or timber posts' length and size. Insert type of treatment and/or desired service life.

Centres of posts: State distances between posts.

Setting posts: Insert the method and the depth (e.g. set in rammed earth to a minimum depth of 600 mm). BS 1722: Part 5 specifies concrete posts to be set in concrete and timber posts to be set in rammed earth or concrete.

Other requirements: State whether a gravel board (concrete or timber) and/or a capping is required (for use with mortised posts only). State whether barbed wire is required, the number of lines and the finish for the mild steel extension arms.

Wooden palisade

Type: Use table 1 from the British Standard and select reference (e.g. WPC 120). The type reference indicates whether oak or other timber is to be used, material of posts, whether posts are mortised or recessed to receive rails and height.

Height: State size. Part 6 specifies heights of 1,050, 1,200, 1,500, 1,650 and 1,800 mm.

Palisades and rails: Give details of the timber required and the design of palisade and rails, e.g. 75 × 20 mm softwood with pointed tops and arris rails. BS 1722: Part 6 specifies palisades of 75 × 20 mm, 65 × 20 mm and triangular section cut from 50 × 50 mm. Arris (triangular section) or rectangular rails can be specified.

Posts: Specify concrete or timber posts, length and size.

Preservation treatment: Insert type of treatment and/or desired service life.

Centres of posts: State distances between posts.

Setting posts: Insert method and depth. The British Standard specifies concrete posts to be set in concrete and timber posts to be set in rammed earth or concrete.

Other requirements: State whether barbed wire is required, the number of lines and the finish of the mild steel extension arms. A single line of barbed wire can be fixed by stapling to the top of timber posts. BS 1722: Part 6 specifies barbed wire for fixing to the top of 1800 mm high fences only.

Wooden post and rail

Type: Use table 1 from the British Standard and select reference (e.g. MPR 11/3). There are two basic constructions – mortised and nailed.

Height: State size. Part 7 specifies only two heights of fence – 1,100 and 1,300 mm.

Timber: Specify type of timber.

Preservation treatment: Insert type of treatment and/or desired service life (e.g. CCA category B).

Centres of posts: BS 1722: Part 7 specifies: 2.85 m for mortised fences, 1.80 m for nailed fences.

Setting posts: BS 1722: Part 7 specifies setting in concrete or rammed earth, or posts can be driven. Mortised fences have an intermediate ('prick') post which is set by driving to a depth of 450 mm.

Wooden panel

Type: Use table 1 from the British Standard and select reference (e.g. WW 60).

Infill: Options include:

- Woven wood
- Waney edged overlapping horizontal boards
- Square sawn overlapping horizontal or vertical boards
- Feather-edged overlapping horizontal or vertical boards.

BS 1722: Part 11 specifies preservative treatment for panels other than those made from Western red cedar. State which is required.

Height: State size. Part 11 specifies heights of 600, 900, 1,200, 1,500 and 1,800 mm.
Posts: Insert details (either timber or concrete).
Preservation treatment: Part 11 specifies preservative treatment for all timber other than Western red cedar.
Setting posts: Insert method and the depth.

Metal types

For metal fences BS 1722 covers the following parts:

Part 1   Chain Link
Part 2   Woven Wire
Part 3   Strained Wire
Part 8   Mild Steel Bar
Part 9   Mild Steel Vertical Bar
Part 10   Anti-Intruder
Part 12   Steel Palisade
Part 13   Tennis Court

Chain link
BS 1722: Part 1 specifies chain link fencing for domestic and commercial use with heights ranging from 900 to 1,800 mm (2,130 mm with barbed wire extension arms).

Type: Select reference from BS 1722: Part 1, tables 1 or 2 (e.g. GLS 140C).
Height: Specify measurements. Heights given in BS 1722: Part 1 are based on commonly available widths of chain link mesh.
Mesh and wire: Insert the type of wire and finish required. Mesh size and wire gauge are specified in BS 1722: Part 1 for each height and application of the fencing and need not be given unless a different size and gauge are required.
Posts and struts: Insert details (e.g. concrete, wood or metal). Proprietary non-standard types of post (e.g. lattice pylons) can be specified as an alternative.
Treatment: Insert (e.g. galvanised). For preservative treated timber insert type of treatment required and/or desired service life (e.g. CCA category B).
Centres of posts: State distances between posts. These requirements are specified in BS 1722: Part 1.

Setting posts: See table and insert details.

Woven wire
Woven wire fencing to BS 1722: Part 2 is mainly used for agricultural and forestry use. It is in two parts:

* General pattern.
* Specialised types (with high tensile spring steel wire support) for rabbit and deer control in forestry protection.

Type: Select reference from BS 1722: Part 2, table 1 (e.g. C6/90/30W).
Height: State size and specify measurements.
Mesh: Insert requirements selected from BS 1722: Part 2, table 6 (e.g. hexagonal mesh above C6/90/30W woven wire).
Posts and struts: See table in BS 1722: Part 2 which specifies:

* Concrete.
* Steel angle, tube and rectangular hollow section.
* Square sawn or round timber.
* Round or sawn timber for posts of high tensile pattern fences.

Treatment: Insert details (e.g. galvanised for metal, creosote for timber).
Centres of posts: Specify dimensions. Intermediate posts should be at not greater than 25 m centres for rabbit fencing and 14 m centres for stock, sheep and deer fencing.
Setting posts: See tables in BS and specify dimensions.

Strained wire
BS 1722: Part 2 specifies two basic forms of strained wire fencing – general pattern and dropper pattern. The use of droppers permits greater spacing of intermediate posts while still maintaining the correct spacing of the wires.

Type: Select from BS 1722: Part 3, table 1 (e.g. SW10.B).
Height: Specify size.
Wire: BS 1722: Part 3 specifies:

* Mild steel wire (4, 4.5 and 5 mm diameter).

- High tensile steel wire (3.15 mm diameter) and steel barbed wire.
- Plastics-coated high tensile steel wire.
- Spring steel wire (dropper pattern fences only).
- Barbed wire.

All wire is required to be zinc coated. The choice of method of fixing the wires to the posts can usually be left to the fencing contractor. However, if a particular method is required (see BS 1722: Part 3, clause 3.3) it should be specified.

Droppers: BS 1722: Part 3 specifies cleft chestnut pale, timber battens and galvanised or zinc-coated steel. If droppers are not required, delete the item.

Posts and struts: See tables in BS 1722: Part 3 which specify:

- Concrete.
- Steel angle, tube and rectangular hollow section.
- Square sawn, round and cleft timber.

Treatment: Insert (e.g. galvanised). For preservative treated timber insert type of treatment required and/or desired service life (e.g. CCA category B).

Centres of posts: Specify dimensions. General pattern intermediate posts are spaced at 3.5 m centres, dropper pattern intermediate posts at 12 m centres.

Setting posts: See table and insert details. If posts for dropper pattern fences are set in concrete, the hole should be filled to the top.

Mild steel continuous bar

Select reference from BS 1722: Part 8, table 1 (e.g. MSCB/105/4).

Height: State size. Part 8 specifies three heights – 1,050, 1,200 and 1,350 mm.

Bars: Insert 'round top bar' and 'flat lower bars' or 'all to be round'.

Posts: Insert 'flats' or 'tee section'. Hollow section pillars would be provided at all ends and may be specified for corners. In soft or loose ground pillars should have thrust plates. Insert details.

Treatment: Insert details (e.g. galvanised).

Centres of posts: Specify dimensions from table 1 in British Standard.

Method of setting: BS 1722: Part 8 specifies the following minimum depths (mm):

Height of fence (mm)	Flat posts with pronged feet	Tee posts	Pillars
1,050	300	400	450
1,200	350	500	550
1,350	350	600	600

Mild steel vertical bar

Also known as 'unclimbable fencing': insert 'welded' or 'self-adjusting' for the type.

Height: Specify size. BS 1722: Part 9 specifies heights ranging from 1,200 to 2,100 mm in 150 mm increments.

Verticals: Dimensions are specified in BS 1722: Part 9. Verticals can be round or square with various tops (e.g. blunt, pointed, spear, bow, double bow, interlaced bow). In addition, square verticals can be fixed 'square to view' or 'angle to view'.

Centres of verticals: Select from Table 5.13.5

Posts: BS 1722: Part 9 specifies flat bar, butt tees, angles and H sections can also be used. If a sufficiently strong section is used for the posts, the stays can be omitted to give a less cluttered appearance.

Treatment: Insert details (e.g. galvanised)

Centres of posts: State dimensions.

Setting posts/stays/legs: There are many proprietary designs of railing, and methods of setting in the ground vary accordingly. BS 1722: Part 9 specifies posts to be driven, stays and legs to be set in rammed earth. If the ground is not suitable, posts, stays and legs can be set in concrete. Posts should be set at the following depths:

Height of fence (mm)	Minimum depth (mm)
1,200, 1,350	530
1,500, 1,650, 1,800	610
1,950, 2,100	760

BS 1722: Part 9 does not specify complete requirements for posts and stays set in concrete. A suggested specification is: 'Concrete in 300 × 300 mm holes filled to not less than half the depth with post holes not less than (e.g.) 600 mm deep.'
Vertical bar railings are often mounted on low walls and can be set between brick pillars instead of posts. In such cases the ends of posts, stays, legs and rails, as appropriate, should be suitable for grouting or running in lead. See BS 5390, Code of Practice for stone masonry, which considers the problems of fixing steel and iron into masonry. Insert appropriate requirements.

Anti-intruder chain link
Type: BS 1722: Part 10 specifies chain link fencing topped with barbed wire, 2.4 m high to the top of the chain link and 2.9 m high to the top line of barbed wire.
Mesh and wire: Insert 'galvanised' or 'plastics coated'. BS 1722: Part 10 specifies plain galvanised wire and Grade A plastics-coated wire (plastics coating on galvanised wire).
Posts and struts: Insert details. State whether posts are to have cranked tops, extension arms or both, to support the barbed wire.
Centres of posts: State dimensions.
Setting posts: From BS 1722: Part 10 specify requirements. Also note:

• Holes for concrete gate posts to be filled up to ground level.
• Holes for steel gate posts to be filled and the foundation brought up to a height of 50 mm above ground level and finished with a weathered top.

Bottom of fencing: Insert details. BS 1722: Part 10 specifies that galvanised mesh, which is to be buried, should be coated with black paint or bitumen solution. The bottom 450 mm is dipped and the bottom 300 mm is then buried vertically. PVC-coated mesh does not need to be dipped.
Other requirements: State any.

Steel palisade
In situations of extreme exposure or abnormal loading it will be necessary to agree special requirements with the manufacturer (e.g. the provision of stays).
Type: Select type from BS 1722: Part 12, table 1 (general-purpose fencing) or table 2 (security fencing) (e.g. SP 30).
Height: State size. BS 1722: Part 12 specifies the following heights:

• General-purpose fencing 1,800 mm and 2,100 mm.
• Security fencing 2,400, 3,000 and 3,600 mm.

Top of pales: Various patterns are available: plain pointed, pointed, split and fanged, rounded, etc. BS 1722: Part 12 specifies tops of pales for security fencing to be pointed, split and fanged.
Treatment. Fencing components and accessories: Provide details. *Fastenings*: Fastenings should be galvanised steel or stainless steel. Sheradised or plated fastenings will normally be adequate if fence is to be painted. BS 1722: Part 12 requires bolts to be burred over to prevent removal and, if galvanised, to be touched up with zinc-rich primer.
Centres of posts: Specify dimensions. BS 1722: Part 12 specifies 2.75 m centres generally and 1.85 m centres for 3,600 mm high fencing.
Post holes: Provide details. Specify the depth as 'equal to one third of the height of the fence above ground level'.
Other requirements: For example, continuous concrete sill to security fencing (see BS 1722: Part 12, clause 4.9, Removable panels).

Tennis court chain link
Height: State size. BS 1722 specifies a minimum of 2,750 mm.
Mesh and wire: Mesh size and wire gauge are specified in the British Standard and need not be given unless a different size and gauge are required. However, it is necessary to specify the type of wire required and finish (e.g. 'green plastics-coated galvanised mesh and line wire').
Posts and struts: BS specifies steel angle and rectangular hollow section (including the sizes).

Centres of posts: State dimensions.
Setting posts: Insert the method and depth. For posts set in concrete insert also the plan size of the post hole and the requirement to fill the hole not less than half full. BS 1722: Part 13 specifies sizes of holes for straining, struts and intermediate posts to be set in concrete. BS 1722: Part 13 permits alternative methods of setting posts when ground conditions vary. All posts can be set in rammed earth and in poor ground intermediate posts can be set in concrete.

Tables 5 to 8

Tables 5 to 8 summarise the detailed requirements of BS 1722 for setting posts in the ground. Specify the method and depth required in the relevant clause. For posts set in concrete, insert also the plan size of the post hole and the requirement to fill the hole to not less than half full.

Acknowledgements to National Building Specification Ltd.

TABLE 5. POSTS FOR CHAIN LINK FENCING

	Straining posts	Struts	Intermediate posts
Method of setting concrete posts	Concrete	Concrete	Concrete
Method of setting steel posts	Concrete or rammed earth	Concrete or rammed earth	1,800 high – concrete Others – concrete, rammed earth or driven
Method of setting timber posts	Concrete or rammed earth	Concrete or rammed earth	Concrete, rammed earth or driven
Plan size of post holes for setting in concrete (mm)	450 × 450 or 300 diameter	300 × 450	To give 75 mm cover all round or 300 diameter
Minimum depth of post holes for any method of setting: Height of fence (mm)	900, 1,200, 1,400 over 1,400	All heights	900, 1,200, 1,400 over 1,400
Depth of hole (mm)	600	750	450 600 750

TABLE 6. POSTS FOR WOVEN WIRE FENCING

	Straining posts	Struts	Intermediate posts
Method of setting concrete posts*	Concrete Concrete	Concrete (loose base plate in rammed earth)	Rammed earth (concrete)
Method of setting steel and timber posts*	Concrete (rammed earth)	Concrete (rammed earth)	Driven
Plan size of post holes for setting in concrete (mm)	450 × 450	300 × 450	To give 75 mm cover all round
Minimum depth of post holes for any method of setting	750	450	600

*BS 1722: Part 2 specifies one method for each type of post. It also suggests alternatives which can be specified if warranted by the ground conditions – these are shown in parentheses.

TABLE 7. POSTS FOR STRAINED WIRE FENCING

	Straining posts	Struts	Intermediate posts
Method of setting concrete posts	Concrete	Concrete	Concrete
Method of setting steel and timber posts	Concrete or rammed earth	Concrete or rammed earth	Concrete, rammed earth or driven
Plan size of post holes for setting in concrete (mm)	450 × 450 or 300 diameter	300 × 450	To give 75 mm cover all round or 300 diameter
Minimum depth of post holes for any method of setting: Height of fence (mm)	900 1,050–1,350 1,800, 2,100	All heights	Less than 1,800 1,800, 2,100
Depth of hole (mm) – for concrete	600 750 900	450	600 750
– for rammed earth	900 1,050 1,200	450	600 750

100

TABLE 8. POSTS FOR CLEFT CHESTNUT PALE FENCING

	Straining posts	Struts	Intermediate posts
Method of setting concrete posts	Concrete	Concrete	Concrete
Method of setting timber posts	Concrete or rammed earth	Concrete or rammed earth	Driven
Plan size of post holes for setting in concrete (mm)	300 × 300 or 300 diameter	300 × 450	To give 75 mm cover all round or 300 diameter
Minimum depth of post holes for any method of setting: Height of fence (mm)	Less than 1,500 1,500, 1,800	All heights	Less than 1,500 1,500, 1,800
Depth of hole (mm)	600	750	450 600 750

DETAIL SHEETS

General
Cappings (2)
Timber post foundations (2)
Osier hurdles
Woven wood
Waney edge board
Close board – medium
Close board – high
Close board – double-sided
Close board – thick and thin board
Close board – with brick
Timber palisade – medium
Timber palisade – high
Timber palisade – double-sided
Timber palisade – diagonal board
Timber palisade – with PVC
Palisade – angled
Horizontal double slatted
Horizontal open slatted
Cleft chestnut
Cleft chestnut and wire
Post and rail – staggered joints
Post and rail – butt joints
Lincolnshire post and rail
Sussex two rail
Post and wire
Plastic mesh

Low mesh (2)
Timber and mesh
Timber poles
Metal
Vertical bar – medium (2)
Vertical bar – tall
Bow topped – low
Bow topped – medium
Metal – flat section (2)
Chain link 1800
Chain link 3000
General
Concrete palisade

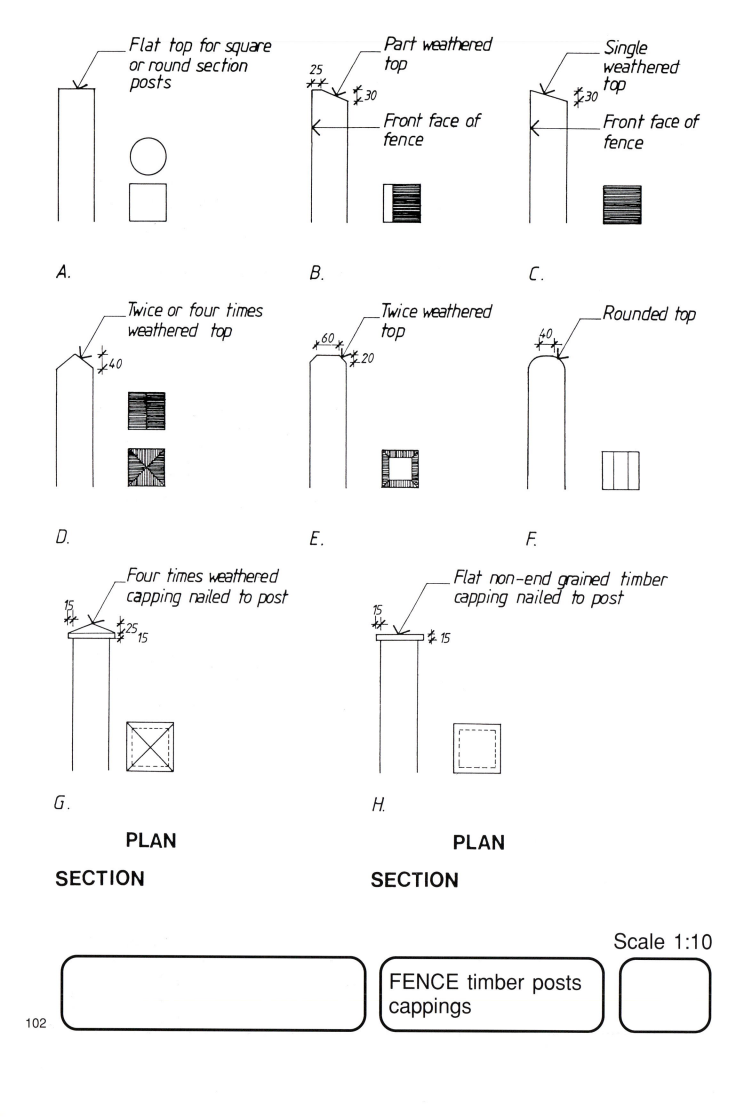

Flat top for square or round section posts

A.

Part weathered top
25
30
Front face of fence

B.

Single weathered top
30
Front face of fence

C.

Twice or four times weathered top
40

D.

Twice weathered top
60
20

E.

Rounded top
40

F.

Four times weathered capping nailed to post
15
25
15

G.

PLAN

SECTION

Flat non-end grained timber capping nailed to post
15
15

H.

PLAN

SECTION

Scale 1:10

FENCE timber posts cappings

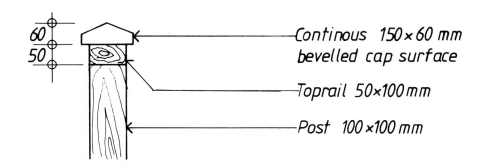

60
50

Continous 150 × 60 mm
bevelled cap surface

Toprail 50×100 mm

Post 100 ×100 mm

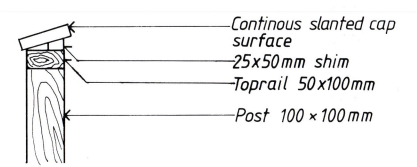

Continous slanted cap
surface

25x50mm shim

Toprail 50 x100mm

Post 100 × 100 mm

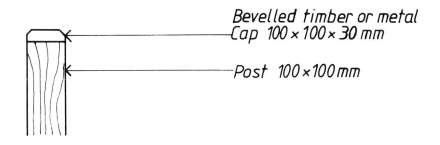

Bevelled timber or metal
Cap 100 × 100 × 30 mm

Post 100 ×100mm

Scale 1:10

FENCE
caps

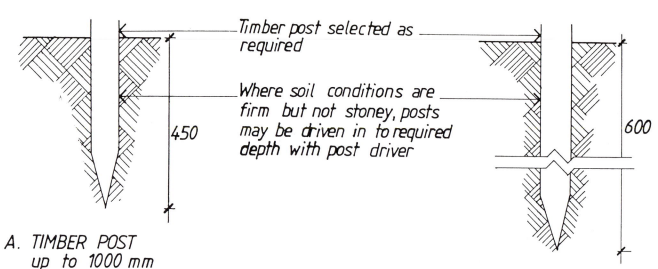

Timber post selected as required

Where soil conditions are firm but not stoney, posts may be driven in to required depth with post driver

450

600

A. TIMBER POST
up to 1000 mm

B. TIMBER POST
1000 to 2000mm

1. DRIVEN

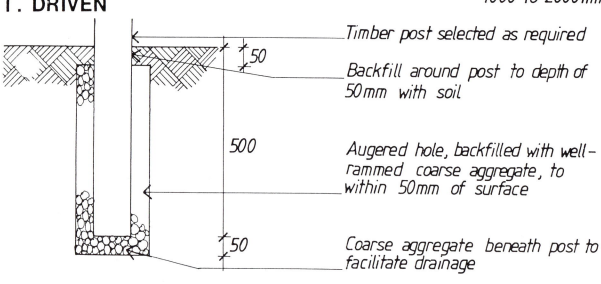

Timber post selected as required

50

Backfill around post to depth of 50mm with soil

500

Augered hole, backfilled with well-rammed coarse aggregate, to within 50mm of surface

50

Coarse aggregate beneath post to facilitate drainage

A. TIMBER POST   upto 1000 mm

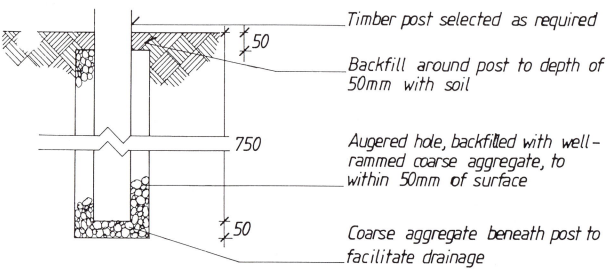

Timber post selected as required

50

Backfill around post to depth of 50mm with soil

750

Augered hole, backfilled with well-rammed coarse aggregate, to within 50mm of surface

50

Coarse aggregate beneath post to facilitate drainage

B. TIMBER POST   1000 to 2000mm

2. RAMMED

Scale 1:10

FENCE timber posts foundations

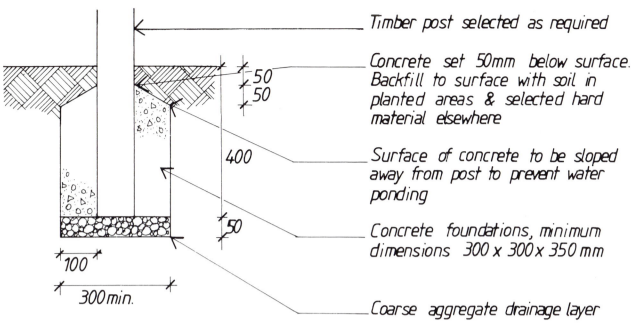

Timber post selected as required

Concrete set 50mm below surface. Backfill to surface with soil in planted areas & selected hard material elsewhere

Surface of concrete to be sloped away from post to prevent water ponding

Concrete foundations, minimum dimensions 300 x 300 x 350 mm

Coarse aggregate drainage layer

50
50
400
50
100
300 min.

A. TIMBER POST upto 1000mm

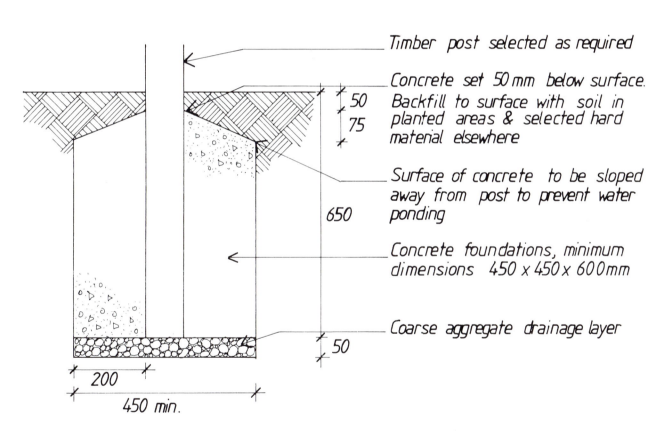

Timber post selected as required

Concrete set 50 mm below surface. Backfill to surface with soil in planted areas & selected hard material elsewhere

Surface of concrete to be sloped away from post to prevent water ponding

Concrete foundations, minimum dimensions 450 x 450 x 600mm

Coarse aggregate drainage layer

50
75
650
50
200
450 min.

B. TIMBER POST 1000 to 2000 mm

3. CONCRETE

Scale 1:10

FENCE timber posts foundations

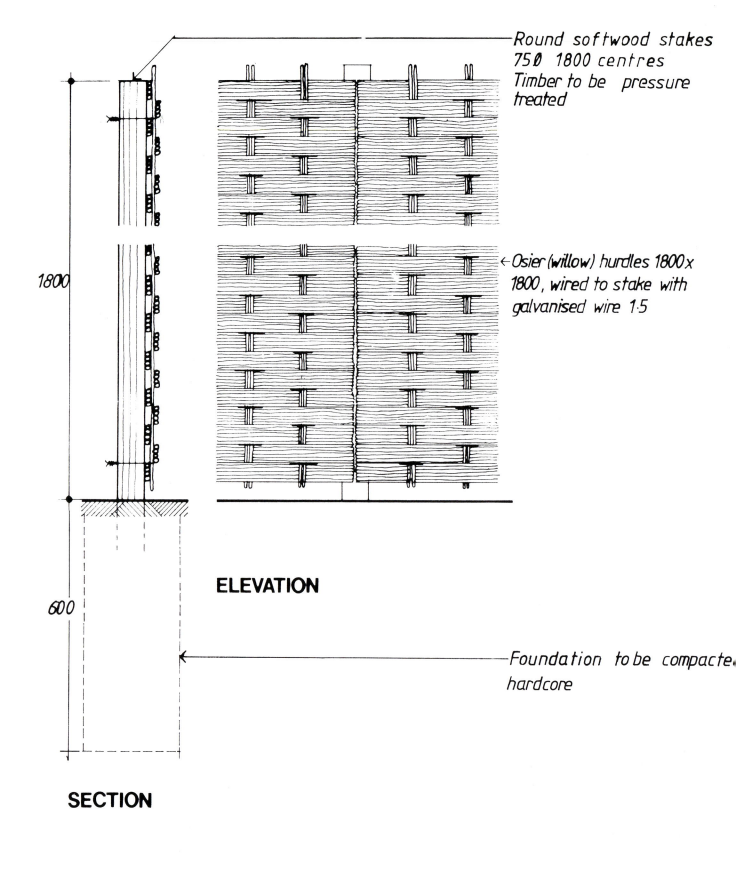

Round softwood stakes
75∅ 1800 centres
Timber to be pressure
treated

←Osier (willow) hurdles 1800 x
1800, wired to stake with
galvanised wire 1·5

1800

600

ELEVATION

Foundation to be compacte.
hardcore

SECTION

Scale 1:10

FENCE
osier hurdles

106

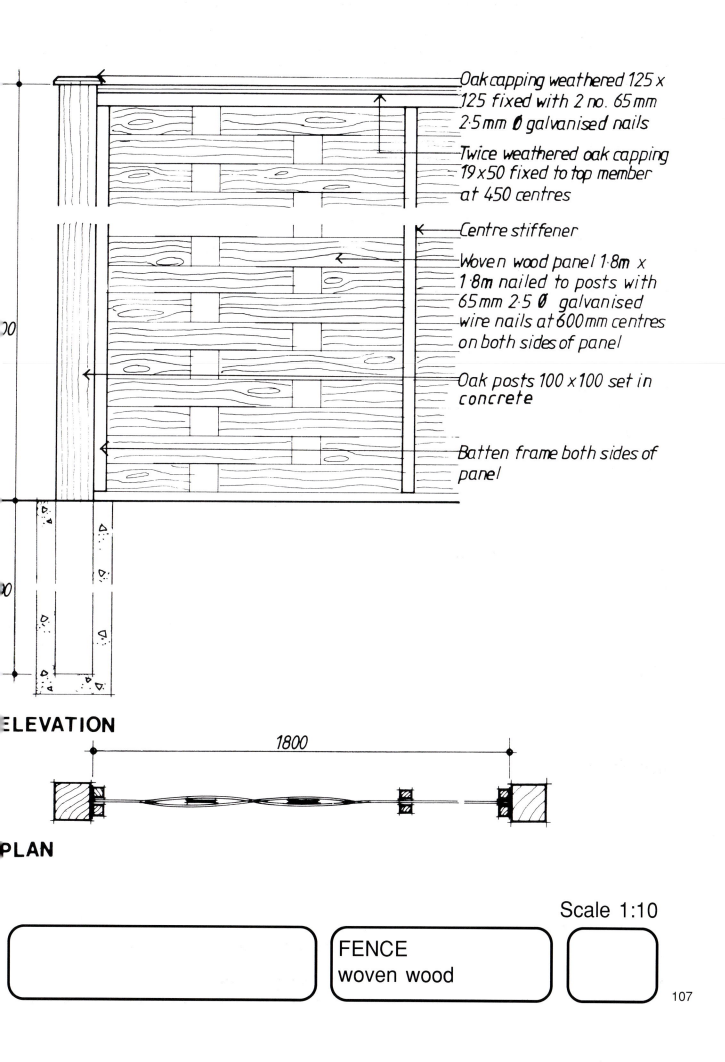

Oak capping weathered 125 x
125 fixed with 2 no. 65 mm
2·5mm Ø galvanised nails

Twice weathered oak capping
19 x 50 fixed to top member
at 450 centres

Centre stiffener

Woven wood panel 1·8m x
1·8m nailed to posts with
65mm 2·5 Ø galvanised
wire nails at 600mm centres
on both sides of panel

Oak posts 100 x 100 set in
concrete

Batten frame both sides of
panel

ELEVATION

1800

PLAN

Scale 1:10

FENCE
woven wood

107

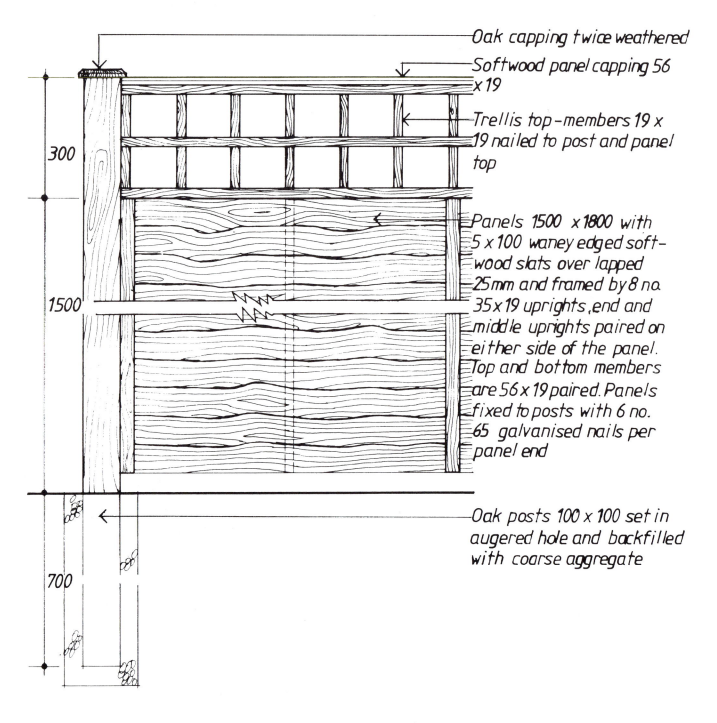

Oak capping twice weathered

Softwood panel capping 56 x 19

Trellis top-members 19 x 19 nailed to post and panel top

300

1500

Panels 1500 x 1800 with 5 x 100 waney edged soft-wood slats over lapped 25mm and framed by 8 no. 35 x 19 uprights, end and middle uprights paired on either side of the panel. Top and bottom members are 56 x 19 paired. Panels fixed to posts with 6 no. 65 galvanised nails per panel end

Oak posts 100 x 100 set in augered hole and backfilled with coarse aggregate

700

ELEVATION

Scale 1:10

FENCE
waney edge board

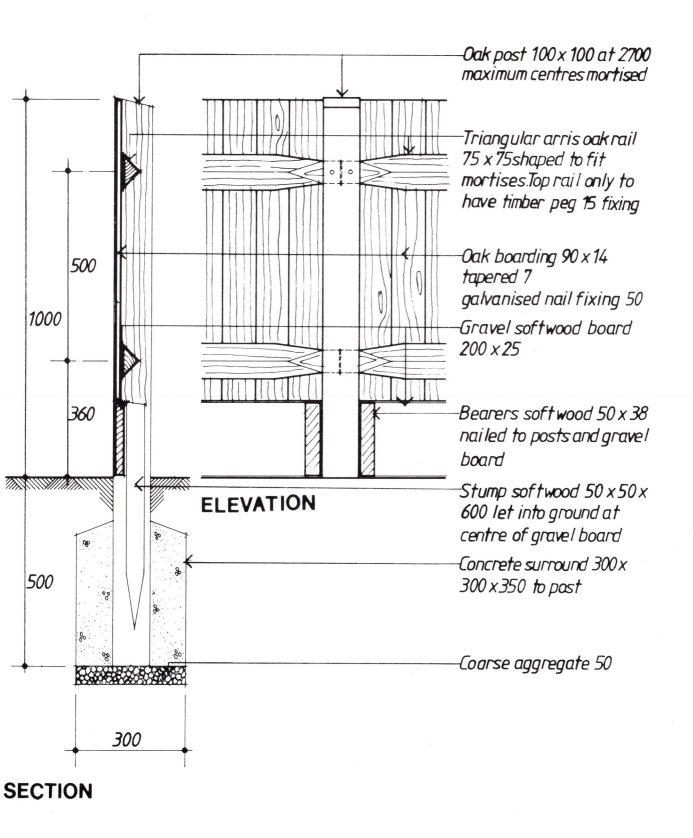

Oak post 100 x 100 at 2700 maximum centres mortised

Triangular arris oak rail 75 x 75 shaped to fit mortises. Top rail only to have timber peg 15 fixing

Oak boarding 90 x 14 tapered 7 galvanised nail fixing 50

Gravel softwood board 200 x 25

Bearers softwood 50 x 38 nailed to posts and gravel board

Stump softwood 50 x 50 x 600 let into ground at centre of gravel board

Concrete surround 300 x 300 x 350 to post

Coarse aggregate 50

500

1000

360

500

300

ELEVATION

SECTION

Scale 1:10

FENCE
close board – medium

109

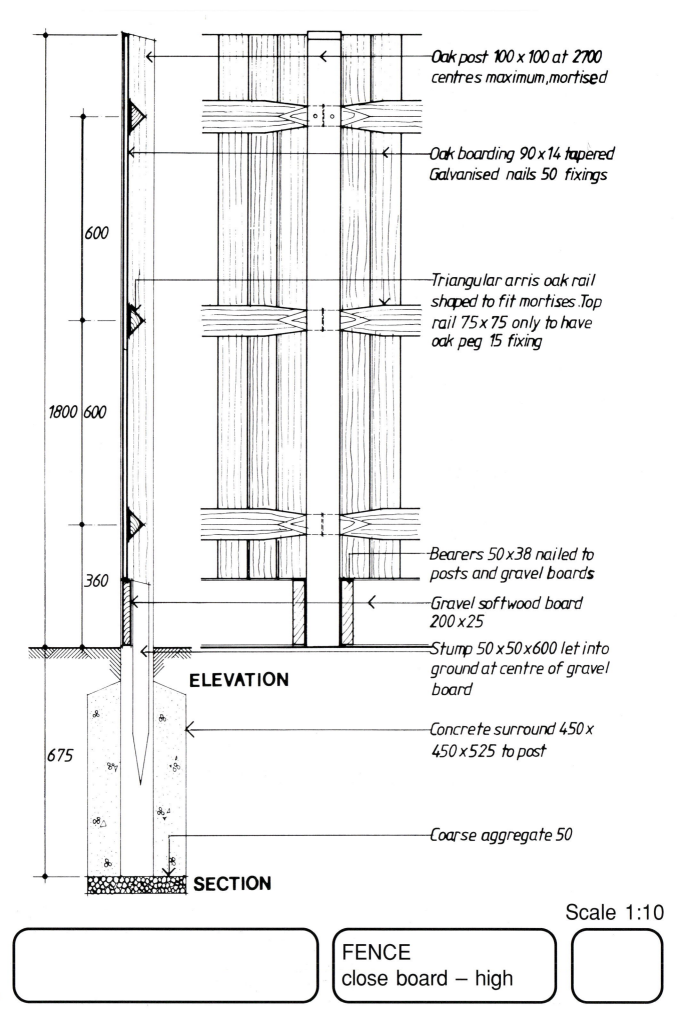

Oak post 100 x 100 at 2700 centres maximum, mortised

Oak boarding 90 x 14 tapered Galvanised nails 50 fixings

Triangular arris oak rail shaped to fit mortises. Top rail 75 x 75 only to have oak peg 15 fixing

Bearers 50 x 38 nailed to posts and gravel boards

Gravel softwood board 200 x 25

Stump 50 x 50 x 600 let into ground at centre of gravel board

Concrete surround 450 x 450 x 525 to post

Coarse aggregate 50

600

1800 600

360

675

ELEVATION

SECTION

Scale 1:10

FENCE
close board – high

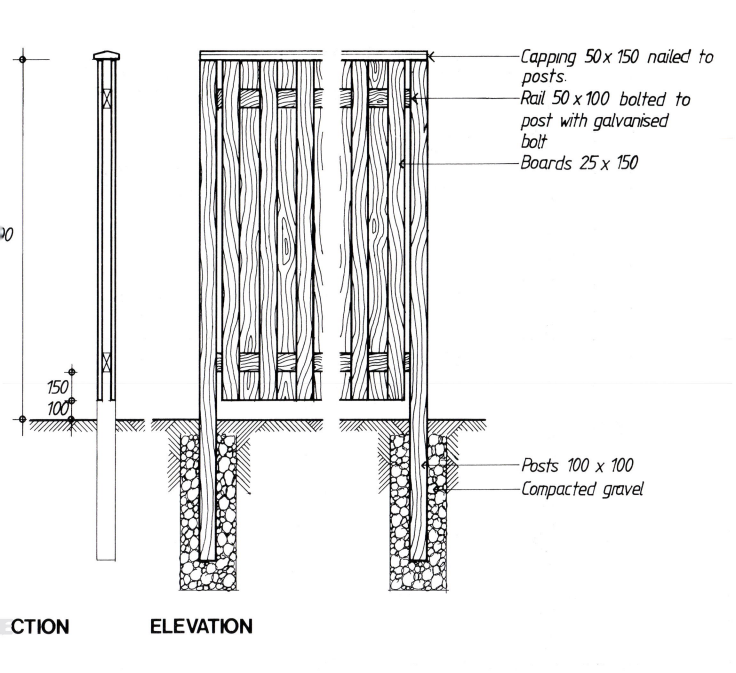

Capping 50 x 150 nailed to posts.

Rail 50 x 100 bolted to post with galvanised bolt

Boards 25 x 150

150

100

Posts 100 x 100

Compacted gravel

CTION   **ELEVATION**

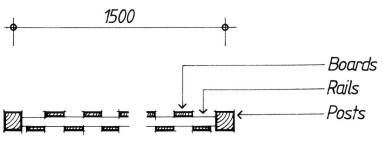

1500

Boards

Rails

Posts

PLAN

Scale 1:20

FENCE
close board –
double-sided

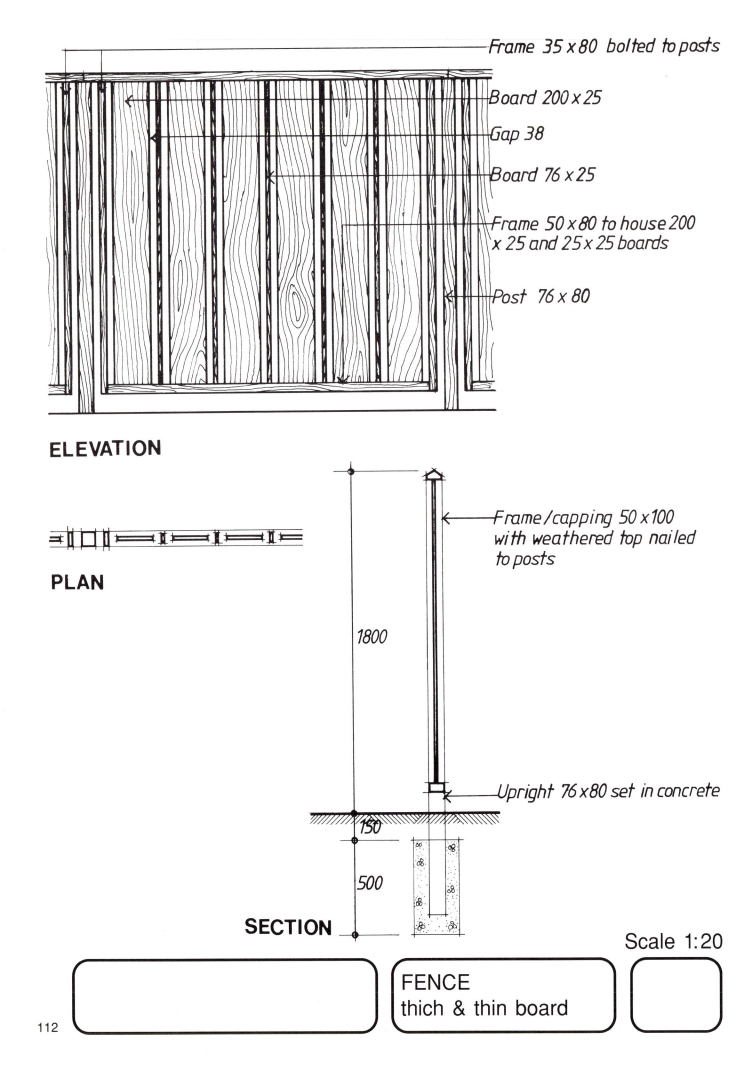

Frame 35 x 80 bolted to posts

Board 200 x 25

Gap 38

Board 76 x 25

Frame 50 x 80 to house 200 x 25 and 25 x 25 boards

Post 76 x 80

ELEVATION

PLAN

Frame/capping 50 x 100 with weathered top nailed to posts

1800

Upright 76 x 80 set in concrete

150

500

SECTION

Scale 1:20

FENCE
thich & thin board

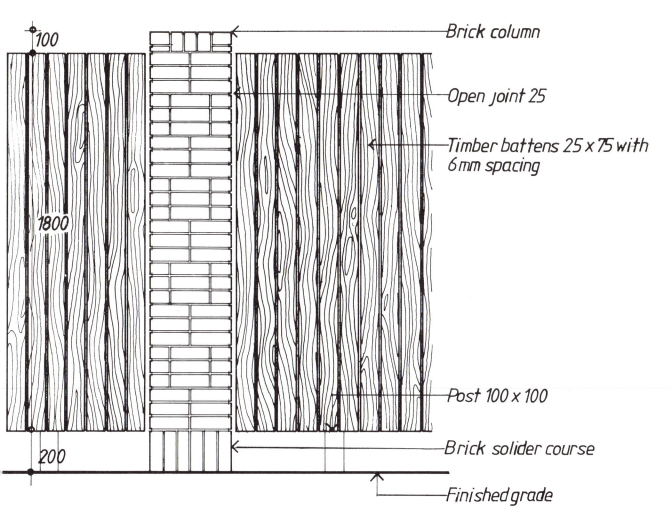

100

1800

200

Brick column

Open joint 25

Timber battens 25 x 75 with
6 mm spacing

Post 100 x 100

Brick solider course

Finished grade

ELEVATION

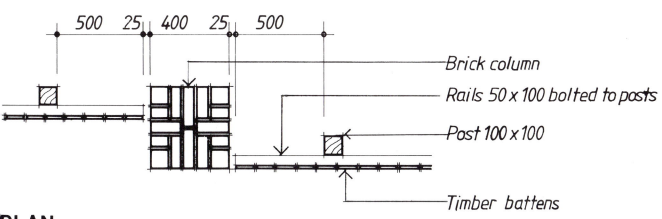

500   25   400   25   500

Brick column

Rails 50 x 100 bolted to posts

Post 100 x 100

Timber battens

PLAN

Scale 1:20

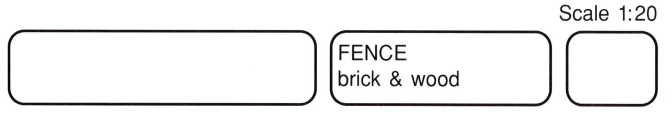

FENCE
brick & wood

113

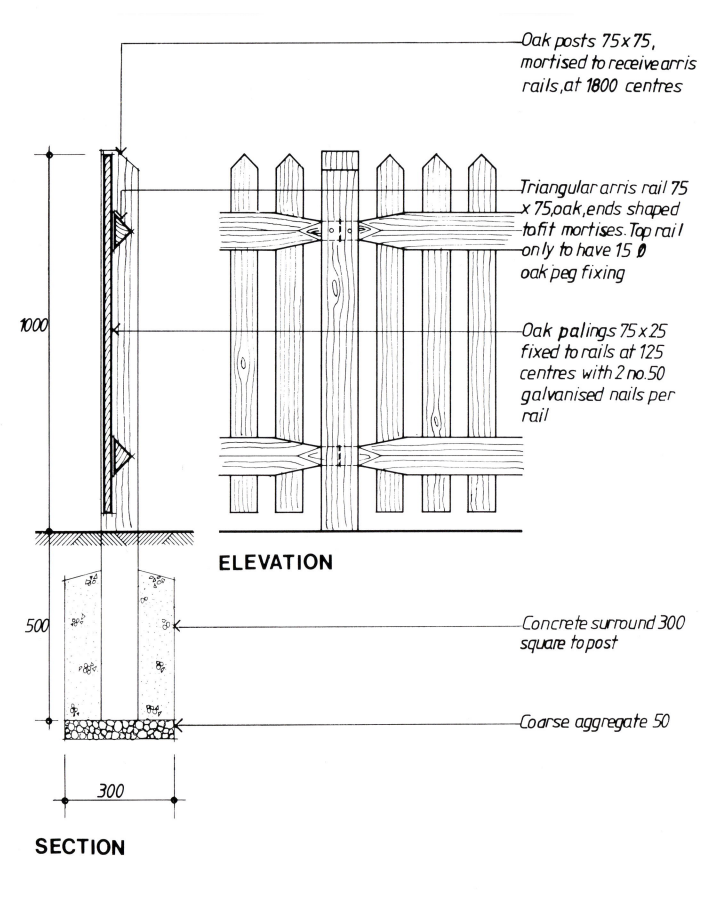

Oak posts 75 x 75, mortised to receive arris rails, at 1800 centres

Triangular arris rail 75 x 75, oak, ends shaped to fit mortises. Top rail only to have 15 ∅ oak peg fixing

Oak palings 75 x 25 fixed to rails at 125 centres with 2 no.50 galvanised nails per rail

1000

ELEVATION

Concrete surround 300 square to post

500

Coarse aggregate 50

300

SECTION

Scale 1:10

114

FENCE
timber palisade –
medium

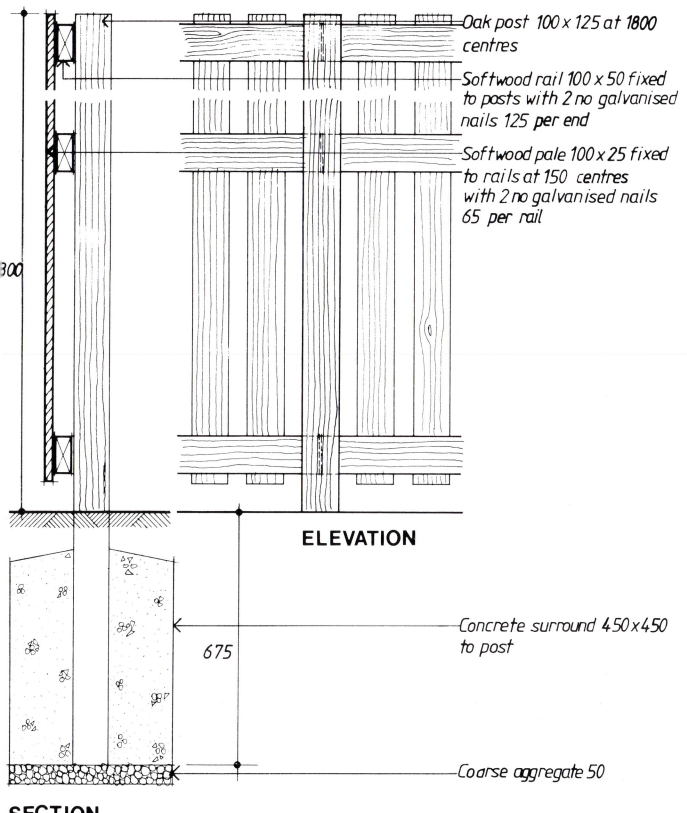

Oak post 100 x 125 at 1800 centres

Softwood rail 100 x 50 fixed to posts with 2 no galvanised nails 125 per end

Softwood pale 100 x 25 fixed to rails at 150 centres with 2 no galvanised nails 65 per rail

300

ELEVATION

Concrete surround 450 x 450 to post

675

Coarse aggregate 50

SECTION

Scale 1:10

FENCE
timber palisade –
high

115

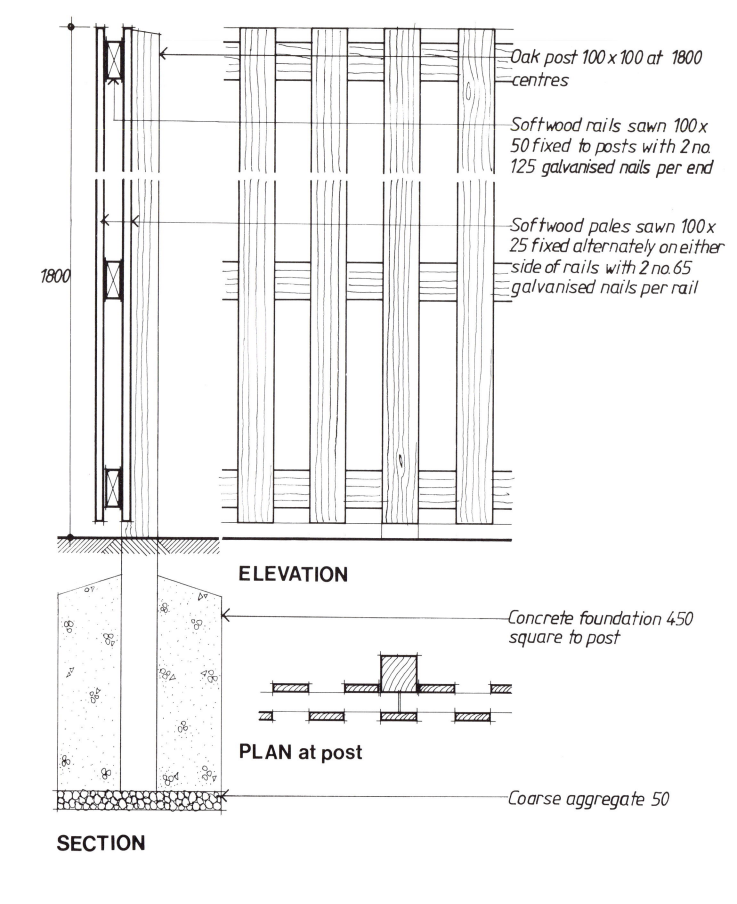

Oak post 100 x 100 at 1800 centres

Softwood rails sawn 100 x 50 fixed to posts with 2 no. 125 galvanised nails per end

Softwood pales sawn 100 x 25 fixed alternately on either side of rails with 2 no. 65 galvanised nails per rail

1800

ELEVATION

Concrete foundation 450 square to post

PLAN at post

Coarse aggregate 50

SECTION

Scale 1:10

FENCE
double sided palisade

116

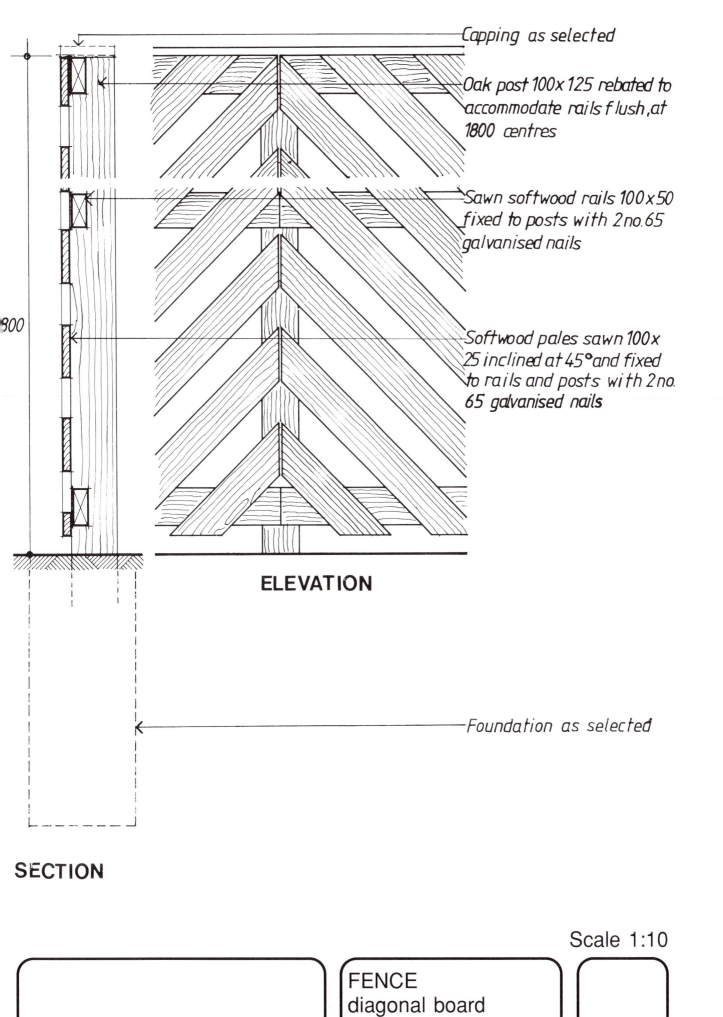

Capping as selected

Oak post 100x125 rebated to accommodate rails flush, at 1800 centres

Sawn softwood rails 100x50 fixed to posts with 2 no. 65 galvanised nails

Softwood pales sawn 100x 25 inclined at 45° and fixed to rails and posts with 2 no. 65 galvanised nails

1800

ELEVATION

Foundation as selected

SECTION

Scale 1:10

FENCE
diagonal board

117

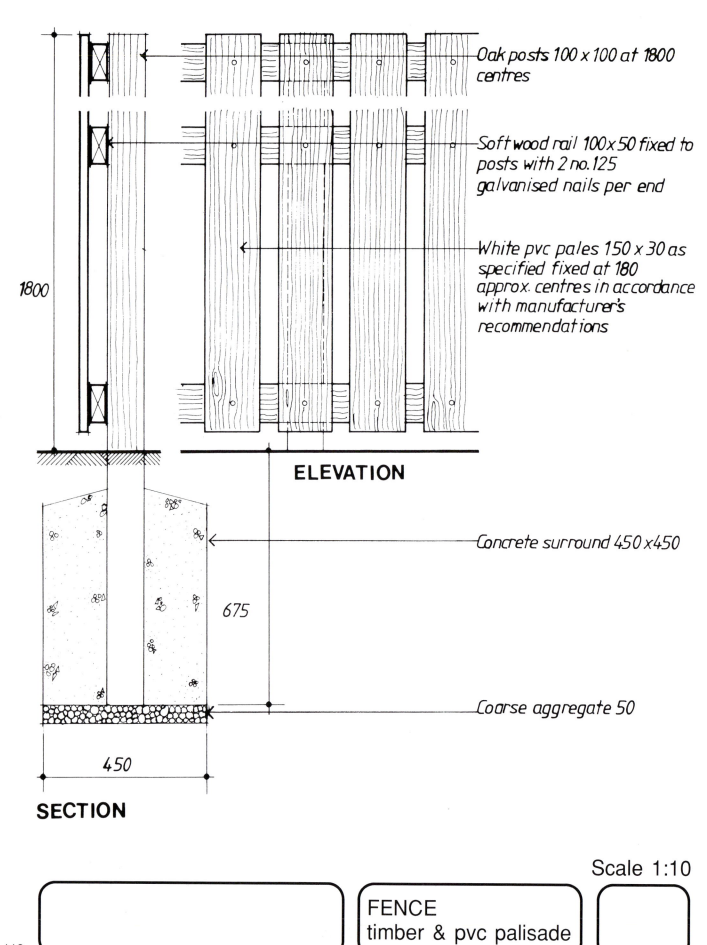

Oak posts 100 x 100 at 1800 centres

Softwood rail 100 x 50 fixed to posts with 2 no. 125 galvanised nails per end

White pvc pales 150 x 30 as specified fixed at 180 approx. centres in accordance with manufacturer's recommendations

1800

ELEVATION

Concrete surround 450 x 450

675

Coarse aggregate 50

450

SECTION

Scale 1:10

FENCE
timber & pvc palisade

118

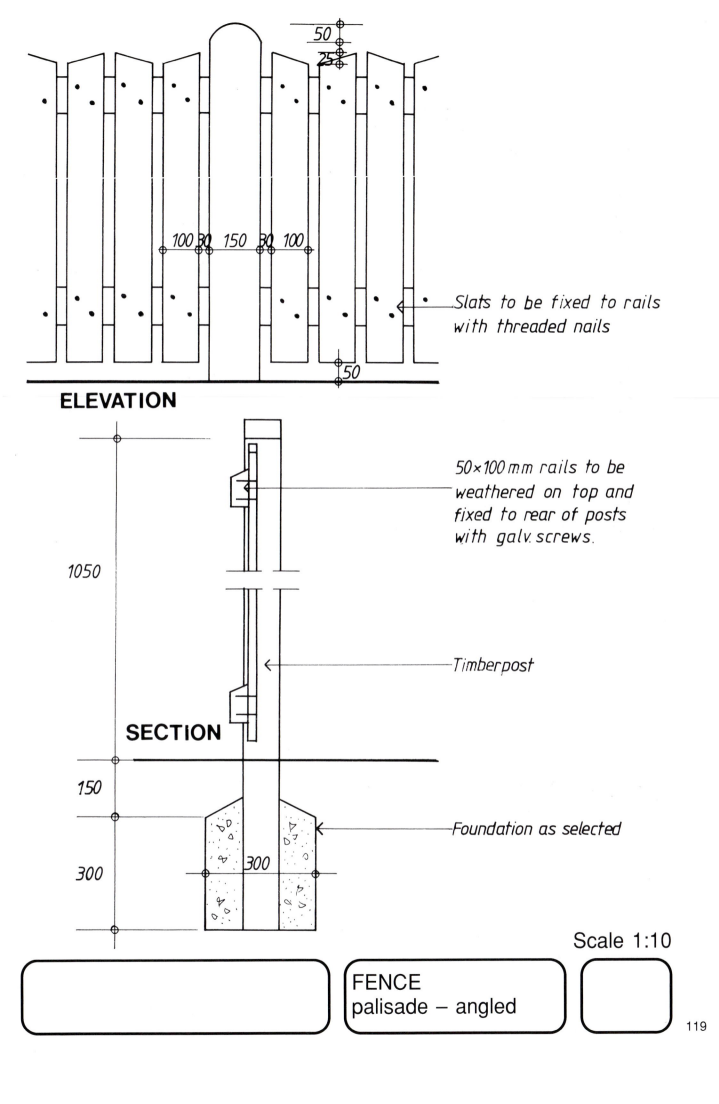

ELEVATION

50
25

100 30 150 30 100

50

Slats to be fixed to rails
with threaded nails

50×100 mm rails to be
weathered on top and
fixed to rear of posts
with galv. screws.

SECTION

1050

150

300

300

Timberpost

Foundation as selected

Scale 1:10

FENCE
palisade – angled

119

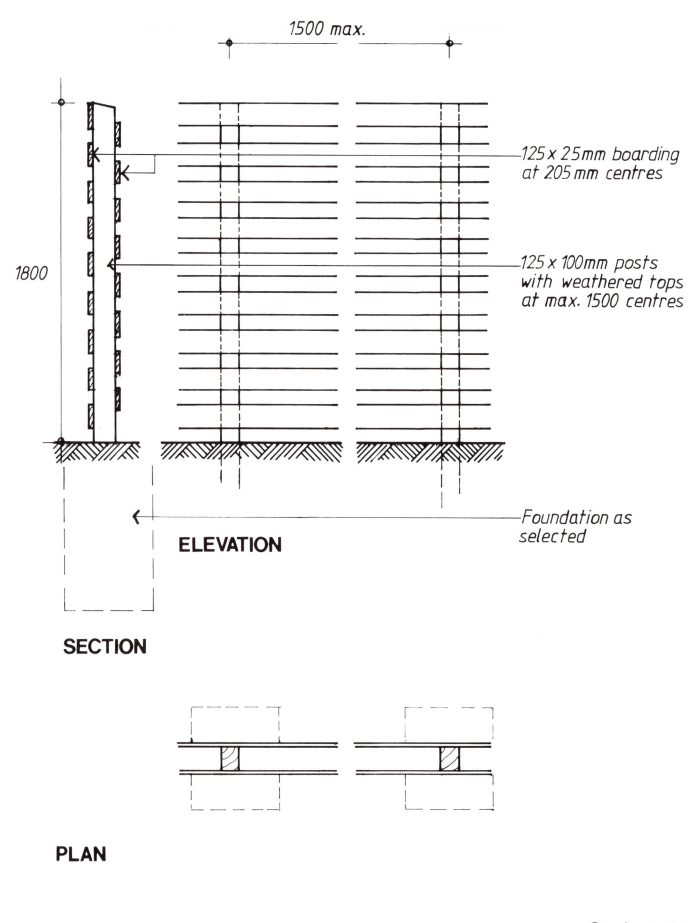

1500 max.

1800

125 x 25mm boarding
at 205mm centres

125 x 100mm posts
with weathered tops
at max. 1500 centres

Foundation as
selected

ELEVATION

SECTION

PLAN

Scale 1:20

FENCE
horizontal double
slatted

120

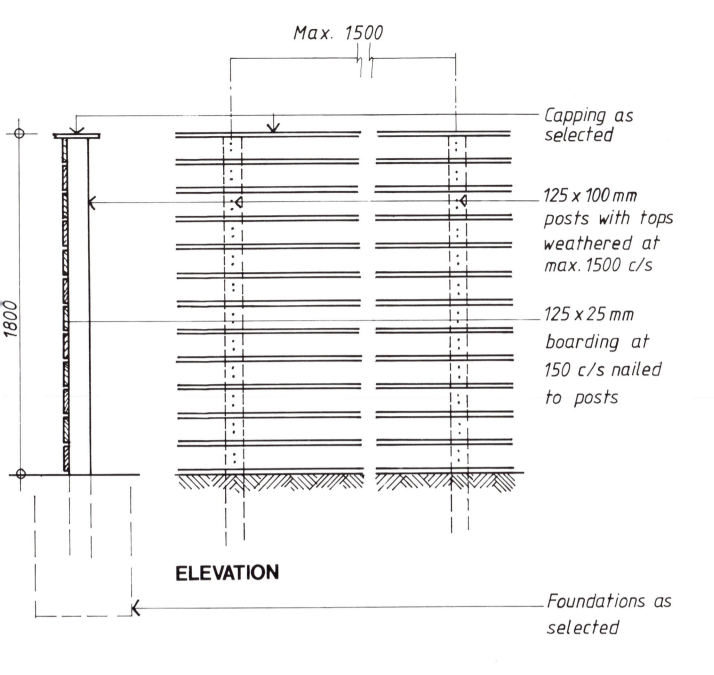

Max. 1500

Capping as selected

125 x 100 mm posts with tops weathered at max. 1500 c/s

125 x 25 mm boarding at 150 c/s nailed to posts

1800

ELEVATION

Foundations as selected

SECTION

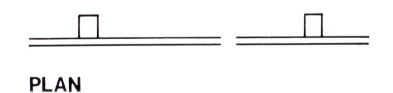

PLAN

Scale 1:20

FENCE
horizontal open
slatted

121

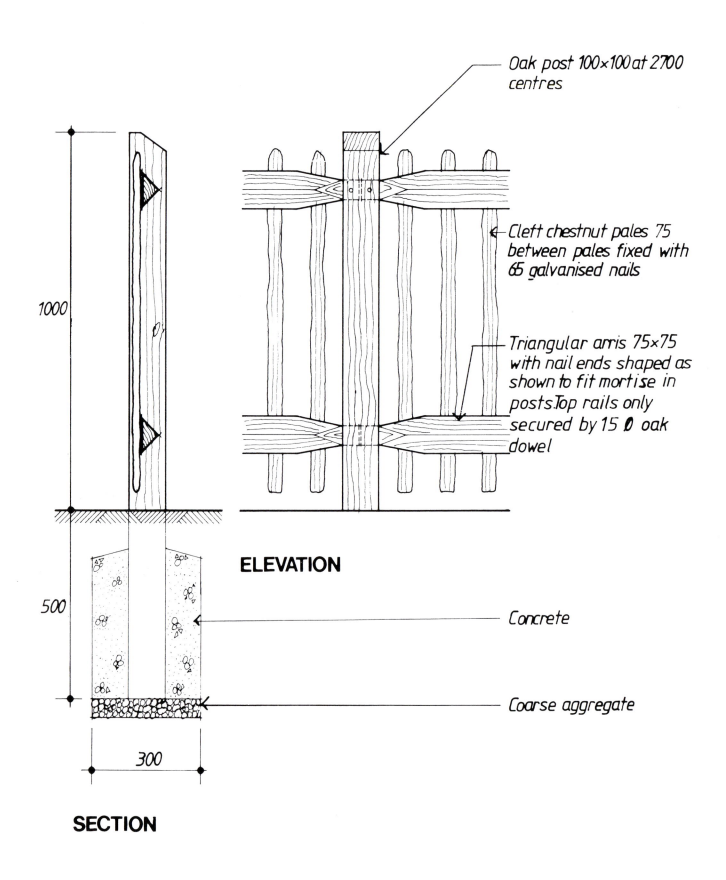

Oak post 100×100 at 2700 centres

Cleft chestnut pales 75 between pales fixed with 65 galvanised nails

Triangular arris 75×75 with nail ends shaped as shown to fit mortise in posts. Top rails only secured by 15 Ø oak dowel

1000

500

300

ELEVATION

SECTION

Concrete

Coarse aggregate

Scale 1:10

FENCE
cleft chestnut

122

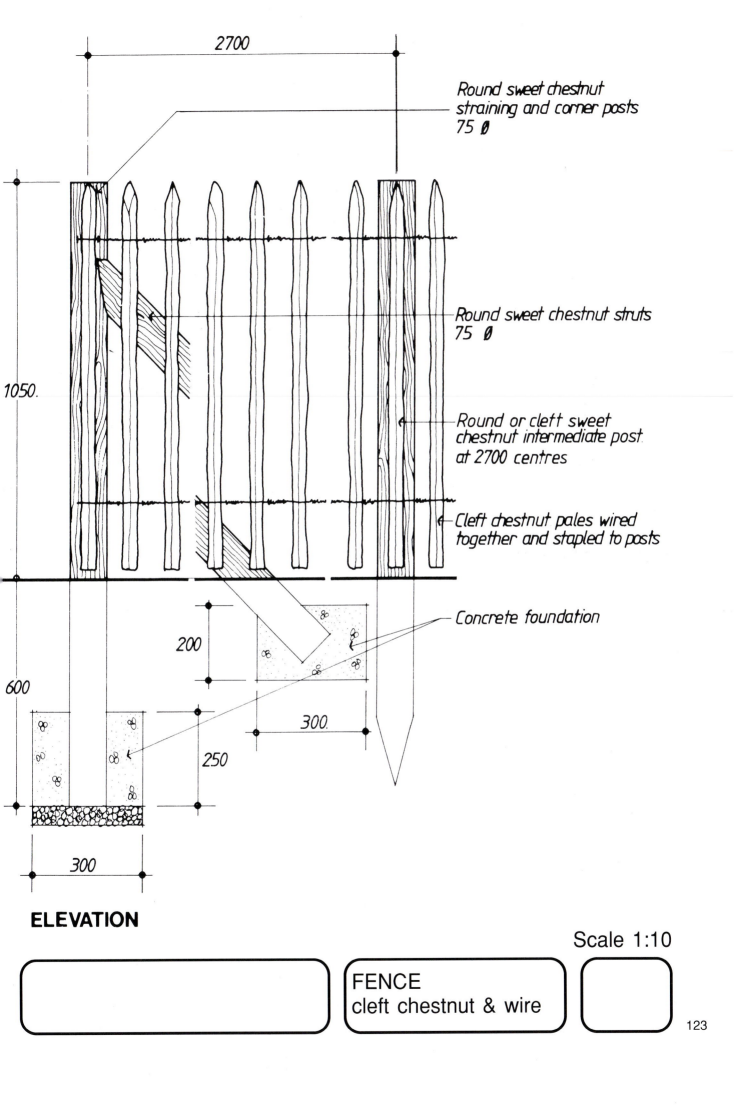

2700

Round sweet chestnut
straining and corner posts
75 Ø

Round sweet chestnut struts
75 Ø

1050.

Round or cleft sweet
chestnut intermediate post
at 2700 centres

Cleft chestnut pales wired
together and stapled to posts

Concrete foundation

200

600

300.

250

300

ELEVATION

Scale 1:10

FENCE
cleft chestnut & wire

123

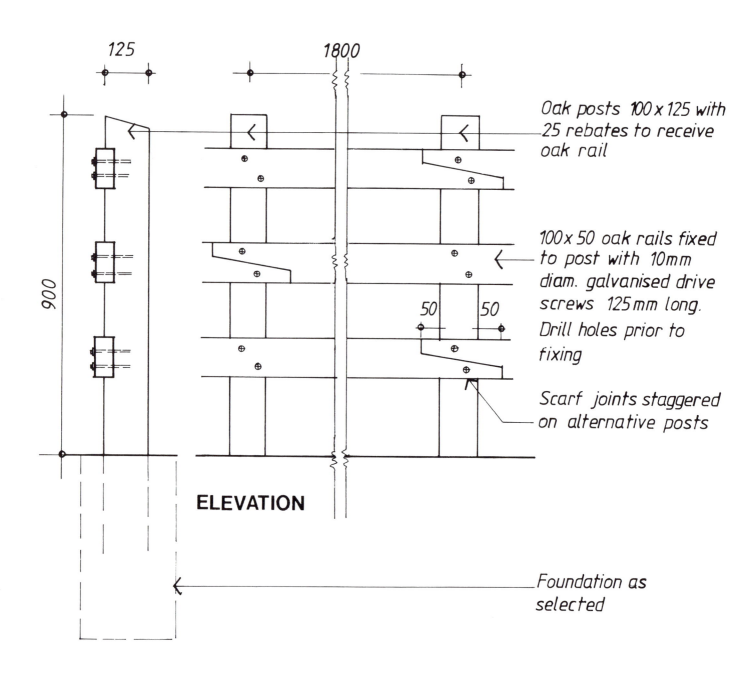

125

1800

Oak posts 100 x 125 with 25 rebates to receive oak rail

100 x 50 oak rails fixed to post with 10mm diam. galvanised drive screws 125mm long. Drill holes prior to fixing

50 50

Scarf joints staggered on alternative posts

900

ELEVATION

Foundation as selected

SECTION

Scale 1:10

FENCE
post & rail –
staggered joints

124

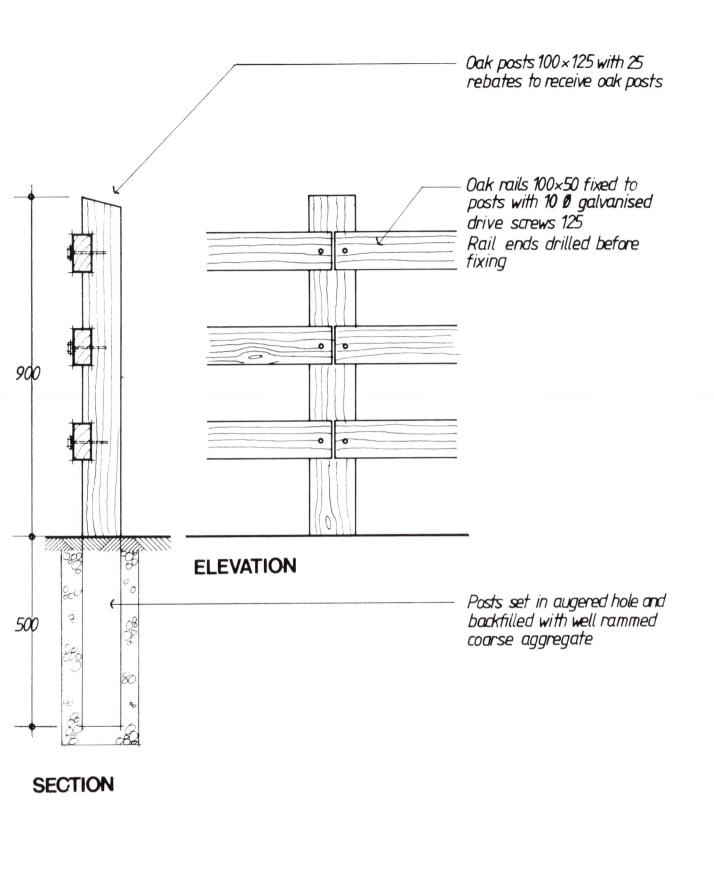

Oak posts 100×125 with 25 rebates to receive oak posts

Oak rails 100×50 fixed to posts with 10 ⌀ galvanised drive screws 125
Rail ends drilled before fixing

900

ELEVATION

Posts set in augered hole and backfilled with well rammed coarse aggregate

500

SECTION

Scale 1:10

FENCE
post & rail –
butt joints

125

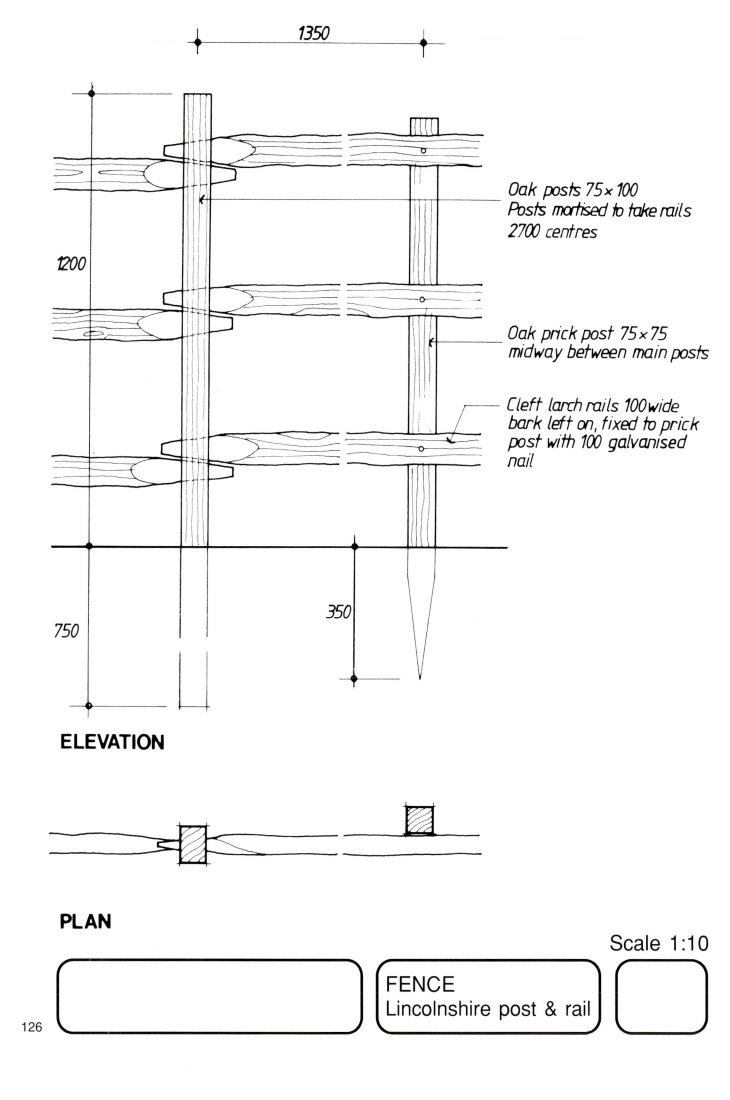

1350

1200

750

350

Oak posts 75 × 100
Posts mortised to take rails
2700 centres

Oak prick post 75 × 75
midway between main posts

Cleft larch rails 100 wide
bark left on, fixed to prick
post with 100 galvanised
nail

ELEVATION

PLAN

Scale 1:10

FENCE
Lincolnshire post & rail

126

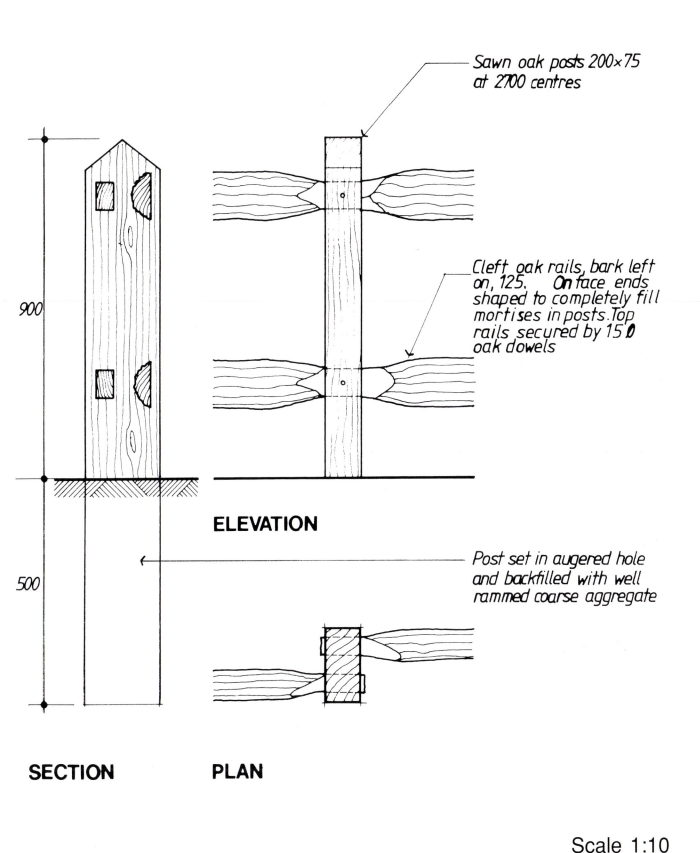

Sawn oak posts 200×75
at 2700 centres

Cleft oak rails, bark left
on, 125. On face ends
shaped to completely fill
mortises in posts. Top
rails secured by 15 ∅
oak dowels

Post set in augered hole
and backfilled with well
rammed coarse aggregate

900

500

ELEVATION

SECTION   **PLAN**

Scale 1:10

FENCE
two rail Sussex

127

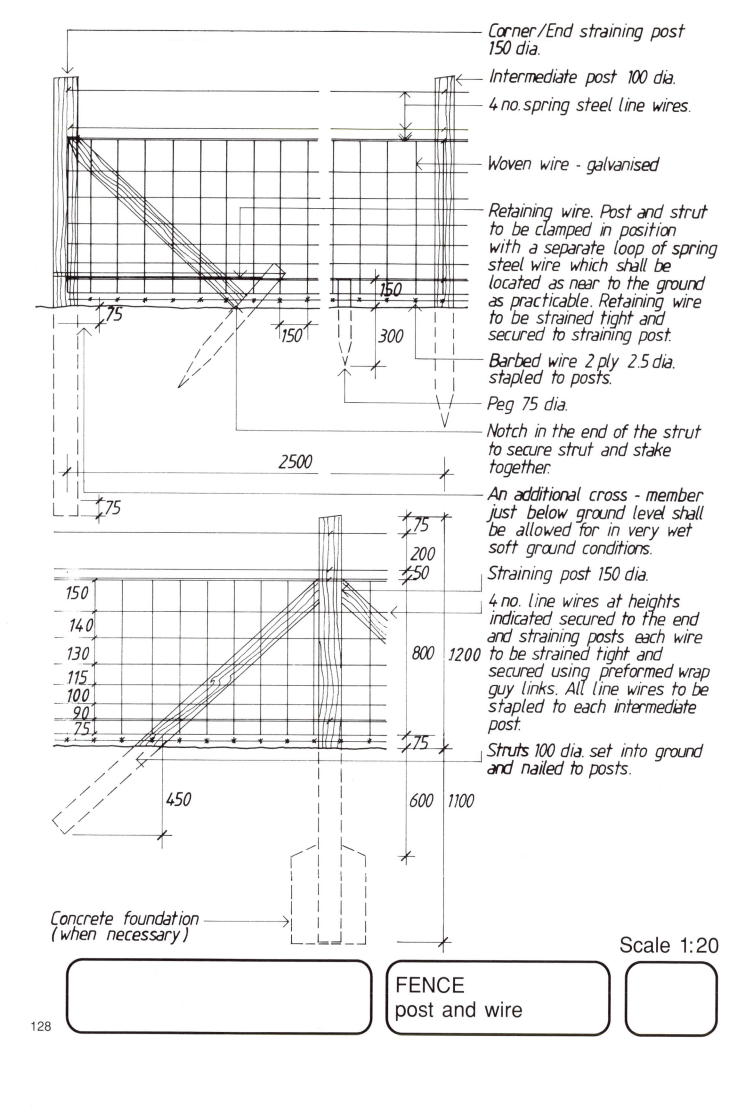

Corner/End straining post 150 dia.

Intermediate post 100 dia.

4 no. spring steel line wires.

Woven wire - galvanised

Retaining wire. Post and strut to be clamped in position with a separate loop of spring steel wire which shall be located as near to the ground as practicable. Retaining wire to be strained tight and secured to straining post.

Barbed wire 2 ply 2.5 dia. stapled to posts.

Peg 75 dia.

Notch in the end of the strut to secure strut and stake together.

An additional cross - member just below ground level shall be allowed for in very wet soft ground conditions.

Straining post 150 dia.

4 no. line wires at heights indicated secured to the end and straining posts each wire to be strained tight and secured using preformed wrap guy links. All line wires to be stapled to each intermediate post.

Struts 100 dia. set into ground and nailed to posts.

Concrete foundation (when necessary)

Scale 1:20

FENCE
post and wire

75   150   2500   300   150

150   140   130   115   100   90   75   450   200   50   75   800   1200   600   1100

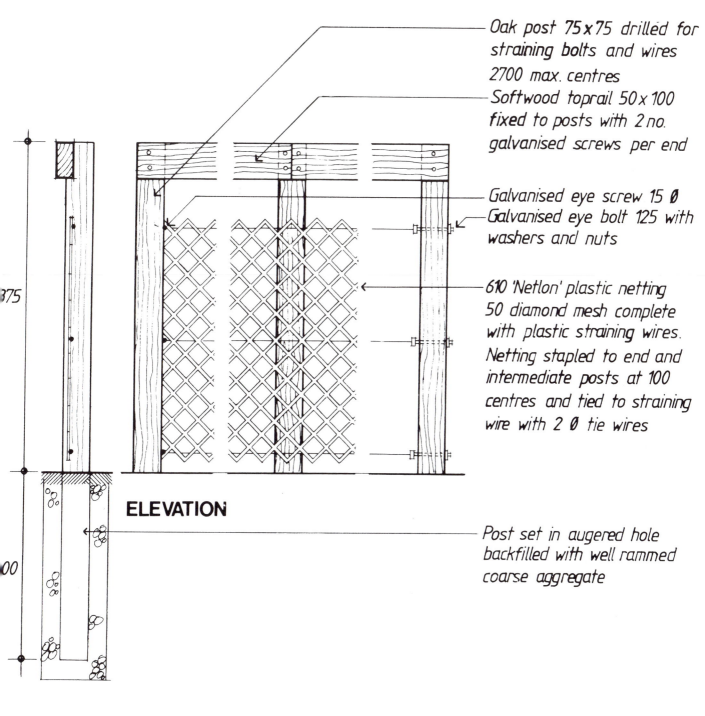

Oak post 75 x 75 drilled for straining bolts and wires 2700 max. centres

Softwood toprail 50 x 100 fixed to posts with 2 no. galvanised screws per end

Galvanised eye screw 15 Ø
Galvanised eye bolt 125 with washers and nuts

610 'Netlon' plastic netting 50 diamond mesh complete with plastic straining wires. Netting stapled to end and intermediate posts at 100 centres and tied to straining wire with 2 Ø tie wires

ELEVATION

Post set in augered hole backfilled with well rammed coarse aggregate

375

00

ECTION

Scale 1:10

FENCE
timber and plastic mesh

129

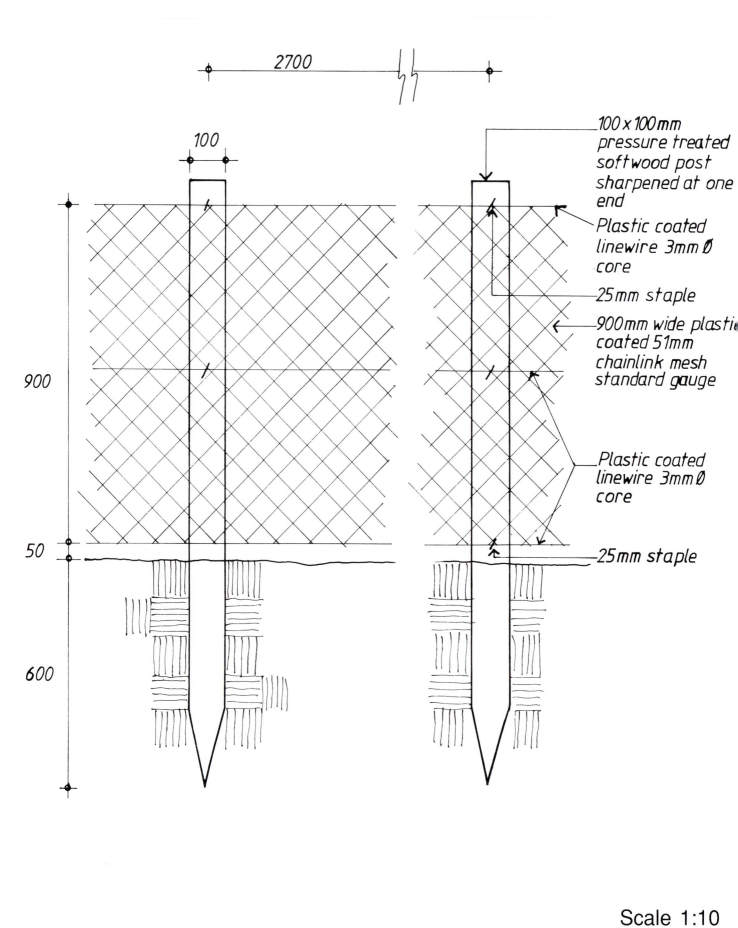

2700

100

900

50

600

100 x 100 mm
pressure treated
softwood post
sharpened at one
end

Plastic coated
linewire 3mm Ø
core

25mm staple

900mm wide plastic
coated 51mm
chainlink mesh
standard gauge

Plastic coated
linewire 3mm Ø
core

25mm staple

Scale 1:10

FENCE
low mesh

130

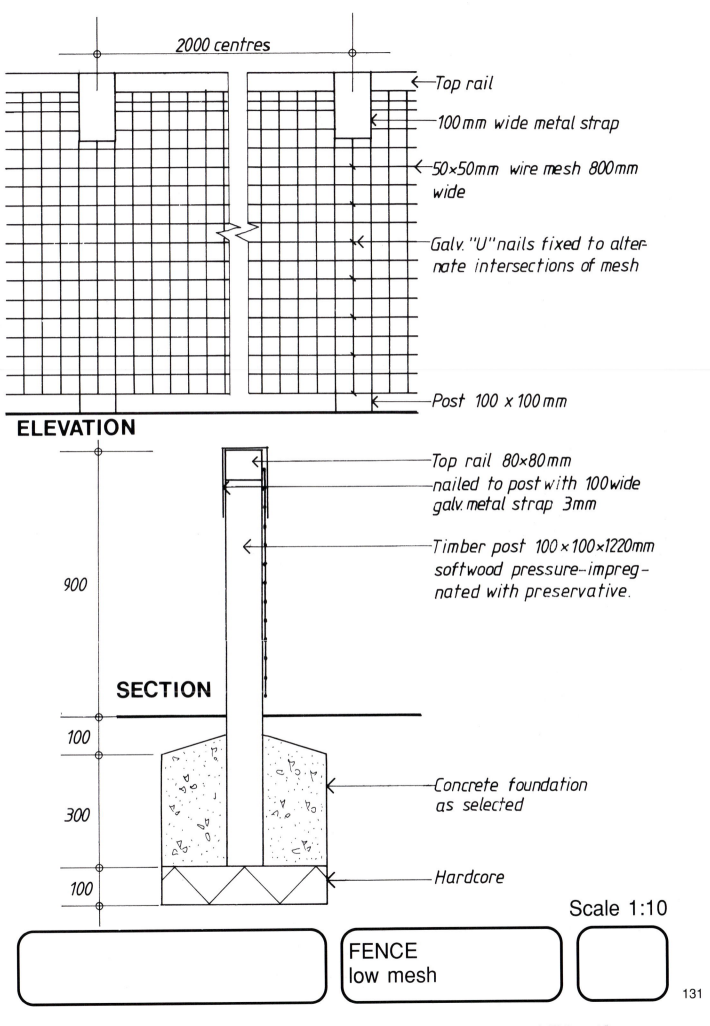

2000 centres

Top rail

100 mm wide metal strap

50×50mm wire mesh 800mm wide

Galv. "U" nails fixed to alternate intersections of mesh

Post 100 × 100 mm

ELEVATION

Top rail 80×80mm nailed to post with 100 wide galv. metal strap 3mm

Timber post 100×100×1220mm softwood pressure-impregnated with preservative.

SECTION

900

100

300

100

Concrete foundation as selected

Hardcore

Scale 1:10

FENCE
low mesh

131

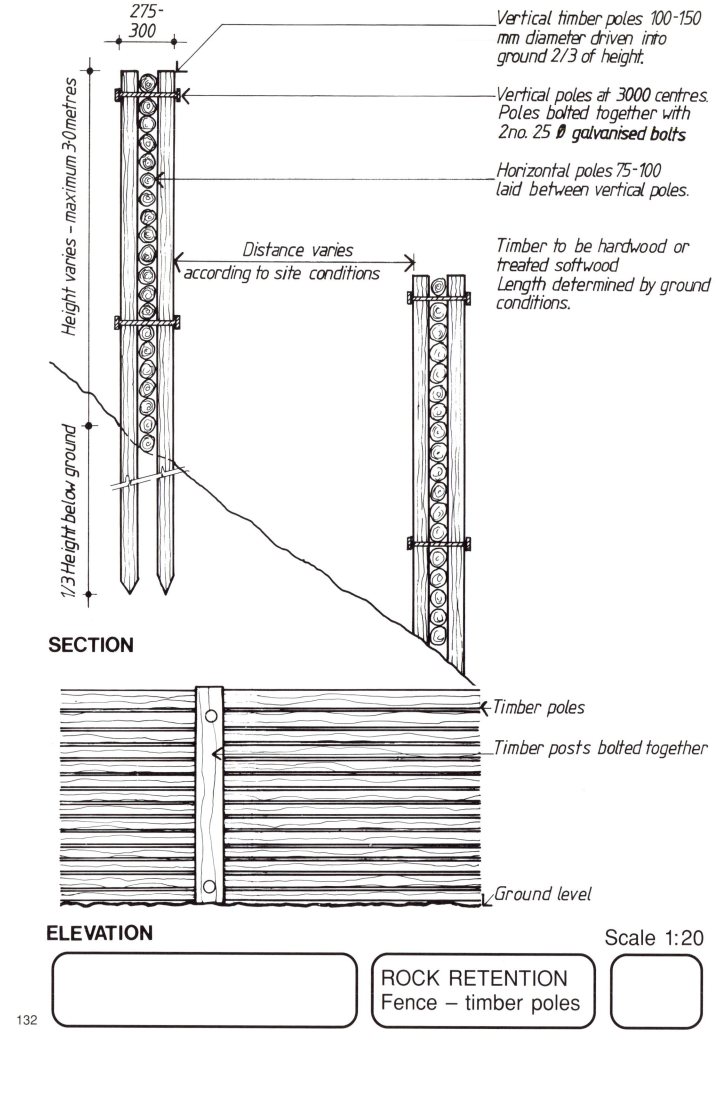

275–300

Vertical timber poles 100-150 mm diameter driven into ground 2/3 of height.

Vertical poles at 3000 centres. Poles bolted together with 2 no. 25 ∅ galvanised bolts

Horizontal poles 75-100 laid between vertical poles.

Timber to be hardwood or treated softwood Length determined by ground conditions.

Height varies – maximum 3·0 metres

1/3 Height below ground

Distance varies according to site conditions

SECTION

Timber poles

Timber posts bolted together

Ground level

ELEVATION

Scale 1:20

ROCK RETENTION
Fence – timber poles

132

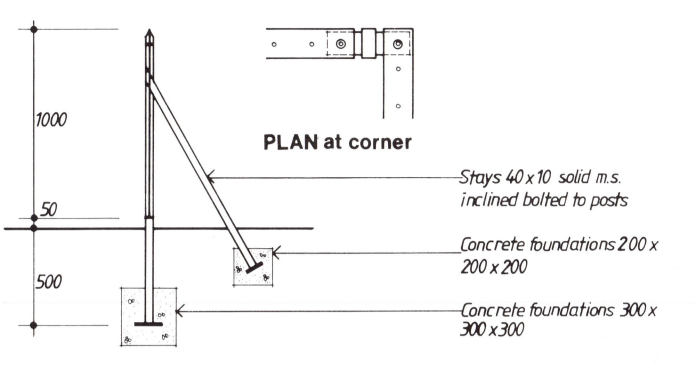

PLAN at corner

1000

50

500

Stays 40 x 10 solid m.s.
inclined bolted to posts

Concrete foundations 200 x
200 x 200

Concrete foundations 300 x
300 x 300

SECTION

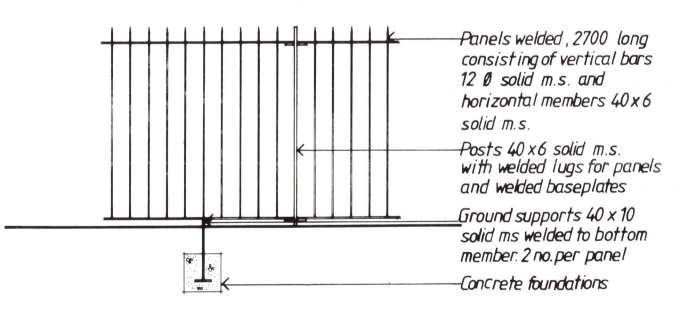

Panels welded, 2700 long
consisting of vertical bars
12 Ø solid m.s. and
horizontal members 40 x 6
solid m.s.

Posts 40 x 6 solid m.s.
with welded lugs for panels
and welded baseplates

Ground supports 40 x 10
solid ms welded to bottom
member. 2 no. per panel

Concrete foundations

ELEVATION

Scale 1:20

FENCE
vertical bar – medium

133

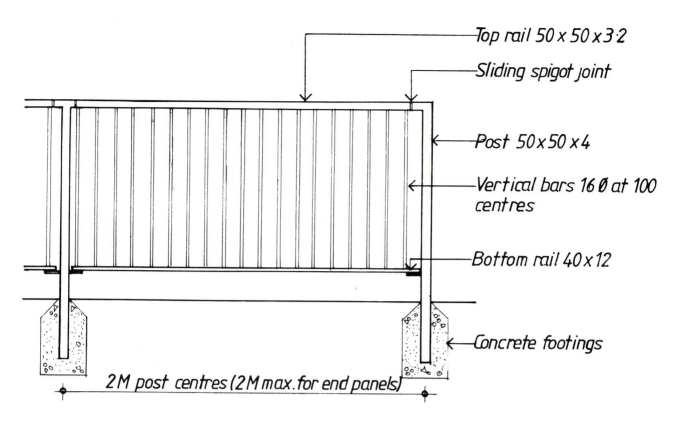

Top rail 50 x 50 x 3·2

Sliding spigot joint

Post 50 x 50 x 4

Vertical bars 16 Ø at 100 centres

Bottom rail 40 x 12

Concrete footings

2M post centres (2M max. for end panels)

ELEVATION

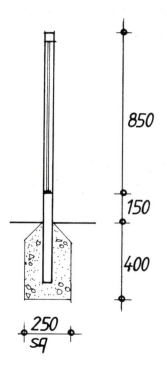

850

150

400

250 sq

SECTION

Scale 1:20

FENCE
vertical bar – medium

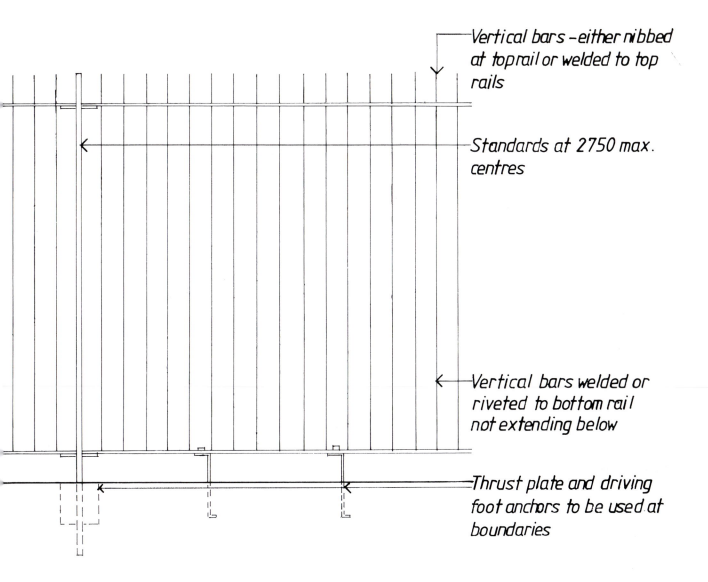

Vertical bars – either nibbed at top rail or welded to top rails

Standards at 2750 max. centres

Vertical bars welded or riveted to bottom rail not extending below

Thrust plate and driving foot anchors to be used at boundaries

ELEVATION

Height of railings vary from approx. 1200 - 2200

Scale 1:20

FENCE
vertical bar – tall

135

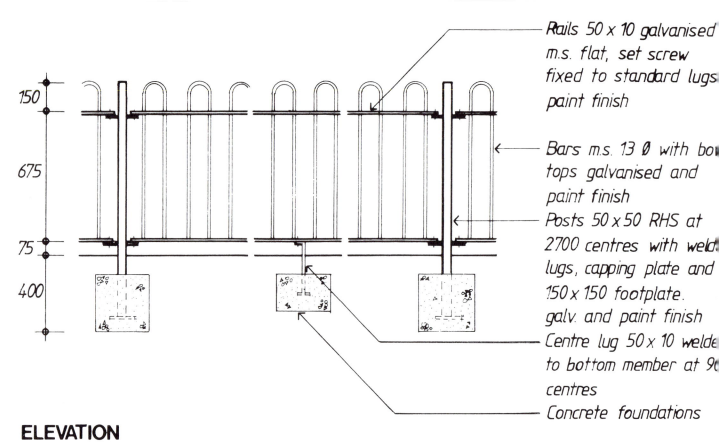

ELEVATION

- 150
- 675
- 75
- 400

Rails 50 x 10 galvanised m.s. flat, set screw fixed to standard lugs paint finish

Bars m.s. 13 Ø with bow tops galvanised and paint finish

Posts 50 x 50 RHS at 2700 centres with weld lugs, capping plate and 150 x 150 footplate. galv. and paint finish

Centre lug 50 x 10 welded to bottom member at 90 centres

Concrete foundations

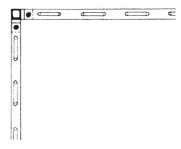

PLAN at corner

Scale 1:20

FENCE
vertical bow topped –

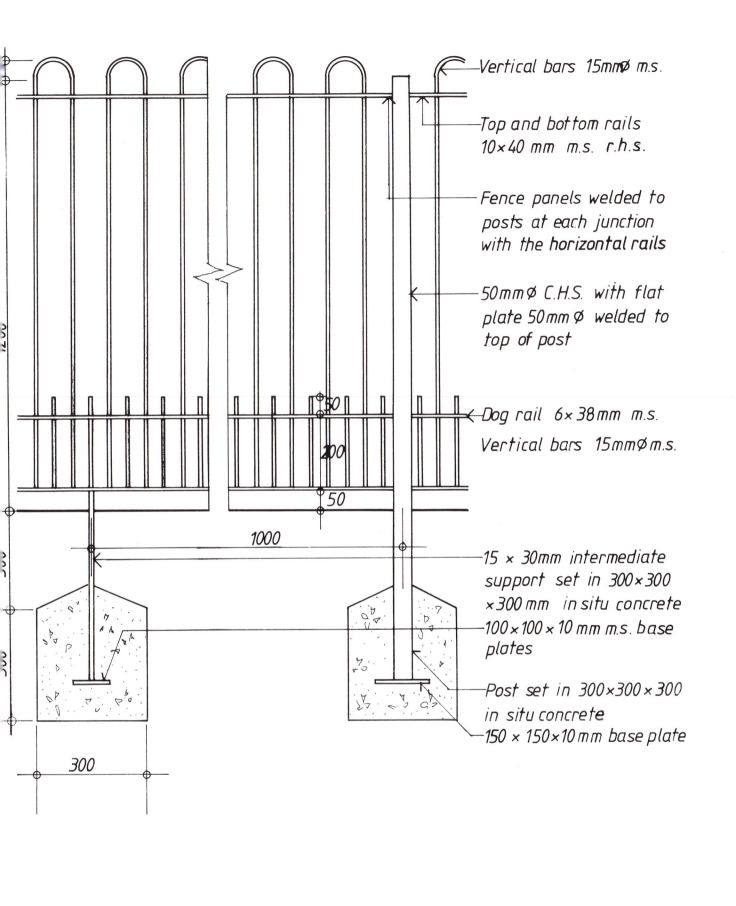

Vertical bars 15mmØ m.s.

Top and bottom rails
10×40 mm m.s. r.h.s.

Fence panels welded to
posts at each junction
with the horizontal rails

50mmØ C.H.S. with flat
plate 50mm Ø welded to
top of post

Dog rail 6×38mm m.s.

Vertical bars 15mmØ m.s.

15 × 30mm intermediate
support set in 300×300
×300 mm in situ concrete

100×100×10 mm m.s. base
plates

Post set in 300×300×300
in situ concrete

150 × 150×10 mm base plate

50

200

50

1000

300

Scale 1:10

FENCE
vertical bow topped –

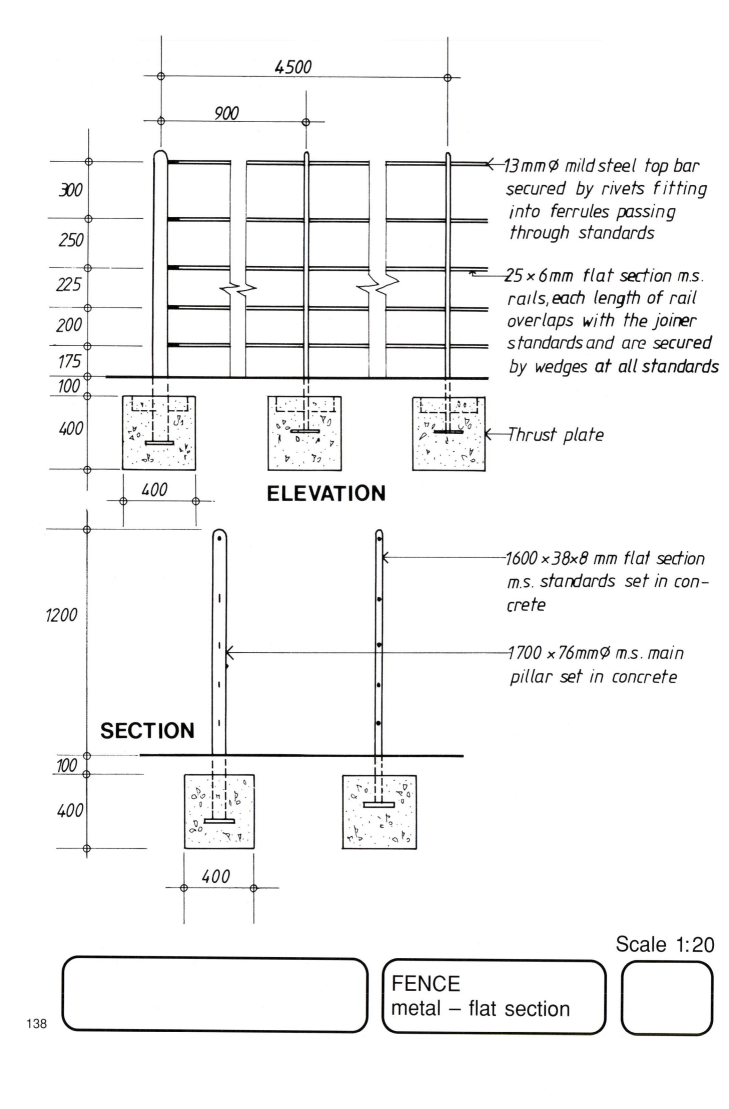

4500

900

300

250

225

200

175

100

400

13 mm Ø mild steel top bar secured by rivets fitting into ferrules passing through standards

25 × 6 mm flat section m.s. rails, each length of rail overlaps with the joiner standards and are secured by wedges at all standards

Thrust plate

400

ELEVATION

1200

1600 × 38×8 mm flat section m.s. standards set in concrete

1700 × 76 mm Ø m.s. main pillar set in concrete

SECTION

100

400

400

Scale 1:20

FENCE
metal – flat section

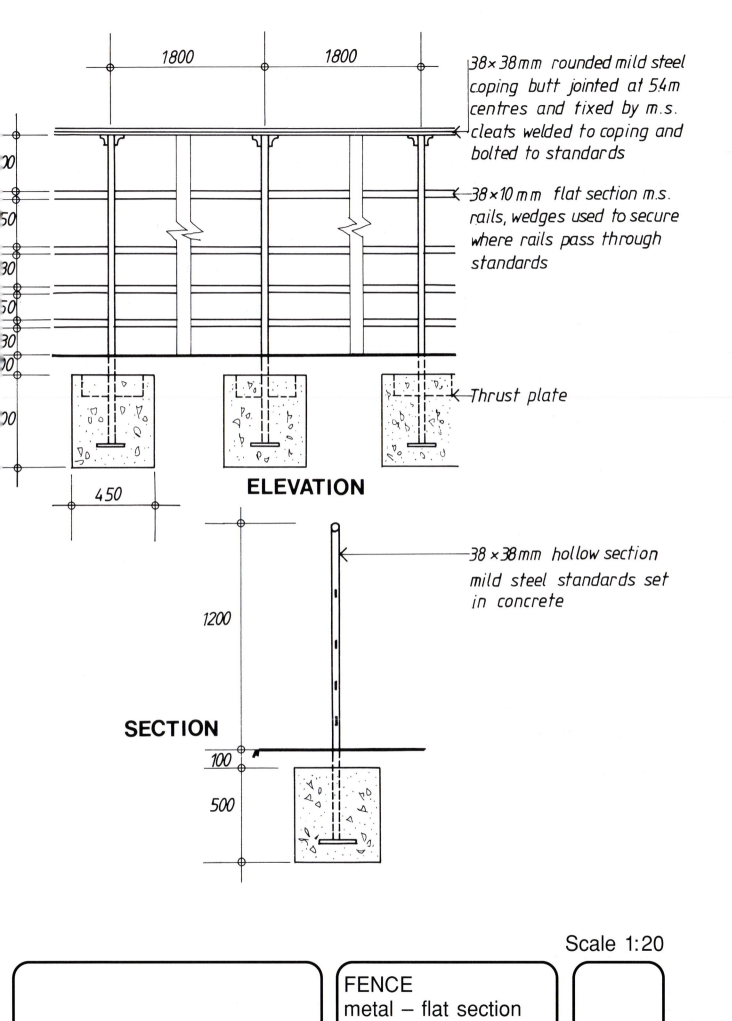

1800   1800

38×38mm rounded mild steel coping butt jointed at 5.4m centres and fixed by m.s. cleats welded to coping and bolted to standards

38×10mm flat section m.s. rails, wedges used to secure where rails pass through standards

Thrust plate

ELEVATION

450

38×38mm hollow section mild steel standards set in concrete

1200

SECTION

100

500

Scale 1:20

FENCE
metal – flat section

139

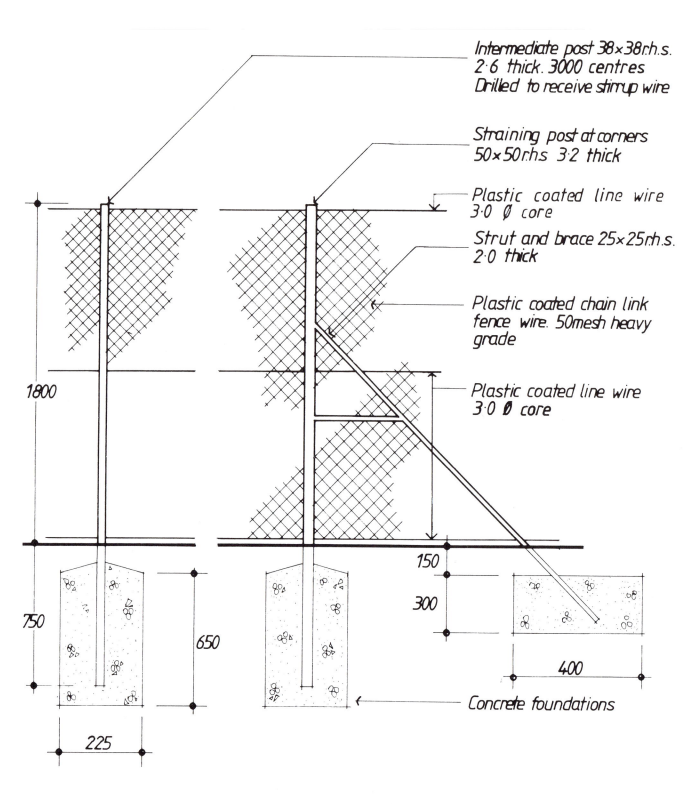

Intermediate post 38×38 r.h.s.
2·6 thick. 3000 centres
Drilled to receive stirrup wire

Straining post at corners
50×50 r.h.s 3·2 thick

Plastic coated line wire
3·0 Ø core

Strut and brace 25×25 r.h.s.
2·0 thick

Plastic coated chain link
fence wire. 50 mesh heavy
grade

Plastic coated line wire
3·0 Ø core

1800

750

225

650

150

300

400

Concrete foundations

ELEVATION   **ELEVATION**

Scale 1:20

FENCE
chain link 1800

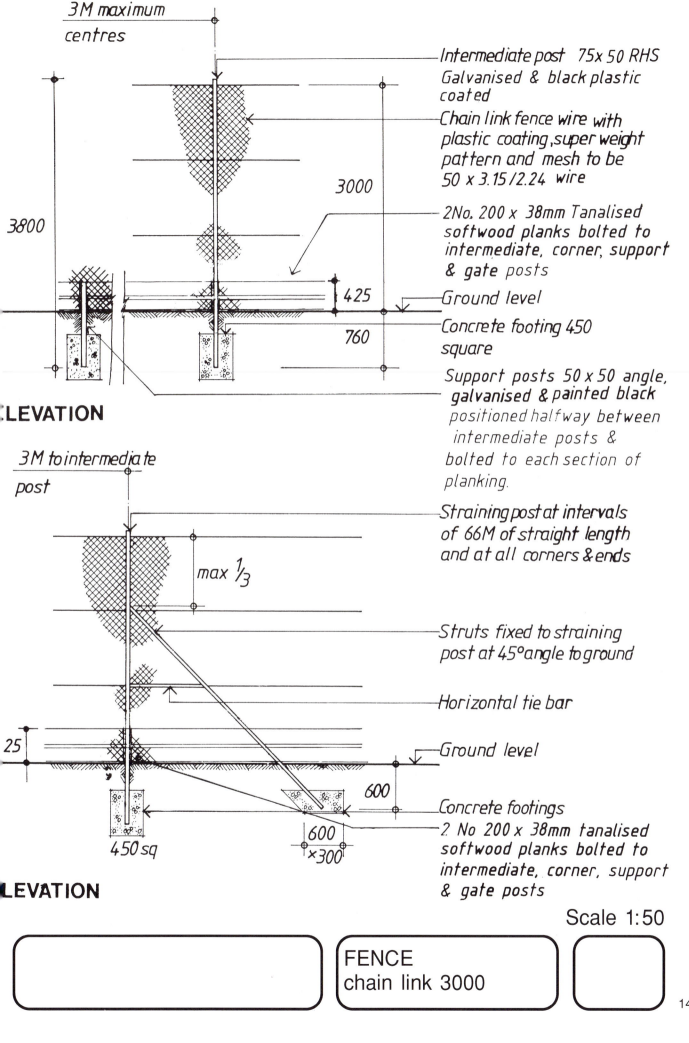

3M maximum
centres

Intermediate post 75 x 50 RHS
Galvanised & black plastic
coated

Chain link fence wire with
plastic coating, super weight
pattern and mesh to be
50 x 3.15/2.24 wire

3000

2No. 200 x 38mm Tanalised
softwood planks bolted to
intermediate, corner, support
& gate posts

3800

425

Ground level

760

Concrete footing 450
square

Support posts 50 x 50 angle,
galvanised & painted black
positioned halfway between
intermediate posts &
bolted to each section of
planking.

ELEVATION

3M to intermediate
post

Straining post at intervals
of 66M of straight length
and at all corners & ends

max ⅓

Struts fixed to straining
post at 45° angle to ground

Horizontal tie bar

25

Ground level

600

Concrete footings

600
x 300

2 No 200 x 38mm tanalised
softwood planks bolted to
intermediate, corner, support
& gate posts

450 sq

ELEVATION

Scale 1:50

FENCE
chain link 3000

141

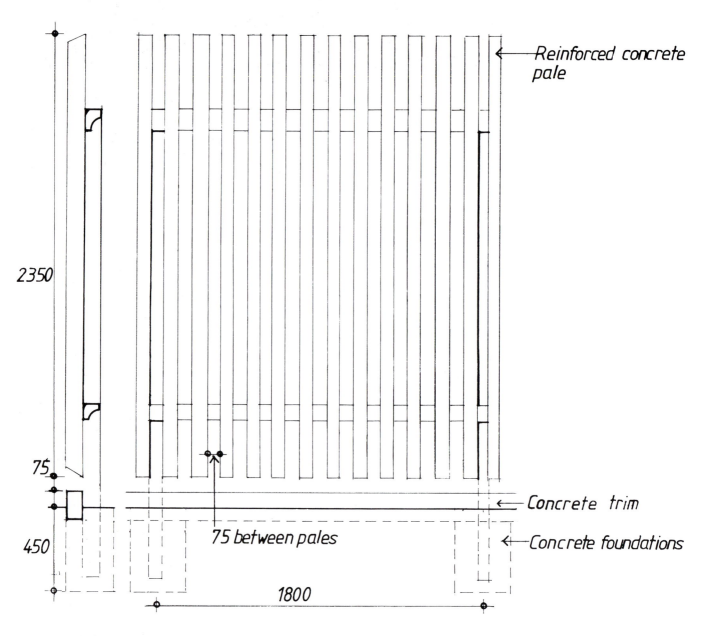

2350

75

450

SECTION

1800

ELEVATION

75 between pales

Reinforced concrete pale

Concrete trim

Concrete foundations

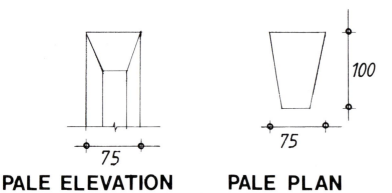

100

75

75

PALE ELEVATION

PALE PLAN

Scale 1:20

RAILINGS
concrete palisade

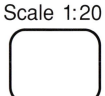

142

GATES AND STILES

GUIDANCE NOTES

Design

The character of a gate also reflects or offsets the character of the enclosure it pierces. The relationship between the proportions of fence or wall to gate is most important. For example, a heavy gate will need a strong post, pier or column to balance it. The material used for a wall will also play a key part in deciding the type of gate and its material.

If a gate looks stronger than the wall it will contradict its function. A gate must appear as a way through a fence or a wall and part of its function is to state this visually. No gate should be higher than the wall or fence which flanks it; there are exceptions to this rule which do work, but usually in the more open landscape.

Standards

BS 3470 covers the requirements for timber and steel field gates, with timber, steel and concrete gate posts. The Standard does not specify any particular design, but does set minimum units on sizes of various members. For gates in chain link and steel palisade fencing, see the relevant BS fence type.

BS 4092: Part 1 covers domestic entrance gates in tubular metal, mild or wrought steel. It specifies dimensions and certain functional requirements, but not detailed design. Part 2 of the same Standard describes domestic wooden gates.

General design requirements of stiles, bridle gates and kissing gates are given in BS 5709: 1979.

Construction

The main point about gate construction is to ensure that adequate cross bracing be provided to prevent the gate from dropping. The usual method of achieving this with timber construction is to provide a diagonal brace from the bottom corner on the hinge side so that the brace is in compression. Tall gates are provided with two separate braces. Metal gates of bolted construction are braced in the same manner. Welded metal gates are not usually cross braced.

Gate stops should be provided. The latch should not be relied on to stop the gate. Double gates should be provided with rebated meeting stiles.

Width

For pedestrian use the structural opening width should not be less than 900 mm. Except for special designs (e.g. gallows gates) the maximum leaf size should be 1,200 mm. For openings larger than this double gates should be used. For large mower access to protected grass areas, a clear opening width of 2,400 mm will be required. Vehicular control of estate roads or parking areas can be affected by the use of gallows gates with opening widths of up to 5,200 mm.

Height

Gate height should be equal to or slightly lower than the adjacent enclosure.

Hinges, locks and latches

Hinges

The usual type of gate hinge is the steel bend hinge. There are two basic types:

1. Hook and band
2. Reversible

Hook and band are available as light or heavy duty, straight or cranked. Reversible hinges are available as light or heavy duty.

Both types are available hot-dip galvanised or sheradised. Tee hinges are also used. These are usually available in a japanned finish, but can be specially ordered with a galvanised finish. All hinge types are described in BS 1227: Part 1A: 1967. They should be strong enough to prevent the gate from sagging.

Locks

Locks for gates usually take the form of barrel bolts. Where these are secured with a padlock they are called padbolts. Double gates should be fitted with bolts to engage in sockets set in concrete or tarmac. A centre stop should be used in conjunction with the bolts. These can be of the fall-down type if the passage of lawn mowers is anticipated. Provision should be made for securing gates in the catches.

Latches

The type of gate latch fitted will depend on the gate height. Low gates can have an automatic latch fitted to the inside of the gate only. High gates can be fitted with a Suffolk-type thumb latch or a ring handle gate latch, both of which are operable from either side of the gate. BS 1331 describes latches suitable for gates.
Either slip-bolts or latches, sometimes called fall-catches, are provided for fastening metal gates; the slip-bolts having the advantage of being capable of receiving a padlock. With double gates a drop-bolt should be fitted to one leaf with a stop let into the ground. Expensive stops have counterbalanced lids which shut as the gate is opened. Catches can be fitted for holding back large gates.

Gate posts

Gate posts of timber or metal can be set in earth or concrete, and BS 3470 specifies the minimum length of post to be used in each case.
They must be on both sides of the opening and be strong enough to support the gates. Dimensions will depend upon the height and weight of the gate. The tops of timber posts should be weathered or rounded. Posts can also be of concrete, brick or masonry.
Brick or stone piers are frequently inserted in fencing to support gates. Large and heavy gates can impose a considerable strain on such piers, which have been known to break off at their base. They should be built with a substantial foundation, taken well into the ground, and with a reinforced concrete core, the reinforcing bars of which should carry down into the foundations.

SPECIFICATION CHECK LIST

BS 3470 specifies requirements for timber and steel field gates with timber, steel and concrete gate posts. The Standard does not specify any particular design but does set minimum limits on sizes of various members. BS 5709 covers Bridle and Kissing Gates. BS 1186 classifies timber.

Drawing reference number: This item can be deleted if a proprietary design of gate is being specified.

Manufacturer and reference: This item can be deleted if a purpose-designed field gate is being specified.

Size(s): The BS for Field Gates specifies a height of 1.1 m and widths of 2.4, 2.7, 3.0, 3.3, 3.6 and 4.2 m. For openings over 4.2 m gates should be made in two leaves. For kissing gates see BS 5709 for minimum height and width.

Materials: BS 3470 specifies timber and steel for gates and timber, steel and concrete for gate posts. State type of material(s). For all gates insert sizes of all component gate parts and posts.

Treatment: If timber gates are to be treated with preservative insert details. Steel gates can be supplied red oxide primed, sprayed with zinc or aluminium, hot-dip galvanised or coated with black bitumen paint.

Fittings: These include strap hinges and hooks, catches and bolts. Fittings can be supplied with various finishes but hot-dip galvanising is strongly recommended.

144

Setting posts: Gate posts can be set in earth or concrete. Specify the minimum length of post to be used in each case. The size of concrete foundation should be shown on a drawing and/or given in the specification.

Finish: Specify type of finish – plain, stained or painted, colour and number of coats.

DETAIL SHEETS

Single gates
Brace detail
Timber palisade (low) (2)
Timber matchboard (low)
Timber matchboard (high)
Timber field
Timber kissing gate
Metal bow topped
Double gates
Timber palisade
Timber matchboard
Timber diagonal
Mild steel bow topped
Metal
Gallows
Stiles
Timber V-shape (2)
Timber stepped (2)
Stone

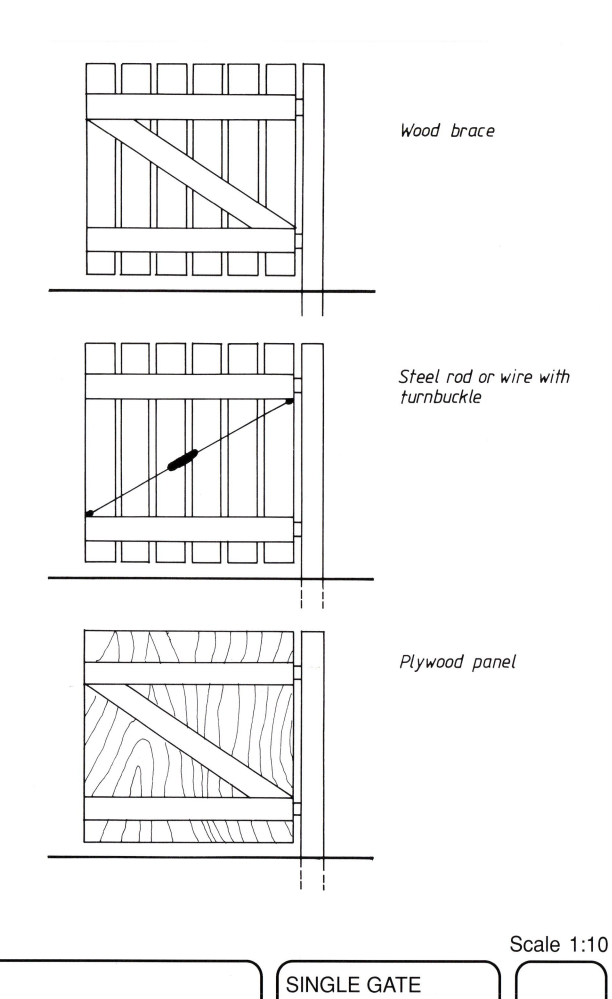

Wood brace

Steel rod or wire with turnbuckle

Plywood panel

Scale 1:10

SINGLE GATE
brace detail

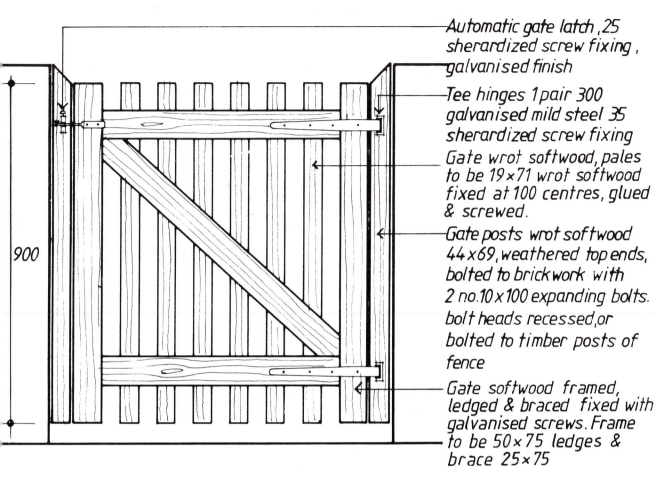

Automatic gate latch, 25 sherardized screw fixing, galvanised finish

Tee hinges 1 pair 300 galvanised mild steel 35 sherardized screw fixing

Gate wrot softwood, pales to be 19×71 wrot softwood fixed at 100 centres, glued & screwed.

Gate posts wrot softwood 44×69, weathered top ends, bolted to brickwork with 2 no.10×100 expanding bolts. bolt heads recessed, or bolted to timber posts of fence

Gate softwood framed, ledged & braced fixed with galvanised screws. Frame to be 50×75 ledges & brace 25×75

900

LEVATION

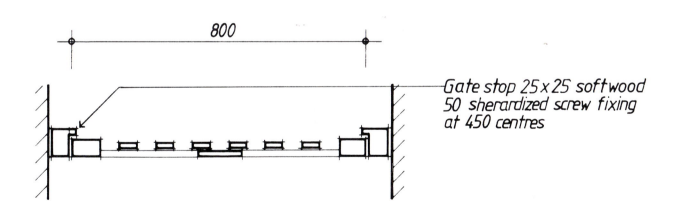

800

Gate stop 25×25 softwood 50 sherardized screw fixing at 450 centres

LAN

Scale 1:10

SINGLE GATE
timber palisade (low)

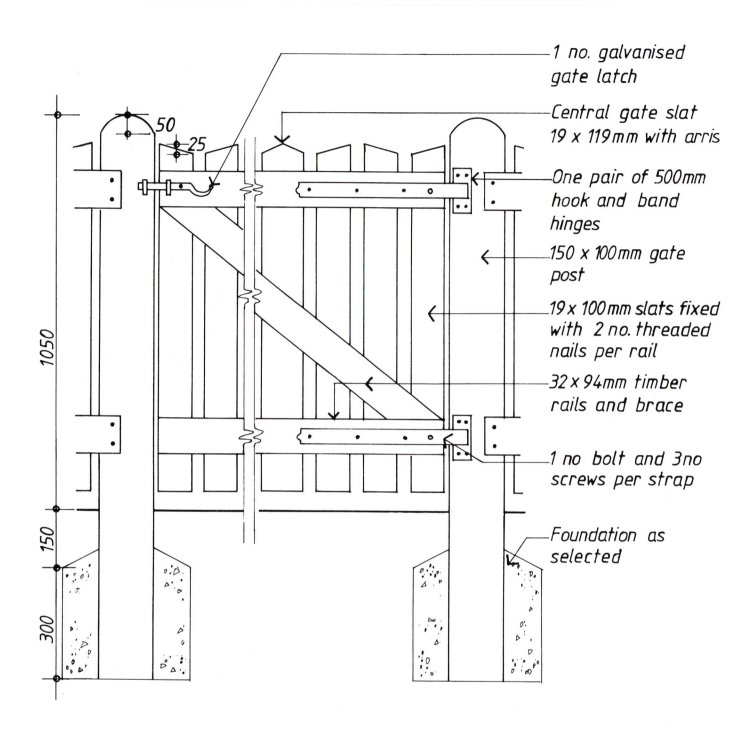

1 no. galvanised
gate latch

Central gate slat
19 x 119mm with arris

One pair of 500mm
hook and band
hinges

150 x 100mm gate
post

19 x 100mm slats fixed
with 2 no. threaded
nails per rail

32 x 94mm timber
rails and brace

1 no bolt and 3no
screws per strap

Foundation as
selected

50

25

1050

150

300

ELEVATION

Scale 1:10

GATE
timber palisade (low)

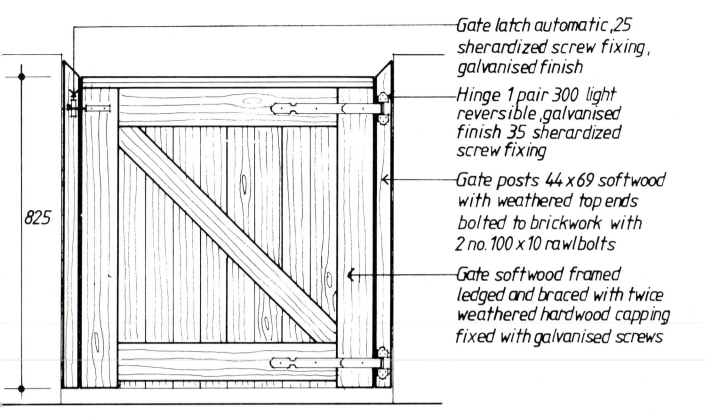

Gate latch automatic,25 sherardized screw fixing, galvanised finish

Hinge 1 pair 300 light reversible,galvanised finish 35 sherardized screw fixing

Gate posts 44 x 69 softwood with weathered top ends bolted to brickwork with 2 no. 100 x 10 rawlbolts

Gate softwood framed ledged and braced with twice weathered hardwood capping fixed with galvanised screws

825

ELEVATION

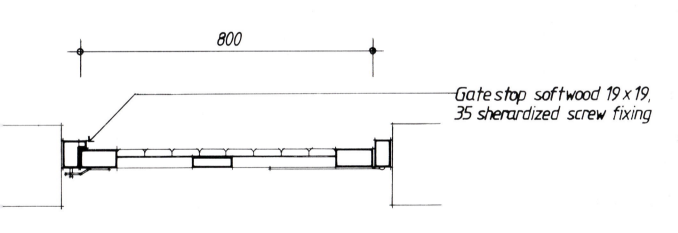

800

Gate stop softwood 19 x 19, 35 sherardized screw fixing

PLAN

Scale 1:10

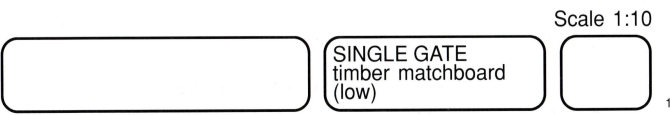

SINGLE GATE
timber matchboard
(low)

149

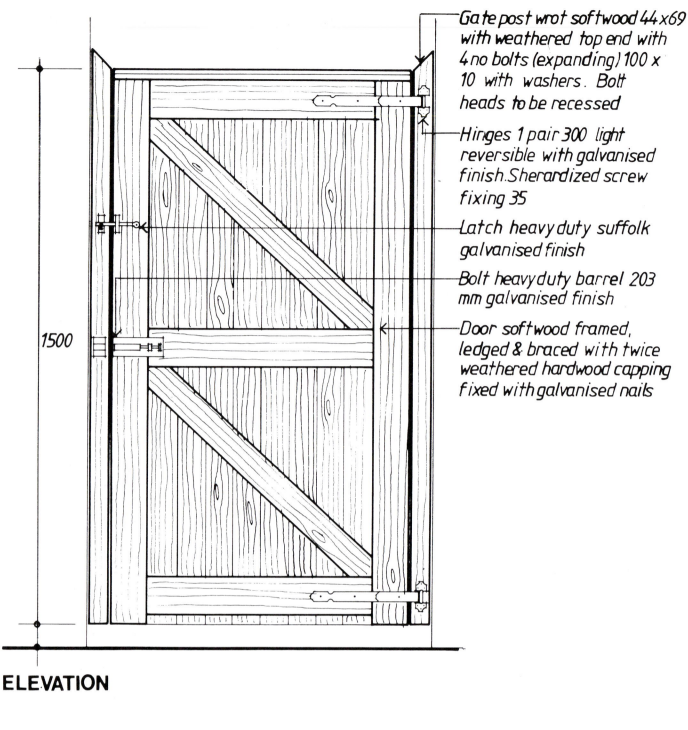

Gate post wrot softwood 44 x 69 with weathered top end with 4 no bolts (expanding) 100 x 10 with washers. Bolt heads to be recessed

Hinges 1 pair 300 light reversible with galvanised finish. Sherardized screw fixing 35

Latch heavy duty suffolk galvanised finish

Bolt heavy duty barrel 203 mm galvanised finish

Door softwood framed, ledged & braced with twice weathered hardwood capping fixed with galvanised nails

1500

ELEVATION

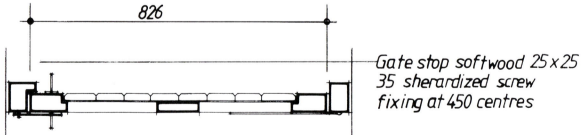

826

Gate stop softwood 25 x 25 35 sherardized screw fixing at 450 centres

PLAN

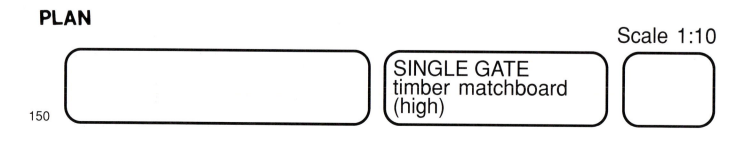

Scale 1:10

SINGLE GATE
timber matchboard
(high)

150

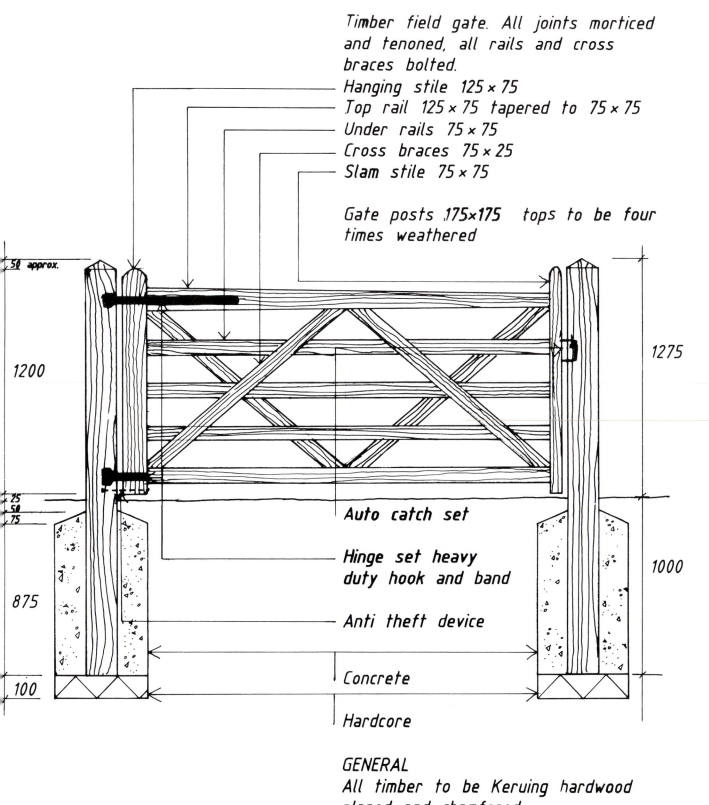

Timber field gate. All joints morticed and tenoned, all rails and cross braces bolted.
Hanging stile 125 × 75
Top rail 125 × 75 tapered to 75 × 75
Under rails 75 × 75
Cross braces 75 × 25
Slam stile 75 × 75

Gate posts 175×175 tops to be four times weathered

50 approx.

1200

1275

25
50
75

Auto catch set

Hinge set heavy duty hook and band

Anti theft device

875

1000

Concrete

100

Hardcore

GENERAL
All timber to be Keruing hardwood planed and chamfered.

Scale 1:20

GATE
timber field

151

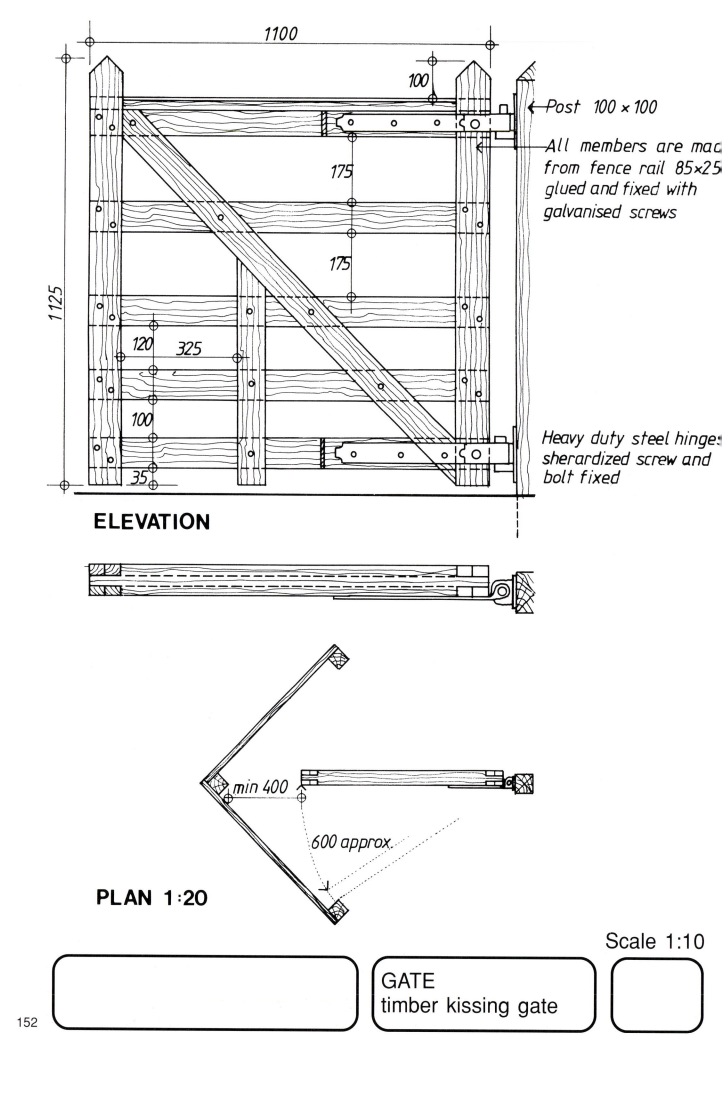

1100

100

1125

175

175

120 325

100

35

ELEVATION

Post 100 × 100

All members are mac
from fence rail 85×25
glued and fixed with
galvanised screws

Heavy duty steel hinge:
sherardized screw and
bolt fixed

min 400

600 approx.

PLAN 1:20

Scale 1:10

GATE
timber kissing gate

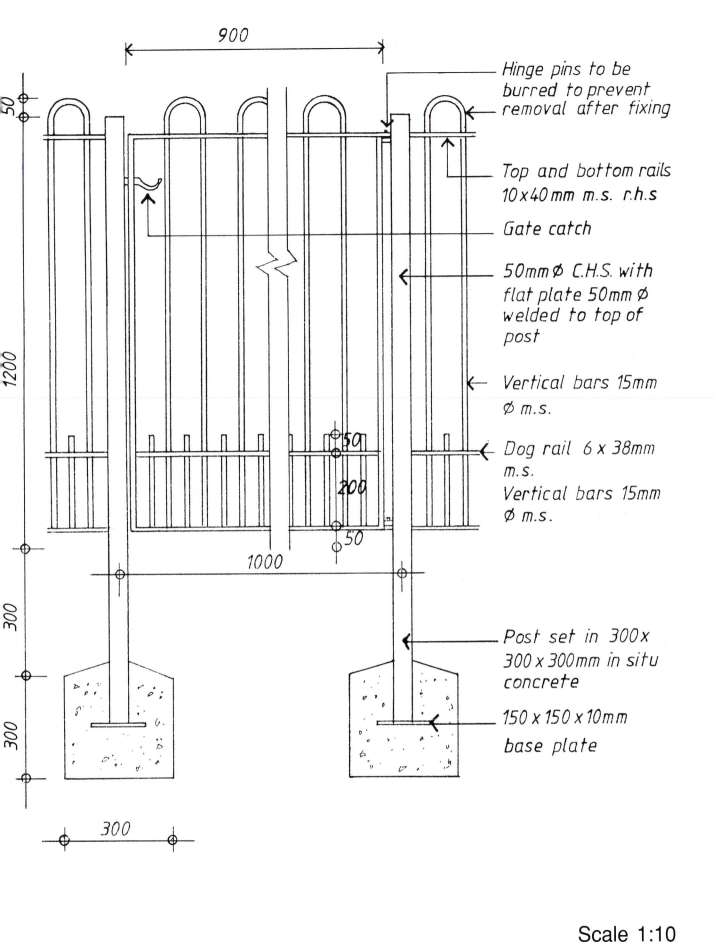

900

50

1200

300

300

300

50

1000

50

200

50

Hinge pins to be
burred to prevent
removal after fixing

Top and bottom rails
10 x 40 mm m.s. r.h.s

Gate catch

50 mm Ø C.H.S. with
flat plate 50 mm Ø
welded to top of
post

Vertical bars 15 mm
Ø m.s.

Dog rail 6 x 38 mm
m.s.
Vertical bars 15 mm
Ø m.s.

Post set in 300 x
300 x 300 mm in situ
concrete

150 x 150 x 10 mm
base plate

Scale 1:10

GATE
metal bow topped

153

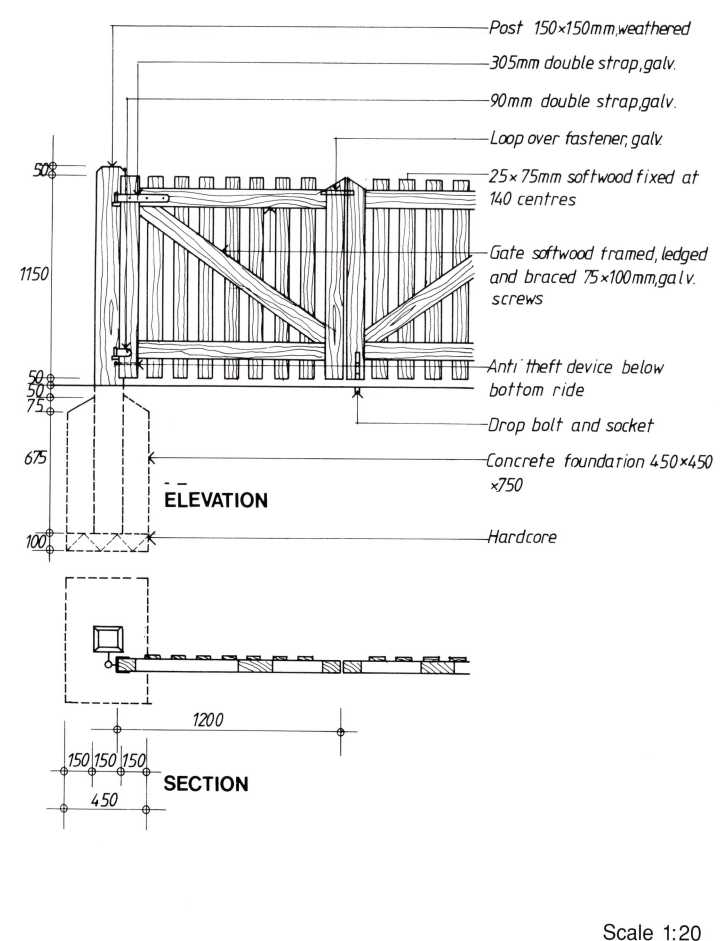

Post 150×150mm, weathered

305mm double strap, galv.

90mm double strap, galv.

Loop over fastener, galv.

25×75mm softwood fixed at 140 centres

Gate softwood framed, ledged and braced 75×100mm, galv. screws

Anti theft device below bottom ride

Drop bolt and socket

Concrete foundation 450×450 ×750

Hardcore

50

1150

50
50
75

675

100

ELEVATION

1200

150 150 150

450

SECTION

Scale 1:20

DOUBLE GATE
timber palisade

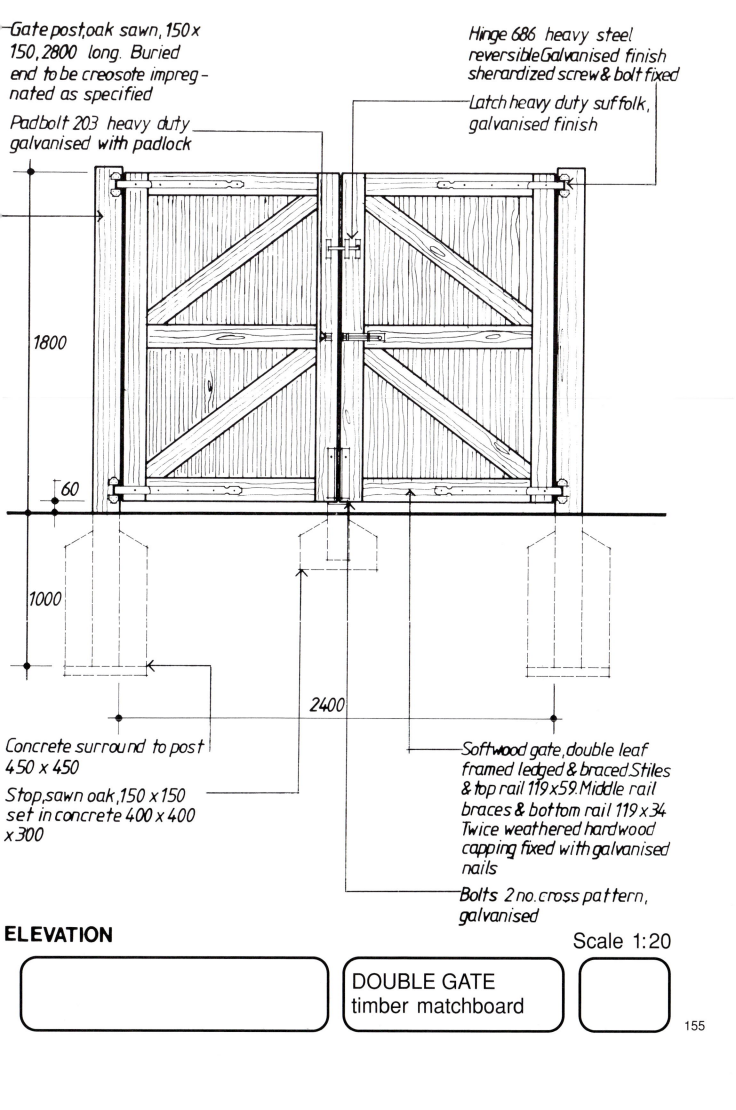

Gate post, oak sawn, 150 x
150, 2800 long. Buried
end to be creosote impregnated as specified

Padbolt 203 heavy duty
galvanised with padlock

Hinge 686 heavy steel
reversible Galvanised finish
sherardized screw & bolt fixed

Latch heavy duty suffolk,
galvanised finish

1800

60

1000

Concrete surround to post
450 x 450

Stop, sawn oak, 150 x 150
set in concrete 400 x 400
x 300

2400

Softwood gate, double leaf
framed ledged & braced. Stiles
& top rail 119 x 59. Middle rail
braces & bottom rail 119 x 34
Twice weathered hardwood
capping fixed with galvanised
nails

Bolts 2 no. cross pattern,
galvanised

ELEVATION

Scale 1:20

DOUBLE GATE
timber matchboard

155

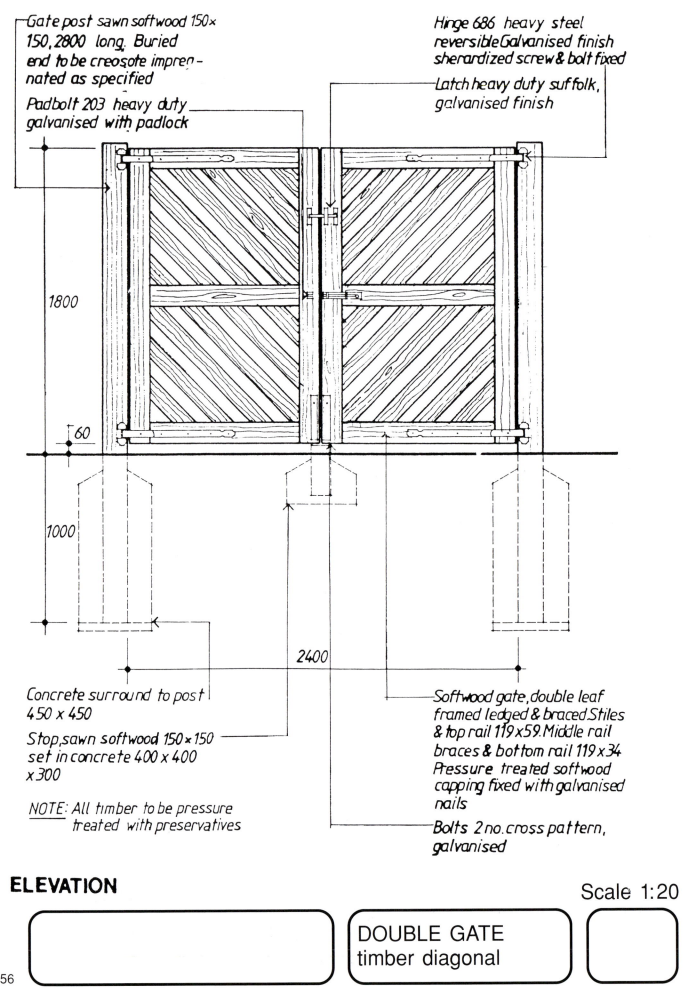

Gate post sawn softwood 150×
150, 2800 long. Buried
end to be creosote impregnated as specified

Padbolt 203 heavy duty
galvanised with padlock

Hinge 686 heavy steel
reversible Galvanised finish
sherardized screw & bolt fixed

Latch heavy duty suffolk,
galvanised finish

1800

60

1000

2400

Concrete surround to post
450 x 450

Stop, sawn softwood 150 × 150
set in concrete 400 x 400
x 300

NOTE: All timber to be pressure
treated with preservatives

Softwood gate, double leaf
framed ledged & braced Stiles
& top rail 119 x 59. Middle rail
braces & bottom rail 119 x 34
Pressure treated softwood
capping fixed with galvanised
nails

Bolts 2 no. cross pattern,
galvanised

ELEVATION

Scale 1:20

DOUBLE GATE
timber diagonal

156

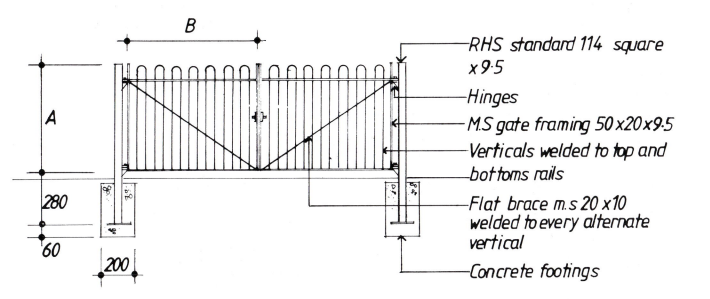

RHS standard 114 square x 9·5

Hinges

M.S gate framing 50 x 20 x 9·5

Verticals welded to top and bottoms rails

Flat brace m.s 20 x 10 welded to every alternate vertical

Concrete footings

B

A

280

60

200

ELEVATION

Nominal Size	A	B	No of verticals/ gate & size (dia)
3800 x 1200	1125	1818	14 x 130
3800 x 1400	1375	1818	14 x 130
3800 x 1800	1725	1818	14 x 190
4400 x 1200	1125	2118	16 x 130
4400 x 1400	1325	2118	16 x 130
4400 x 1800	1725	2118	16 x 190

Scale 1:20

DOUBLE GATE
mild steel bow topped

157

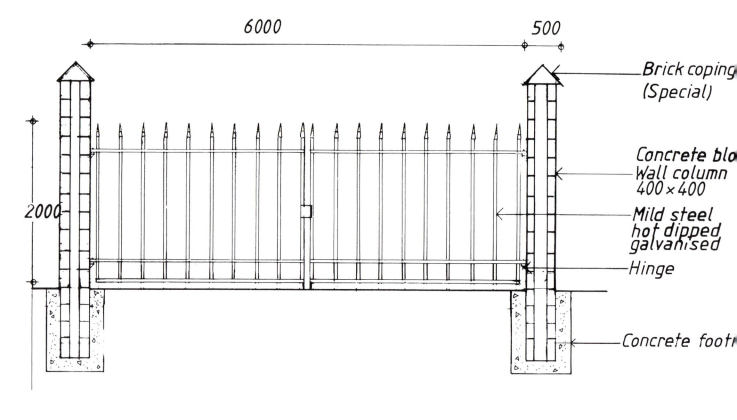

ELEVATION

6000

500

Brick coping
(Special)

Concrete blo
Wall column
400 × 400

Mild steel
hot dipped
galvanised

Hinge

Concrete foot

2000

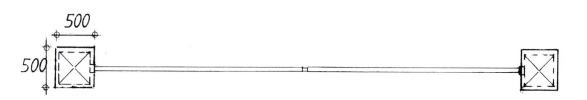

500

500

PLAN

Scale 1:50

GATES
metal

158

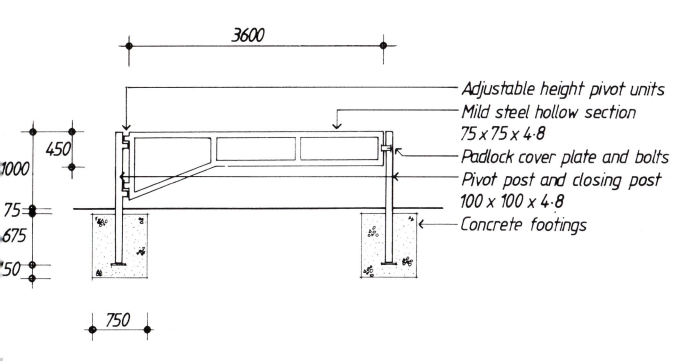

3600

Adjustable height pivot units
Mild steel hollow section
75 x 75 x 4·8
Padlock cover plate and bolts
Pivot post and closing post
100 x 100 x 4·8
Concrete footings

450

1000

75

675

50

750

ELEVATION

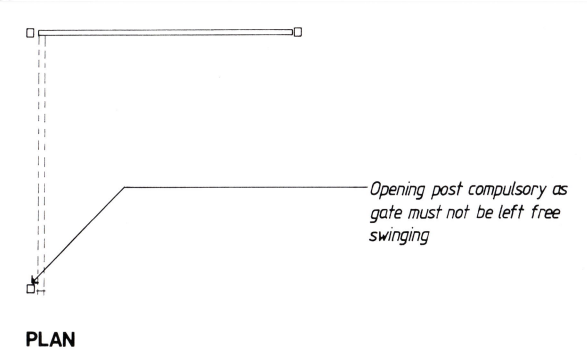

Opening post compulsory as
gate must not be left free
swinging

PLAN

Scale 1:50

GALLOWS GATE
metal

159

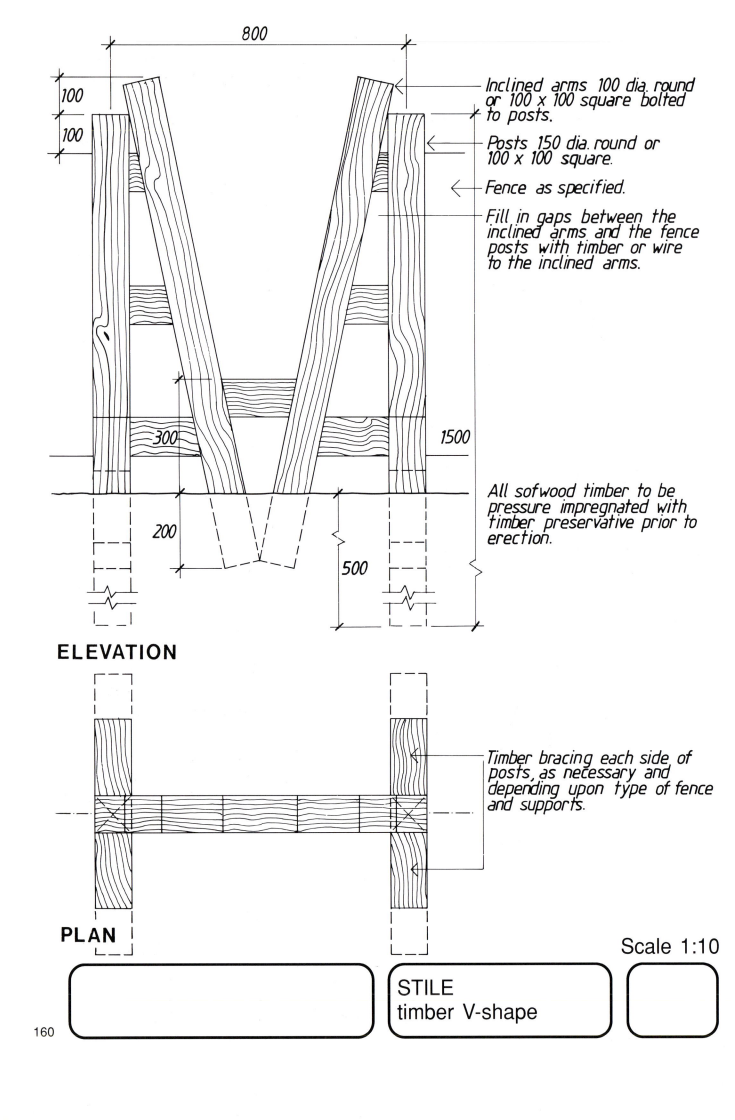

800

100

100

Inclined arms 100 dia. round
or 100 x 100 square bolted
to posts.

Posts 150 dia. round or
100 x 100 square.

Fence as specified.

Fill in gaps between the
inclined arms and the fence
posts with timber or wire
to the inclined arms.

1500

300

All sofwood timber to be
pressure impregnated with
timber preservative prior to
erection.

200

500

ELEVATION

Timber bracing each side of
posts, as necessary and
depending upon type of fence
and supports.

PLAN

Scale 1:10

STILE
timber V-shape

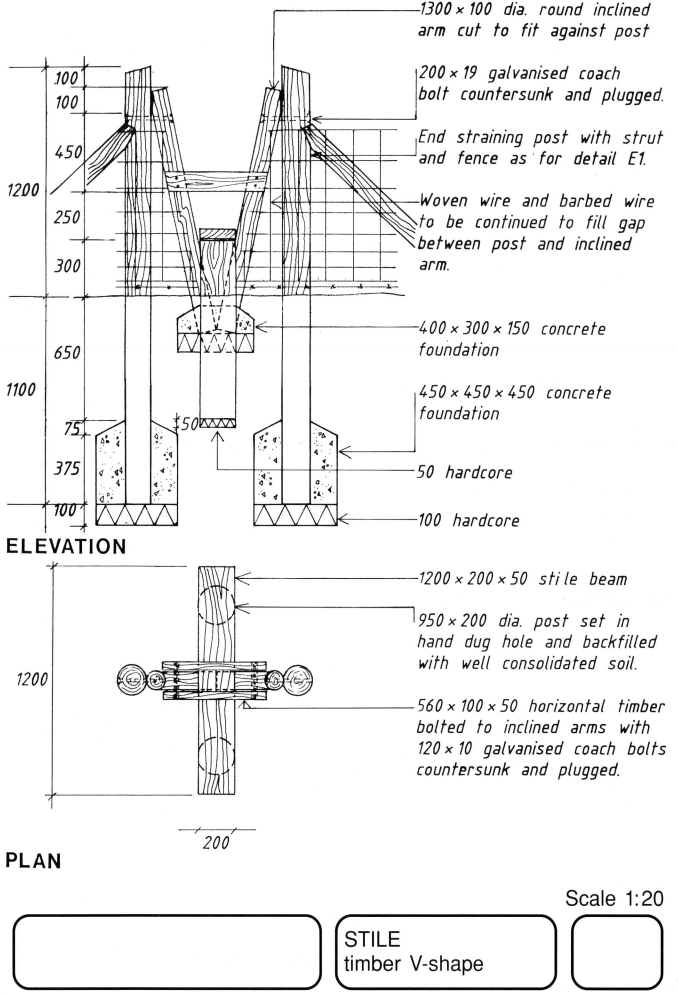

ELEVATION

1300 × 100 dia. round inclined arm cut to fit against post

200 × 19 galvanised coach bolt countersunk and plugged.

End straining post with strut and fence as for detail E1.

Woven wire and barbed wire to be continued to fill gap between post and inclined arm.

400 × 300 × 150 concrete foundation

450 × 450 × 450 concrete foundation

50 hardcore

100 hardcore

PLAN

1200 × 200 × 50 stile beam

950 × 200 dia. post set in hand dug hole and backfilled with well consolidated soil.

560 × 100 × 50 horizontal timber bolted to inclined arms with 120 × 10 galvanised coach bolts countersunk and plugged.

Scale 1:20

STILE
timber V-shape

161

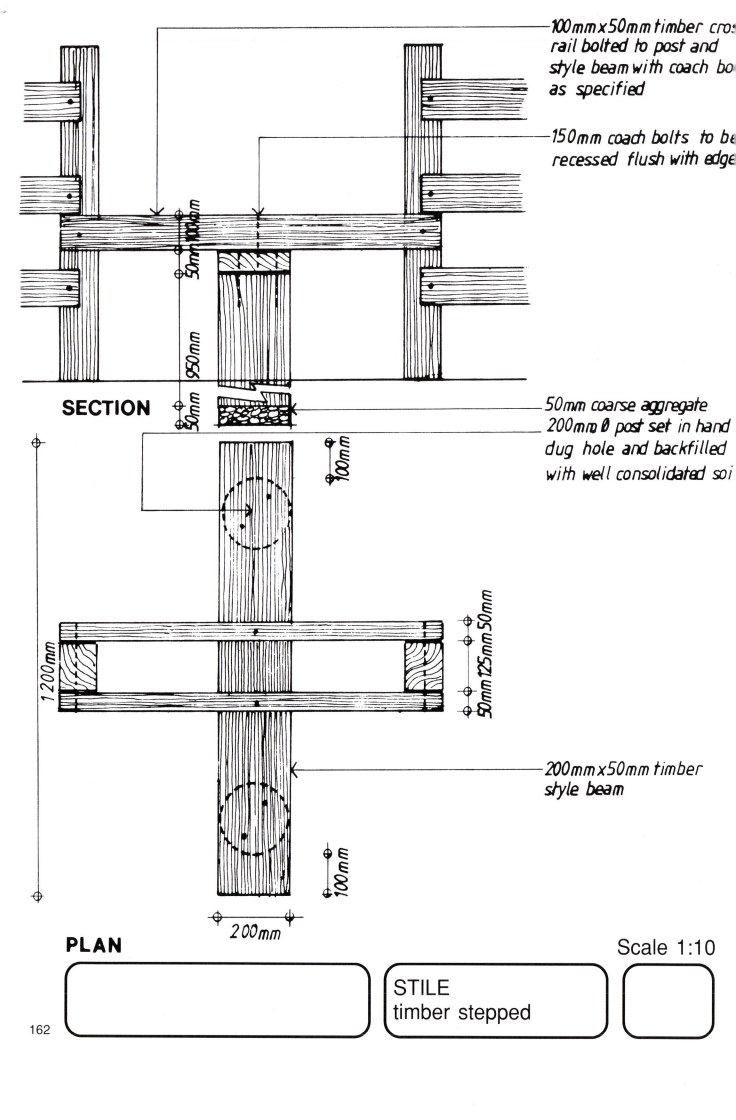

100mm x 50mm timber cross rail bolted to post and style beam with coach bolts as specified

150mm coach bolts to be recessed flush with edge

SECTION

100mm

50mm

950mm

50mm

50mm coarse aggregate

200mm Ø post set in hand dug hole and backfilled with well consolidated soil

1200mm

100mm

50mm 125mm 50mm

200mm x 50mm timber style beam

100mm

200mm

PLAN

Scale 1:10

STILE
timber stepped

162

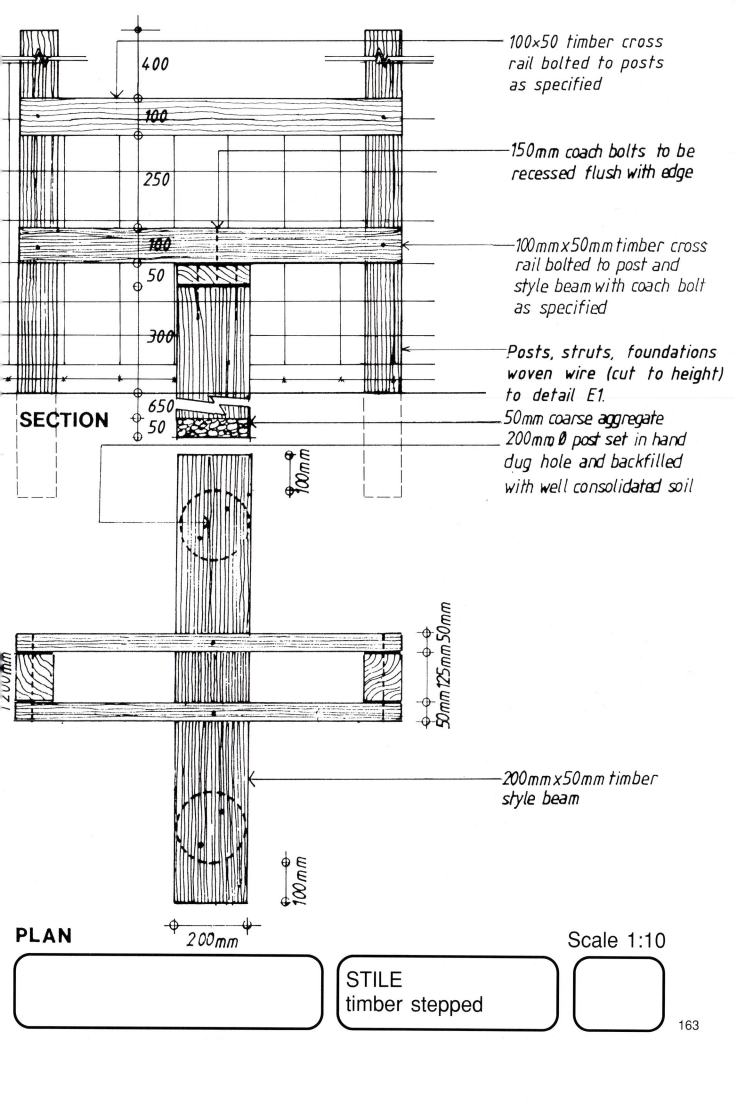

100×50 timber cross
rail bolted to posts
as specified

400

100

150mm coach bolts to be
recessed flush with edge

250

100

100mm×50mm timber cross
rail bolted to post and
style beam with coach bolt
as specified

50

300

Posts, struts, foundations
woven wire (cut to height)
to detail E1.

650

50mm coarse aggregate

50

200mm ∅ post set in hand
dug hole and backfilled
with well consolidated soil

SECTION

100mm

50mm 125mm 50mm

200mm×50mm timber
style beam

100mm

PLAN

200mm

| | STILE | Scale 1:10 |
| timber stepped | |

163

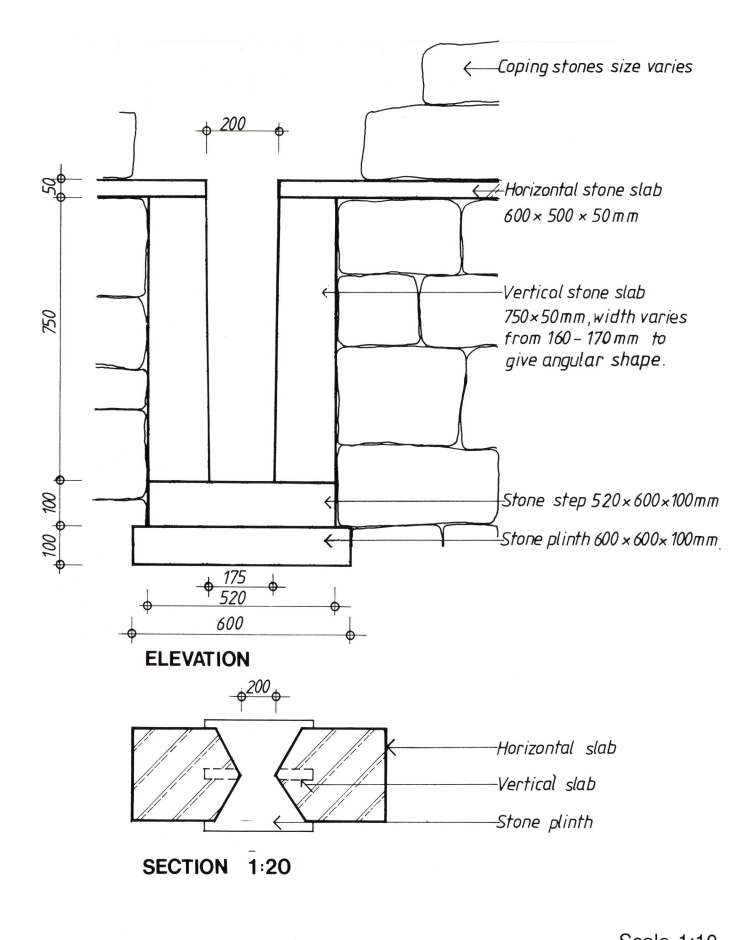

Coping stones size varies

200

50

Horizontal stone slab
600 × 500 × 50 mm

750

Vertical stone slab
750 × 50 mm, width varies
from 160 – 170 mm to
give angular shape.

100 100

100

Stone step 520 × 600 × 100 mm

Stone plinth 600 × 600 × 100 mm.

175
520
600

ELEVATION

200

Horizontal slab

Vertical slab

Stone plinth

SECTION 1:20

Scale 1:10

STILE
stone

BARRIERS

GUIDANCE NOTES

Low rails

Low rails are used as barriers to protect grass or planted areas from pedestrians, except when some are used as traffic barriers in certain circumstances. As they are not more than 600 mm high they are a visual rather than a physical deterrent and whenever possible are preferable to standard fencing, because they are far less conspicuous.

When the posts of low rails are set in grass they should be set in a concrete mowing strip to avoid hand trimming. Low rails, particularly those in metal, will take curves more easily and cheaply than other materials.

Appearance

The advantage of having a low rail is that it enables a barrier to be used which does not visually intrude to any great extent, depending upon its design. Some rails have to be built to withstand the impact of vehicles and therefore they must have far greater strength than a light rail used to keep pedestrians away from an area. The height of a rail also plays an important part.

Low timber rails

Size

Because of their height (up to 400 mm), the designer of low rails should bear in mind their potential for being sat or balanced upon. The design should either cater for, or discourage, such use.

Post spacing, depth of insertion

In view of the factors mentioned above, post centres should be closer (usually 1,000–1,500 mm) than in fencing intended solely as a barrier.

For pedestrian use, a post insertion depth of 300 mm is sufficient if a concrete surround is provided. For controlling vehicular traffic, an insertion depth of 750 mm is required.

When used as a barrier for vehicles or for wheel stops in a car park, timber posts and rails are preferable. The rail must be strong, i.e. 150 × 50 mm with half-lapped joints over stout posts (100 × 75 mm or 100 × 100 mm), chamfered on top. A far stronger barrier is required to prevent vehicles running off a main road.

Joints in top rail

The solution to the problem will vary with the design. The following general points should be observed:

1. Lapped or scarfed joints are preferable.
2. Bolts or screws should not be inserted within 25 mm of board ends.
3. Where the rail consists of two or more members; the joints in each should be staggered.

Corner detail and changes in direction

Where corners and changes in direction are infrequent, the best solution is to duplicate the post support. Where a top rail is used, adequate bearing must be arranged for a mitred joint.

Low metal rails

Size

The remarks made in regard to timber low rails apply equally to metal low rails.

Spacing of standards

The standards for low metal rails are generally spaced at 1,200 mm centres. A surround of concrete must be used because of the small surface area of metal sections.

Metal protection and finish

BS 1722: Part 8 specifies a range of ex-works finishes, the usual finish being a red-oxide primer or hot-dip galvanising after fabrication.

The finished element should be shop welded, construction made with a loose end

to the rail, which is jointed on-site using a screwed sleeve or plate.

With metal rails, changes in direction are usually made in the rail; the space between standards should be closed in order to increase support at this point.

Bollards

These are vertical barriers and are one of the most unobtrusive ways of preventing access by vehicles encroaching on to pedestrian areas. Bollards can sub-divide paved areas into those for people to move quickly and those where they can congregate in a more leisurely manner. Bollards also mark boundaries and protect property, such as corners of buildings.

There are a variety of bollards in different materials: metal, wood, concrete, cast iron and natural stone.

As a barrier to vehicles, bollards should be located at 1,500 mm minimum centres. Bollards should be set 300–450 mm in the ground on a concrete or consolidated hardcore base and surrounded by concrete. If bollards are set in precast paving, careful cutting of the units will be required, unless cobbles are used around them.

Precast concrete

Precast concrete bollards are used more frequently in urban areas because they are relatively cheap and also very strong. There is a variety of pleasant proprietary designs on the market obtainable in different finishes and colours.

Timber

Timber is used more in rural areas and should not be less than 100 mm diameter or square. Hardwood should always be used and the top capped or weathered to shed water.

Metal

Steel and cast iron bollards are becoming more popular in urban areas, especially in historic towns and cities. Removable bollards are usually made of steel.

SPECIFICATION CHECK LISTS

Low rails

General
State purpose – pedestrian or vehicular.

Height
Specify height of rail above ground level.

Material
Timber. Specify type, e.g. hardwood (oak) or softwood (pine). Insert method of treatment and/or desired life (e.g. CCA category 13). State size of timbers to be used for posts and rails.
Metal: Specify type, i.e. RHS – rectangular/round hollow section, RSA – rectangular section angled, etc. Insert if metal is to be hot-dipped galvanised or primed with red-oxide primer. State size of posts and rails.

Workmanship
Centres of posts: State distances between posts.
Setting of posts: Insert method and depth depending upon use, e.g. pedestrian low rail timber posts could be set in rammed earth but metal posts should be set in concrete as should all vehicular rails/barriers timber and metal.
Construction: Describe method of construction of rails to posts, especially joining lengths of rails.
Finish: Specify type of finish, e.g. timber to be stained, metal to be painted.

Bollards

General
State purpose of bollard, especially if it is for a vehicular barrier. Fixed or removable.

Height
Specify height above ground level.

Material
Timber. Specify type, e.g. hardwood (oak) or softwood (pine). Insert method of treatment and/or desired life (e.g. CCA category 13). State size of timbers to be used. Describe any special type of shaping or grooving.

Metal: Specify type and shape.

Workmanship
Centres of bollards: State distances between bollards.
Setting of bollards: Insert method and depth depending upon use, i.e. pedestrian or vehicular.
Finish: Specify type of finish, e.g. timber to be stained or painted, metal to be primed and painted.
Removable: Describe method of making bollard removable.

DETAIL SHEETS

Barriers
Timber foundations – 300 high
– 350 high
– 400 high (4)
– 500 high
– 550 high
Metal (300–500 high) (3)
Metal and timber (450 high)
Bollards
Fixed timber – 750 high
– 950 high
– 1,000 high
– 1,200 high
Concrete – 600 high
– 600 high
– 750 high
– 1200 high
Metal – 750 high
Removable timber – 400 high
– 900 high
– 1,000 high

PEDESTRIAN

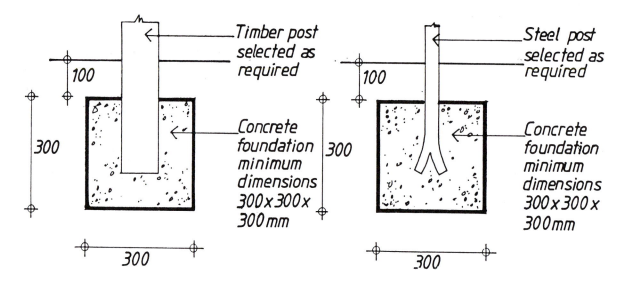

Timber post selected as required

100

300

300

Concrete foundation minimum dimensions 300 x 300 x 300 mm

TIMBER POST

Steel post selected as required

100

300

300

Concrete foundation minimum dimensions 300 x 300 x 300 mm

STEEL POST

VEHICULAR

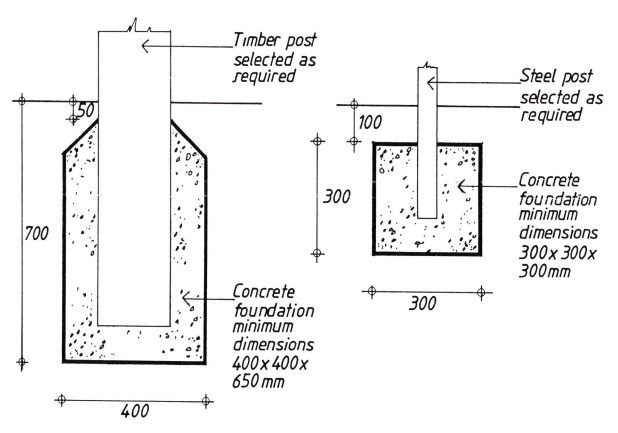

Timber post selected as required

50

700

400

Concrete foundation minimum dimensions 400 x 400 x 650 mm

TIMBER POST

Steel post selected as required

100

300

300

Concrete foundation minimum dimensions 300 x 300 x 300 mm

STEEL POST

Scale 1:10

LOW RAILS/BARRIERS
foundations

168

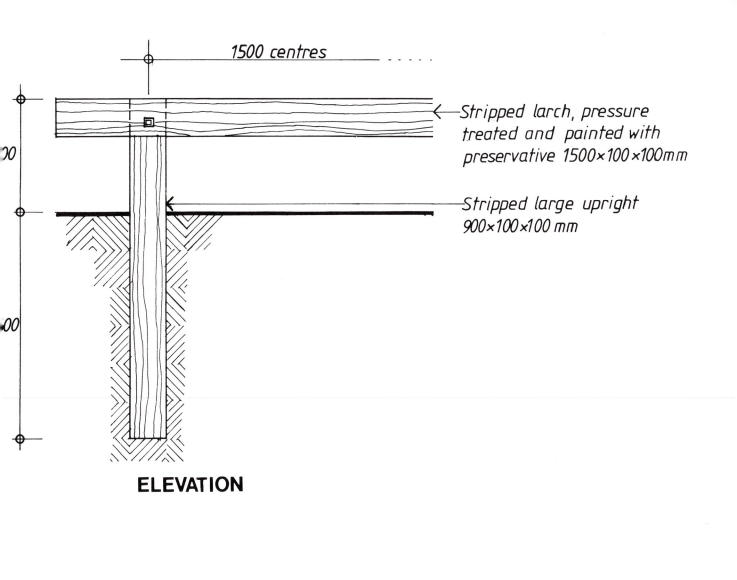

ELEVATION

1500 centres

Stripped larch, pressure treated and painted with preservative 1500×100×100mm

Stripped large upright 900×100×100 mm

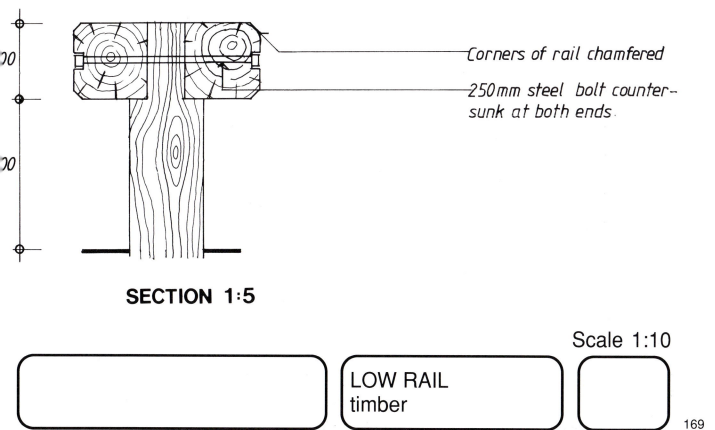

SECTION 1:5

Corners of rail chamfered

250mm steel bolt counter-sunk at both ends.

Scale 1:10

| | LOW RAIL timber | |

169

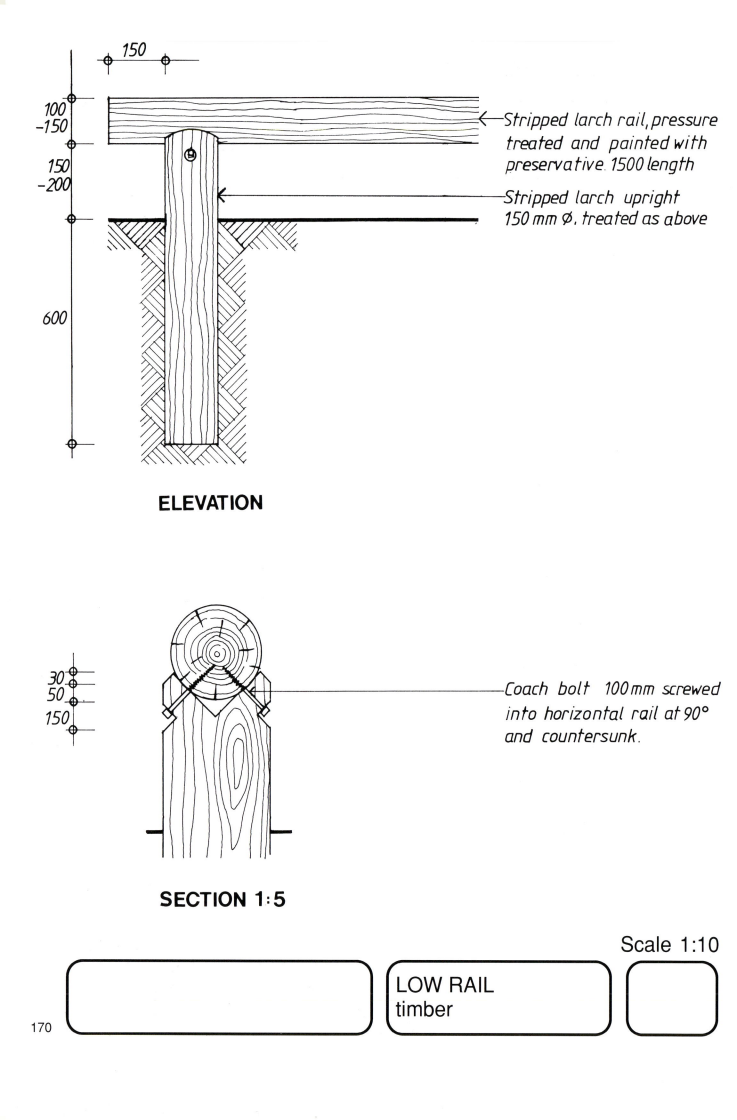

150

100
-150

150
-200

600

→ Stripped larch rail, pressure treated and painted with preservative. 1500 length

— Stripped larch upright 150 mm Ø, treated as above

ELEVATION

30
50
150

— Coach bolt 100mm screwed into horizontal rail at 90° and countersunk.

SECTION 1:5

Scale 1:10

LOW RAIL
timber

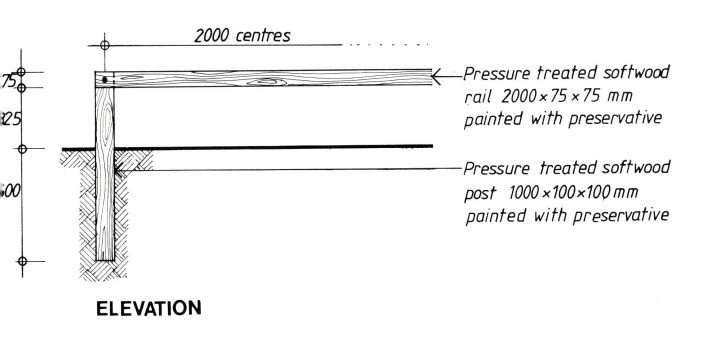

2000 centres

75

25

00

Pressure treated softwood rail 2000 × 75 × 75 mm painted with preservative

Pressure treated softwood post 1000 × 100 × 100 mm painted with preservative

ELEVATION

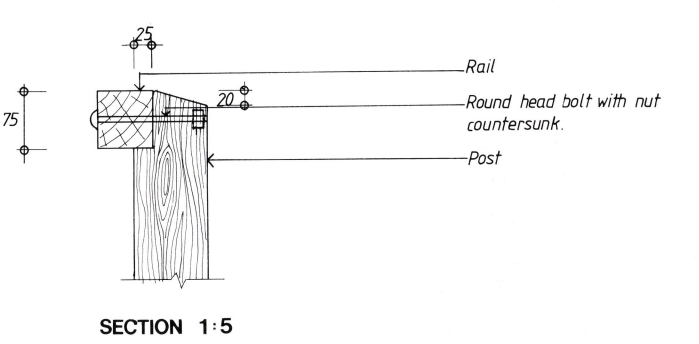

25

75

20

Rail

Round head bolt with nut countersunk.

Post

SECTION 1:5

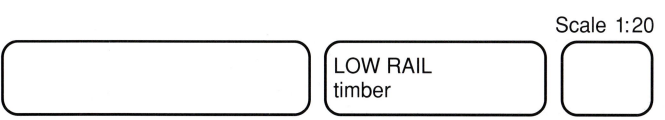

Scale 1:20

LOW RAIL
timber

171

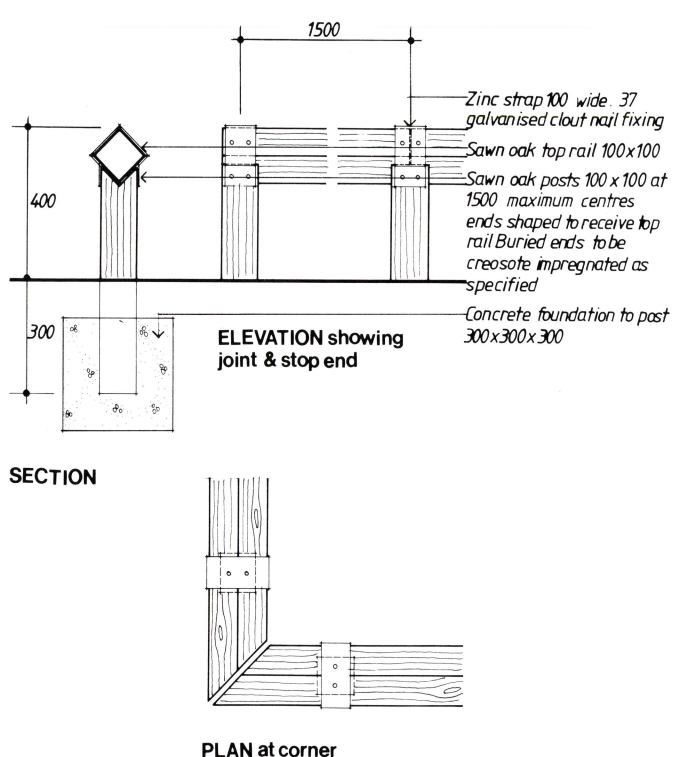

1500

Zinc strap 100 wide. 37 galvanised clout nail fixing

Sawn oak top rail 100 x 100

Sawn oak posts 100 x 100 at 1500 maximum centres ends shaped to receive top rail Buried ends to be creosote impregnated as specified

Concrete foundation to post 300 x 300 x 300

400

300

ELEVATION showing joint & stop end

SECTION

PLAN at corner

Scale 1:10

LOW RAIL
timber

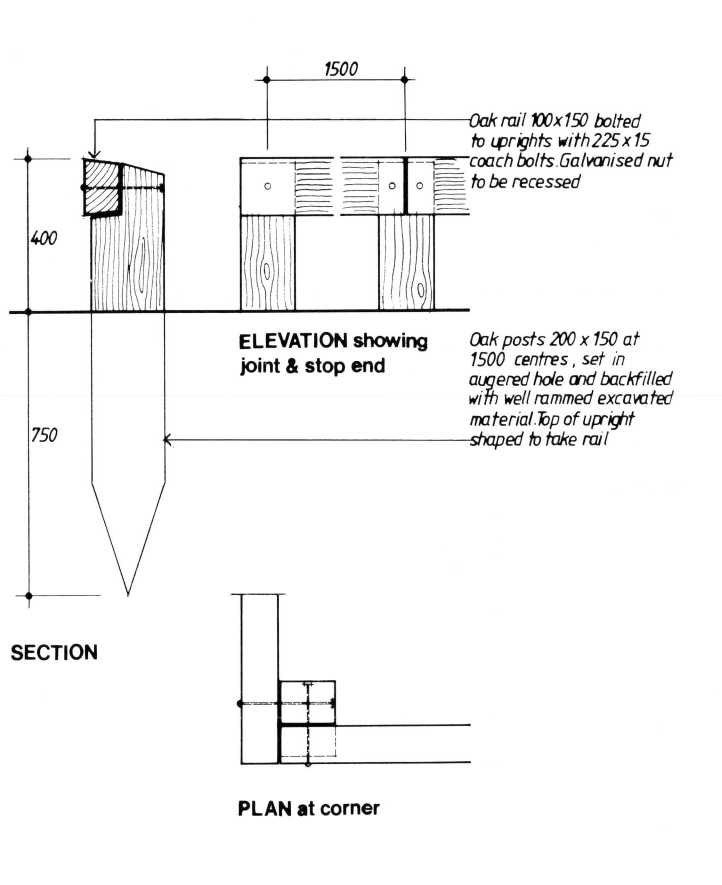

1500

Oak rail 100x150 bolted to uprights with 225x15 coach bolts. Galvanised nut to be recessed

400

ELEVATION showing joint & stop end

Oak posts 200 x 150 at 1500 centres, set in augered hole and backfilled with well rammed excavated material. Top of upright shaped to take rail

750

SECTION

PLAN at corner

Scale 1:10

LOW RAIL
timber

173

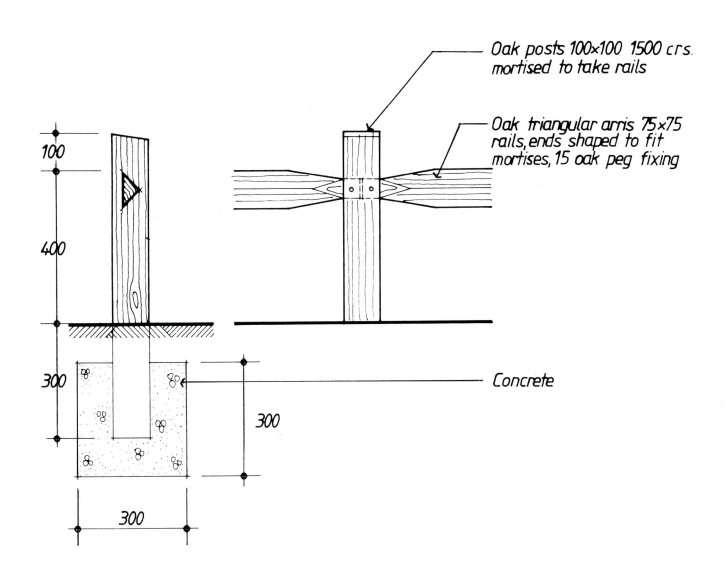

Oak posts 100×100 1500 crs.
mortised to take rails

Oak triangular arris 75×75
rails, ends shaped to fit
mortises, 15 oak peg fixing

100

400

300

300

300

Concrete

Scale 1:10

LOW RAIL
timber

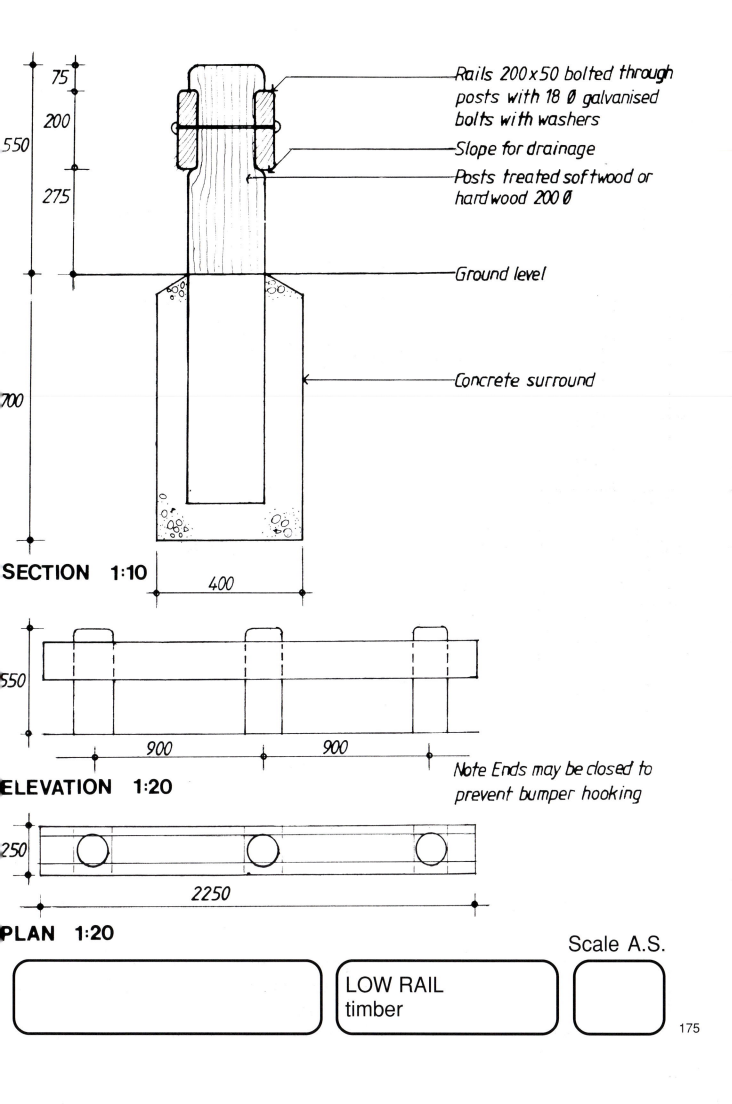

SECTION 1:10

75
200
550
275
700
400

Rails 200×50 bolted through posts with 18 ∅ galvanised bolts with washers

Slope for drainage

Posts treated softwood or hardwood 200 ∅

Ground level

Concrete surround

ELEVATION 1:20

550
900   900

Note Ends may be closed to prevent bumper hooking

PLAN 1:20

250
2250

Scale A.S.

LOW RAIL
timber

175

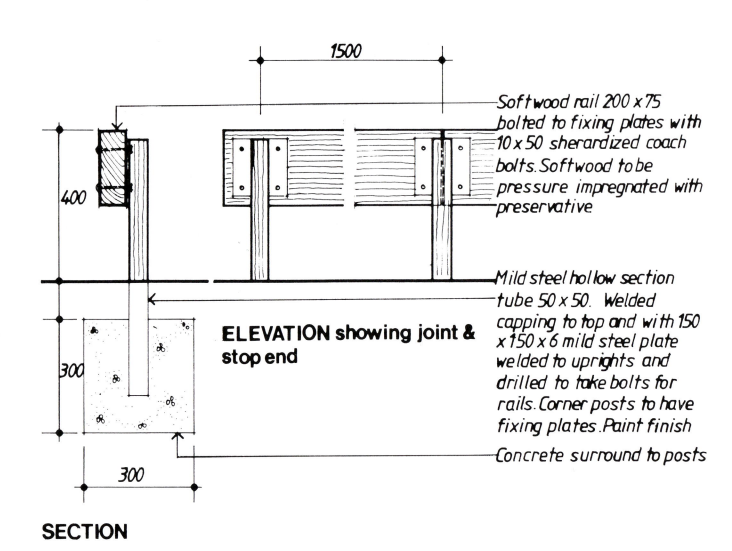

1500

Softwood rail 200 x 75 bolted to fixing plates with 10 x 50 sherardized coach bolts. Softwood to be pressure impregnated with preservative

400

ELEVATION showing joint & stop end

Mild steel hollow section tube 50 x 50. Welded capping to top and with 150 x 150 x 6 mild steel plate welded to uprights and drilled to take bolts for rails. Corner posts to have fixing plates. Paint finish

300

Concrete surround to posts

300

SECTION

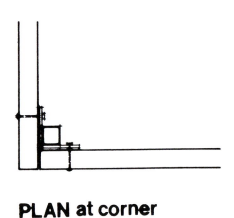

PLAN at corner

Scale 1:10

LOW RAIL
timber & steel

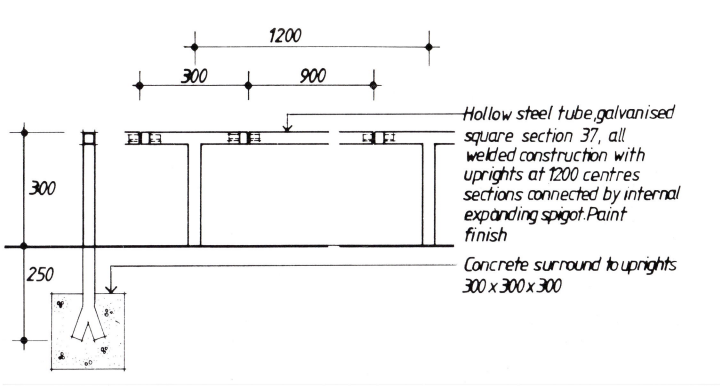

1200

300 900

300

250

Hollow steel tube, galvanised square section 37, all welded construction with uprights at 1200 centres sections connected by internal expanding spigot. Paint finish

Concrete surround to uprights 300 x 300 x 300

ELEVATION

Scale 1:10

LOW RAIL
steel tube

177

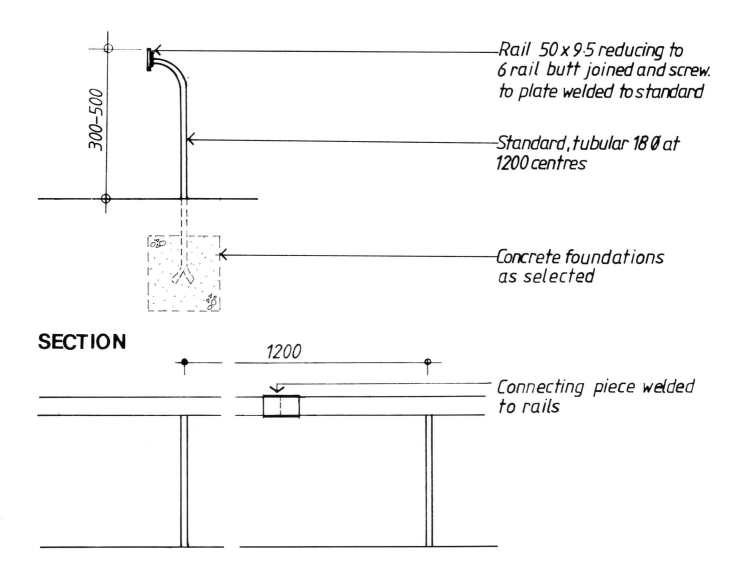

SECTION

300–500

Rail 50 x 9·5 reducing to
6 rail butt joined and screw.
to plate welded to standard

Standard, tubular 18 Ø at
1200 centres

Concrete foundations
as selected

ELEVATION

1200

Connecting piece welded
to rails

Scale 1:10

LOW RAIL
metal

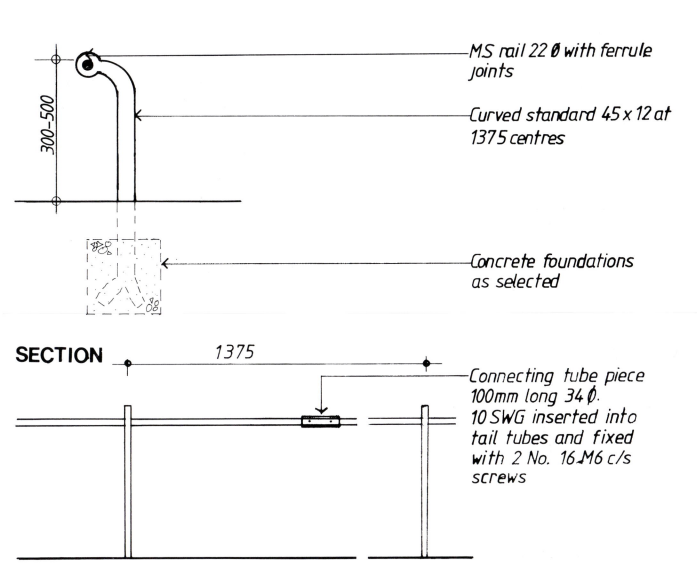

MS rail 22 Ø with ferrule joints

Curved standard 45 x 12 at 1375 centres

300–500

Concrete foundations as selected

SECTION

1375

Connecting tube piece 100mm long 34 Ø. 10 SWG inserted into tail tubes and fixed with 2 No. 16 M6 c/s screws

ELEVATION

Scale 1:10

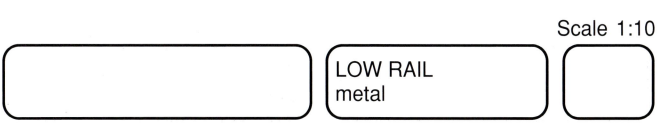

LOW RAIL
metal

179

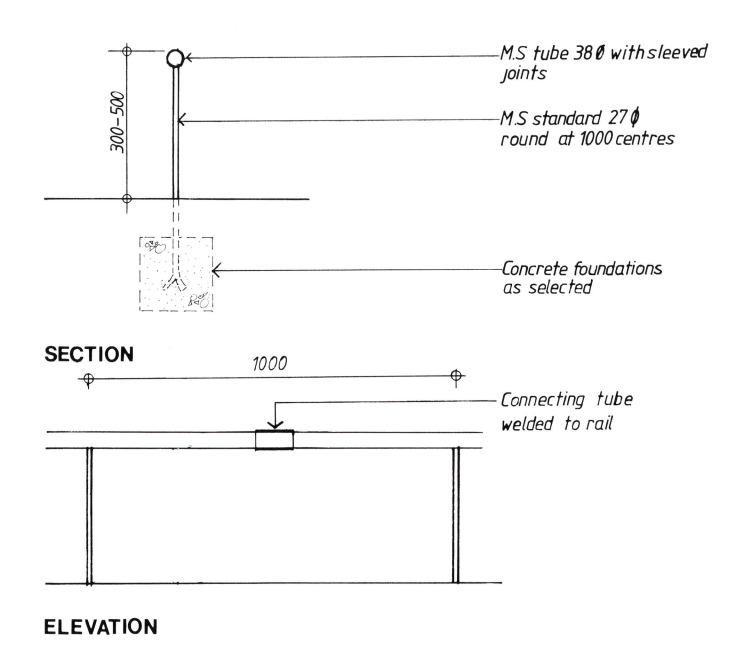

M.S tube 38∅ with sleeved joints

M.S standard 27∅ round at 1000 centres

300–500

Concrete foundations as selected

SECTION

1000

Connecting tube welded to rail

ELEVATION

Scale 1:10

LOW RAIL
metal round

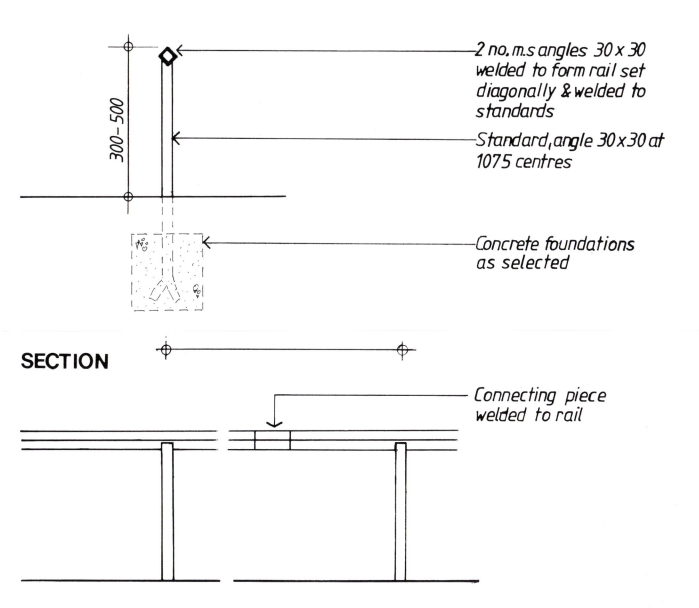

2 no. m.s angles 30 x 30 welded to form rail set diagonally & welded to standards

Standard, angle 30 x 30 at 1075 centres

Concrete foundations as selected

300-500

SECTION

Connecting piece welded to rail

ELEVATION

Scale 1:10

LOW RAIL
metal angular

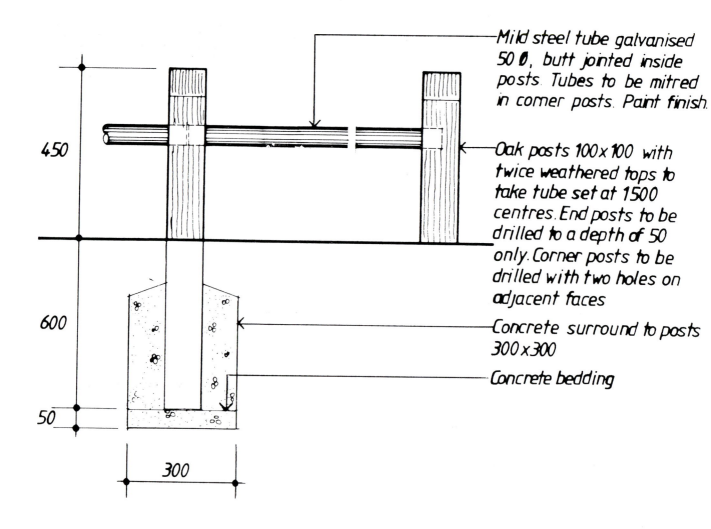

450

600

50

300

Mild steel tube galvanised 50 Ø, butt jointed inside posts. Tubes to be mitred in corner posts. Paint finish.

Oak posts 100 x 100 with twice weathered tops to take tube set at 1500 centres. End posts to be drilled to a depth of 50 only. Corner posts to be drilled with two holes on adjacent faces

Concrete surround to posts 300 x 300

Concrete bedding

ELEVATION

Scale 1:10

LOW RAIL
timber & steel tube

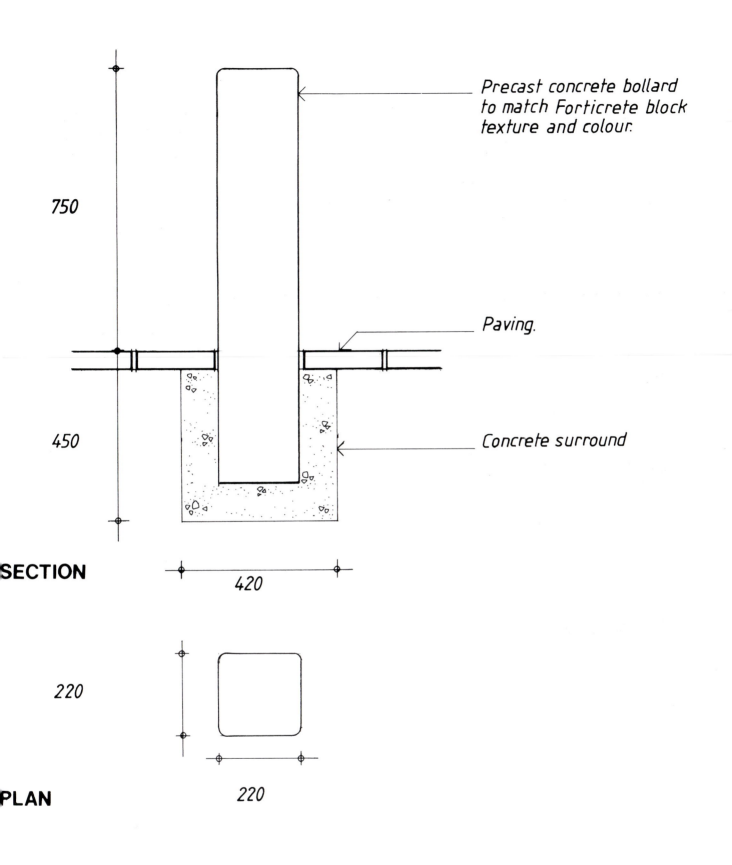

750

450

SECTION

420

Precast concrete bollard
to match Forticrete block
texture and colour.

Paving.

Concrete surround

220

PLAN

220

Scale 1:10

BOLLARD
concrete

183

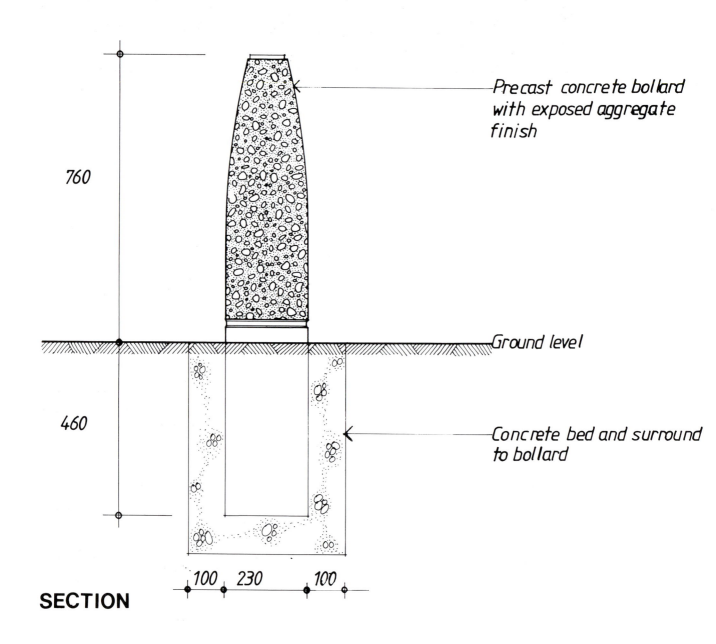

760

Precast concrete bollard
with exposed aggregate
finish

Ground level

460

Concrete bed and surround
to bollard

100   230   100

SECTION

230

PLAN

Scale 1:10

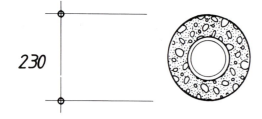

BOLLARD
exposed aggregate

184

REFERENCES

APPENDIX A

Walls

British Cement Association (BCA)
formerly C&CA
A.K. Tovey, *Concrete Masonry for the Designer*, 1981

Brick Development Association (BDA)
Practical Notes:
5 *Overhand bricklaying*
6 *Damp proof courses and flashings with brickwork and blockwork*
7 *Repointing of brickwork*
Design Notes:
6 *Brick cladding to timber frame construction*
10 *Designing for movement in brickwork*
Design Guide:
9 *Brickwork domestic fireplaces and chimneys*
Publications:
Brickwork Retaining Walls, August 1981
External Walls: Design of Wind Loads
The Design of Free-standing Brick Walls, February 1983
Mortars for Brickwork, September 1973
J.O.A. Korff, *Design of Freestanding Walls*, 1985
W.G. Curtin, G. Shaw, J.K. Beck and W.A. Bray
Design of Brick Diaphragm Walls, 1982

British Precast Concrete Federation
Design of Urban Space: a GLC manual, R. Cartwright (ed.), Architectural Press, 1980

National House Building Council (NHBC)
Practice Note 5 *Timber frame dwellings*

British Ceramic Research Association
Design Guide for Reinforced and Pre-stressed Clay Brickwork,
SP 91:1977
Architects' Journal
Products in practice supplements:
Concrete blocks 27.2.85
Bricks 27.11.85
Salvage and reuse of bricks 6.4.77

Building Research Establishment (BRE)
Digests:
65, 66 *The selection of clay building bricks*
89 *Sulphate attack on brickwork*
77 *Damp proof courses*
160 *Mortars for bricklaying*
165 *Clay brickwork, Part 2*
200 *Repairing brickwork*
214 *Cavity barriers and firestops, Part 1 (withdrawn)*
246 *Strength of brickwork and blockwork walls: design for vertical load*
250 *Concrete in sulphate bearing soils and ground water*
277 *Built-in cavity wall insulation for housing*
Defect Action Sheets:
12 *Cavity trays in external cavity walls: preventing water penetration*
17 *External masonry walls insulated with mineral fibre cavity-width batts: resisting rain penetration*
Information Paper:
7/83 Window to wall jointing
Current Paper:
16/73 Long term unrestrained expansion of test bricks
92/74 Expansion of unrestrained Fletton brickwork
Publications:
Thermal insulation: Avoiding risks, 1988
C.W. Newberry and K.J. Eaton,
Wind loading handbook, BRE Report, HMSO

Cement and Concrete Association
Concrete Block Walls, 1966
Screen Walls of Pierced Concrete
A.K. Tovey, *Concrete Masonry for the Designer*, 1981

Fences and gates

Timber Research and Development Association
Timber Fences and Gates

BIBLIOGRAPHY

APPENDIX B

Walls

J. Ashurst and F.G. Dimes, *Stone in Building*, Architectural Press, 1977

E. Beazley, *Design and Detail of the Space between Buildings*, Architectural Press, 1960

Brick in Landscape Architecture Garden Walls, Technical Notes 29A, Structural Clay Products Institute, 1750 Old Meadow Road, McLean, VA 22101, 1968

B.A. Heseltine and J.N. Tutt, *Brickwork Retaining Walls*, BDA, 1981

R.M. Cartwright, *The Design of Urban Space*, Architectural Press, 1980

M.F. Downing, *Landscape Construction*, E & F N Spon, 1977

John Duell and Fred Lawson, *Damp proof course Detailing*, Architectural Press, 1983

Earth retaining structures, Civil Engineering Code of Practice No. 2 (1951), Institution of Civil Engineers

M. Gage and T. Kirkbride, *Design in Blockwork*, 2nd Edition, Architectural Press, 1976

M. Gage and M. Vandenberg, *Hard Landscape in Concrete*, Architectural Press, 1975

J.O.A. Korff, *Design of freestanding walls*, 1985

A.E. Munson, *Construction Design for Landscape Architects*, McGraw-Hill, 1974

C. Tandy, *AJ Handbook of Urban Landscape*, Information Sheet 35, Architectural Press, 1972

Structural Design of Serpentine Walls, Technical Notes 33, Brick Institute of America

Walls and Fences, Brick Association of North Carolina, PO Box 6305, Greensboro, NC 27405

Fences

Central Electricity Generating Board, *Design Memorandum on the Use of Fences*, January 1966

D. Lovejoy & Partners, *Spon's Landscape Handbook*. E & F N Spon, 1983

A. Pinder and A. Pinder, *Beazley's Design and Detail of the Space between Buildings*, E & F N Spon, 1990

Spon's Landscape Handbook, E & F N Spon

C. Tandy, *AJ Handbook of Urban Landscape*, Information Sheet 34, 1972

G.S. Thomas, *Plants for Ground Cover*, Dent, 1970

A.E. Weddle (ed.), *Techniques of Landscape Architecture*, Heinemann, 1967

A.E. Weddle, *Landscape Techniques*, Heinemann, 1979

Fences and gates

T. Blackwell, *Walls and Fences in Japan*, Landscape Australia, 2/1988, pp. 208–210

British Trust for Conservation Volunteers, *Fencing: A Practical Conservation Handbook*, Wallingford, 1986

J. Brookes, *The Garden Book* (includes a short section on fences for domestic garden), Dorley Kindersley, 1984

Central Electricity Generating Board, *Design Memorandum on the Use of Fences*, January 1966

J. Clarke and R. Boswell, *Tests on Round Timber Fence Posts*, Forestry Commission, HMSO, 1976

M.F. Downing, *Landscape Construction*, E & F N Spon, 1977

Forestry Commission, *Forest Fencing*

Greater London Council, Finishes for External Softwood Joinery: A Warning, *Development and Materials Bulletin 79*, Use of Pigmented Water-repellent, October/November 1974

G. Jaffa, *Fencing Requirements in the Eyes of the Law: Parks and Sports Grounds* (especially maintenance rights), January 1985, pp. 10–11

T. Jemison, Railings, *Landscape Design*, June 1983, pp. 27–30; August 1983, pp. 33–36; October 1983, pp. 33–36; February 1984, pp. 43–44

A. Lisney and K. Fieldhouse, *Landscape Design Guide*, Vol. 2, *Hard Landscape: The Design of Paved Spaces, Landscape Enclosure and Landscape Furniture*, Gower, 1990 (Chapters 12–14 deal with fences)

Derek Lovejoy Partnership, *Spon's Landscape and External Works Price Book: 10th Edition*, E & F N Spon, 1991

Monmouthshire County Council, *Fences in the Countryside*. 1974

National Building Agency, External Works Detail Sheet, Architectural Press, 1977, Chapter 3

A. Pinder and A. Pinder, *Beazley's Design and Detail of the Space between Buildings*, E & F N Spon, 1990

Judith Rowe, *Badger Gates*, Forestry Commission, HMSO, 1976

C. Tandy (ed.), *Handbook of Urban Landscape*, Architectural Press, 1972

A.E. Weddle (ed.), *Techniques of Landscape Architecture*, 2nd Edition, Heinemann, 1979

Stone

J. Ashurst and F.G. Dimes, *Stone in Building*, Architectural Press, 1984

Building Research Establishment (BRE), *The selection of natural building stone*, BRE Digest 269

Natural Stone Directory, 7th Edition, Ealing Publications, April 1987

Specifications

NBS specification

BRITISH STANDARDS

APPENDIX C

Walls generally

BS 12: 1978 Ordinary and rapid-hardening Portland cement
BS 146: 1973 Part 2: Portland blast furnace cement
BS 743: 1970 Materials for damp-proof courses
BS 890: 1972 Building limes
BS 1178: 1982 Milled lead sheet
BS 1200: 1976 Sands for mortar
BS 1217: 1986 Cast stone
BS 1449: 1983 Part 2: Stainless steel strip
BS 1470: 1987 Aluminium and aluminium alloy strip
BS 2870: 1980 Rolled copper and copper alloy strip
BS 2989: 1982 Zinc and Iron – Zinc alloy coated steel strip
BS 4027: 1980 Sulphate-resisting Portland cement
BS 4729: 1971 Shapes and dimensions of special bricks
BS 5642: 1983 Part 2: Coping units

Brick and block walls

CP 121: 1973 Part 1: Brick and block masonry
BS 187: 1978 Calcium silicate bricks
BS 3921: 1985 Clay bricks and blocks
BS 4729: 1971 Shapes and dimensions of special bricks
BS 6073: 1981 Precast concrete masonry units

In-situ concrete walls

BS 1881: 1970 Methods of testing concrete
BS 4482: 1985 Hard drawn mild steel wire for reinforcing concrete
BS 4483: 1983 Steel fabric for reinforcing concrete
BS 5328: 1981 Methods of specifying concrete
BS 5328: 1981 Ready-mixed concrete
BS 5896: 1989 High tensile steel wire for reinforcing concrete
BS 6100: 1984 Glossary of terms for concrete and reinforced concrete and other appropriate standards listed in earlier sections

Rendered walls

BS 1199: 1976 Sands for external renderings
BS 4764: 1986 Powder cement paints
BS 5262: 1976 Code of practice for external rendered finishes
BS 6213 1982 Guide to selection of constructional sealants and other appropriate standards listed in previous sections and those defining specific sealant types

Stone walls

BS 5390: 1976 Code of practice for stone masonry
BS 6100: 1984 Glossary of terms for stone used in building and other appropriate standards already listed above

Retaining walls

BS 3921: 1974 Clay bricks and blocks
BS 5628: 1978 The structural use of masonry: Part 1

Unreinforced Masonry
Civil Engineering CP 2: 1951 Earth retaining structures
CP 110: 1972 The structural use of concrete
CP 111: 1970 Structural recommendations for loadbearing walls
CP 121: Part 1: 1973 Walling: Brick and block masonry
BS 187: Part 2: 1978 Calcium silicate (sand lime and flint lime) bricks
BS 729: 1971 Hot dip galvanised coatings on iron and steel articles

Timber fences

BS 144/3051: 1972/7 Coal tar creosote for the preservation of timber
PA 532: 1980 A paint system comprising an undercoat and gloss finish
BS 565: 1972 Glossary of terms relating to timber and woodwork
BS 881/589: 1974: Nomenclature of commercial timbers
BS 913: 1973 Wood preservation by means of pressure creosoting

BS 1201: 1963 Wood screws
BS 1202: 1974 Nails
BS 1282: 1975 Guide to the choice, use and
application of wood preservatives
BS 1336: 1971 Knotting
BS 1722: 1986 Part 4 Cleft Chestnut Pale Fences
Part 5 Close Boarded Fences
Part 6 Wooden Palisade Fences
Part 7 Wooden Post and Rail Fences
Part 11 Woven Wood and Lap
Boarded Panel Fences
BS 2015: 1985 Glossary of paint terms
BS 2521/2523: 1966   Lead-based priming paints
BS 3452/3453: 1962   Waterborne wood
preservatives and their
application
BS 4102: 1986 Steel wire for fences
BS 4261: 1985 Glossary of terms relating to timber
preservation
BS 4471: 1971/73 Dimensions for softwood
BS 4756: 1971 Aluminium priming paints for
woodwork
BS 5056: 1970 Copper naphthenate wood
preservatives
BS 5082: 1974 Water-thinning priming paints for wood
BS 5450: 1977 Sizes of hardwoods and methods of
measurement
BS 5358: 1976 Low-lead solvent-thinned priming paint
for wood
BS 5705: 1979/80 Solutions of wood preservatives in
organic solvents
BS 6150: 1982 Code of practice for painting of
buildings

Metal fences

BS 4:   1980 Part 1: Hot-rolled steel sections
BS 405: 1987 Expanded metal (steel)
BS 481: 1972 Part 2: High tensile steel wire mesh
BS 729: 1986 Hot-dip galvanized coatings on iron
and steel
BS 1052: 1980 Mild steel wire
BS 1449: 1983 Steel plate, sheet and strip
BS 1474: 1988 Wrought aluminium bars, tubes and
sections
BS 1485: 1983 Galvanized wire netting
BS 1554: 1986 Stainless steel round wire
BS 1615: 1987 Anodic oxidation coatings on
aluminium
BS 1722: Part 1 1986 Chain Link Fences
Part 2 1989 Rectangular Wire Mesh and
Hexagonal Wire Netting
Fences

Part 3 1986 Strained Wire Fences
Part 8 1978 Mild Steel (low carbon steel)
Part 9 1979 Mild Steel (low carbon steel)
Fences with round or square
verticals and flat posts and
horizontals
Part 10 1990 Anti-intruder Fences in Chain
Link and Welded Mesh
Part 12 1990 Steel Palisade Fences
Part 13 1978 Chain Link Fences for Tennis
Court Surroundings
BS 3830: 1973 Vitreous enamelled steel
BS 3987: 1974 Anodic oxide coatings on aluminium
for external applications
BS 4102: 1986 Steel wire for fences
BS 4483: 1985 Steel fabric
BS 4842: 1984 Storing organic finishes on aluminium
BS 4848: 1975 Part 2: Hot-rolled hollow steel sections
BS 4921: 1988 Sheradized coatings on iron and steel
BS 6323: 1982 Seamless and welded steel tubes
BS 6722: 1986 Recommendations for metal wire and
the standards for paints listed under
Timber fencing above

Gates and stiles

BS 1186: 1986 Part 1: Specification for timbers
BS 1227: 1967 Part 1: Hinges for general building
purposes
BS 3470: 1975 Field gates and posts
BS 4092: 1966 Domestic front entrance gates
BS 5707: 1979 Stiles, bridle gates and kissing gates

Changes of level (ramps)

BS 5810: Access for the disabled to buildings
BSI Education Information, Aid for the disabled

MANUFACTURERS AND SUPPLIERS

(FENCES, RAILINGS, GATES, WALLS)

APPENDIX D

Abacus Municipal Ltd
Sutton-in-Ashfield
Notts NG17 5FT
(0623 511111)

Akzo Coatings
99 Station Road
Didcot
Oxon OX11 7NQ
(0235 815141)

Amstad Systems
Amstad House
Cliftonville Road
Northampton NN1 5BU
(0604 29721)

Anda Crib
Oaklands House
Solartron Road
Farnborough
Hampshire GU14 7QL
(0252 549334)

Ballantine Bo'ness Iron Co. Ltd
Bo'ness
West Lothian
Scotland EH15 9PW
(0506 822721)

Blenheim Estate Sawmills
Combe
Witney
Oxford OX8 8ET
(0993 881206)

Blue Circle Industries Ltd
Church Road
Murston
Sittingbourne
Kent ME10 3TN
(0795 21066)

Bolton Brady Ltd
Turton Street
Bolton
BL1 2SP
(0204 32111)

Braby Group Ltd
Ashton Gate Works
Bristol BS3 2LQ
(0272 664041)

British Gates and Timber Ltd
Castletons Oak Sawmill
Biddenden
Nr Ashford
Kent TN27 8DD
(0580 291555)

Brookbrae Ltd
53 St Leonard's Road
London SW14 7NQ
(081 8769238)

Broxap and Corby Ltd
Walker Street
Radcliffe
Manchester M26 9JH
(061 796 5600)

Bruce and Hyslop Ltd
Well Lane
Park Street
Bootle
Merseyside L20 3BS

Buffalo Fence Ltd
19 Mill Lane
Benson
Oxford OX9 5SA
(0491 38368)

Dorothea Ltd
Pearl House
Hardwick Street
Buxton
Derbyshire SK17 6DH
(0298 79121)

Dimex
Dimex House
116 High Street
Solihull
West Midlands B91 3SD
(021 704 3551)

Durafencing Ltd
37 Nightingale Grove
London SE13
(081- 318 1215)

Ferrous Gate Company
Acorn Works
Green-Street-Green Road
Dartford
Kent
(032 72119)

Forest Fencing Ltd
Stanford Court
Stanford Bridge
Nr Worcester
(08865 451)

Graepel-Barrier
BSA Guns Ltd
Armoury Road
Smallheath
Birmingham B11 2PX
(021 772 8543)

Grassphalte-Gaze
Old House Lane
Bisley
Surrey GU24 9DS
(04867 80284)

Hill and Smith
PO Box 4
Canal Street
Brierley Hill
West Midlands DY5 1JL
(0384 480084)

ICI Fibres
Hookstone Road
Harrogate
North Yorkshire
(0423 68021)

H. S. Jackson & Son (Fencing)
Stowting Common
Near Ashford
Kent TN25 6BN
(023-375 393)

Joint Technology Ltd
Unit 12, Claydon Industrial Park
Greater Blakenham
Suffolk IP6 0JD
(0473 831000)

KUFA Plastics Ltd
2 Lyon Close
Chantry Estate
Kempston
Bedford MK42 7SB
(0234 854464)

Lionweld Kennedy Ltd
Marsh Road
Middlesbrough
Cleveland T51 5JS
(0642 245151)

Marley Building Products
Peasmarsh
Guildford
Surrey GU3 1LS
(0483 69922)

Non-Corrosive Metal Products Ltd
(Street Furniture Ltd)
Horton Road
West Drayton
Middlesex
(0895 42607)

Orsogril UK Ltd
Southwood Summit Centre
83 Apollo Rise
Farnborough
Hampshire
(0252 521212)

Permafix Products
72-74 Bath Road
Cheltenham
Gloucestershire GL53 7JT
(0242 573202)

PJP Trading Ltd
151 Dixons Hill Road
North Mimms
Hatfield
Herts AL9 7JE
(070 72 66726)

Ranalah Gates
Gloucester Road Trading Estate
Malmesbury
Wiltshire SN16 9JT
(0666 823001)

Reinforced Concrete Construction
Co. Ltd
Delph Road
Brierley Hill
Staffs DY5 2RW
(0384 78079)

River and Sea Gabions (London)
2 Swallow Place
Princes Street
London W1R 85Q
(071 629 8528)

James W. Shenton Ltd
Edison Works
Tinsley Street
Great Bridge
Tipton
West Midlands DY4 7LQ
(021-557 2531)

Sloan Davidson Ltd
Carrick Foundry
Stanningley
Pudsey
Yorkshire LS28 7XE
(0532 571892)

SMP (Playgrounds) Ltd
Pound Road
Chertsey
Surrey KT16 8EJ
(0932 568081)

J. Starkie Gardner Ltd
Lady Lane Industrial Estate
Hadleigh
Ipswich
Suffolk IP7 9DG
(0473 822525)

Steelway-Fensecure Glynwed
Steels & Engineering Ltd
Queensgate Works
Bilston Road
Wolverhampton WV2 2NJ
(0902 451733)

UAC Timber (Wragby)
Wragby
Lincoln LN3 5NE
(067 34 304)

Woodscape Ltd
Upfield
Pike Lowe
Brinsall
Nr Chorley
Lancs PR6 8SP
(0254 830886)

INSTITUTIONS AND ASSOCIATIONS

APPENDIX E

Aluminium Federation
Broadway House
Calthorpe Road
Five Ways
Birmingham B15 1TN
Tel: (021) 455 0311
Technical information and advice.

Association of Safety Fencing Contractors
7 Woodgates Close
North Ferriby
North Humberside HU14 3JS
Tel: (0482) 633569

British Constructional Steelwork Association Limited
4 Whitehall Court
Westminster
London SW1A 2ES
Tel: (071) 839 8566

Fencing Industry Association Ltd
Timbers House
35 Oakwood Avenue
Purley
Surrey CR2 1AR

The Fencing Contractor's Association
St John's House
23 St John's Road
Watford, Herts
Tel: (0923) 248895

National Corrosion Service
National Physical Laboratory
Teddington
Middlesex TW11 0LW
Tel: (081) 977 3222

NBS Services Ltd
Mansion House Chambers
The Close
Newcastle upon Tyne NE1 3RE
Tel: (091) 232 9594
Fax: (091) 232 5714

Timber Research and Development Association (TRADA)
Stocking Lane
Hughenden Valley
High Wycombe
Buckinghamshire HP14 4ND
Tel: (0240) 24 (Naphill) 3091/2771/3956

The Welding Institute
Abington Hall
Abington
Cambridge
CB1 6AL

Zinc-Lead Development Association (ZDA)
34 Berkeley Square
London W1X 6AJ
Tel: (071) 499 6636
Technical advice and publications.

Gravel

Hardcore

Hoggin

Rock

Rubble

Sand

Topsoil

Water

UNIT MATERIALS

Brick paving

Brickwork

Cobbles

Concrete-p.c. blockwork

section

Concrete-p.c. paving units

Metal

Setts

Stone-natural, cut

Stone-reconstituted

Rubble stone-random

Rubble stone-coursed

Timber-dressed (wrot)

Timber-rough (unwrot)

IN-SITU MATERIALS

Asphalt

Concrete-in-situ

Mortar

Grass

Gravel

Hoggin

Sand

Soil

Rock

Rubble

Water

UNIT MATERIALS

Brick-stretcher bond

Brick-basket weave

Brick-stack bond

Brick-herringbone

Cobbles-random laid

Cobbles-coursed

Cobbles-flat, parallel laid

Concrete-p.c. paving slabs

Concrete-p.c. blocks

Concrete-p.c. hexagonal slabs

Setts-stack bond

Setts-stretcher bond

Stone-natural

Stone-reconstituted

Stone-random paving

Tiled paving

Timber

IN-SITU MATERIALS

Asphalt

Concrete-i.s. broom finish

Concrete-i.s. exposed aggregate

Concrete-i.s. trowelled finish

Concrete-i.s. marked finish

192

plan

APPENDIX G
Conversion tables

Rates

Imperial unit	Metric unit	Conversion factor (×)	Reciprocal (×)
lb/sq yd	kilogram/m² (kg/m²)	0.54	1.83
lb/acre	gram/m² (g/m²)	0.112	8.922
lb/acre	kilogram/ha (kg/ha)	1.121	0.892
ton/acre	tonne/ha (t/ha)	2.511	0.398
cwt/cu yd	kilogram/m³	66.5	0.015
lb/cu ft	kilogram/m³	16.018	0.062
oz/sq yd	gram/m² (g/m²)	33.906	0.0295
oz/sq yd	kiloram/ha (kg/ha)	339.057	0.00295
gal/sq yd	litre/m² (l/m²)	5.437	0.1839
gal/acre	cubic metre/ha (m³/ha)	0.01123	0.089
gal/acre	litre/ha (l/ha)	11.233	0.089
gal per min	litre/sec (l/s)	0.0757	13.158
gal per sec	litre/sec (l/s)	4.5461	0.220
million gal per day	cubic metre/sec (m³/s)	0.0526	19.011
miles per hour	metre/sec (m/s)	0.447	2.237
ft/sec	metre/sec (m/s)	0.305	3.281
cub ft/sec	cubic metre/hr (m³/h)	102	0.0098
lb/sq in	kilogram/m² (kg/m²)	703.07	0.00142
btu/lb	kilojoule/kilogram (kJ/kg)	2.325	0.430

Gradients

Ratio rise: horizontal distance	Angle	Grade (%)
1 in 1	45°	100
1 in 2	26° 34′	50
1 in 3	18° 26′	33(1/3)
1 in 4	14° 02′	25
1 in 5	11° 19′	20
1 in 10	5° 43′	10
1 in 15	3° 49′	6(2/3)
1 in 20	2° 52′	5
1 in 40	1° 25′	2(1/2)
1 in 50	1° 09′	2
1 in 60	0° 57′	1(2/3)
1 in 80	0° 43′	1(1/4)
1 in 100	0° 34′	(2/3)